T0034635

MUSLIMS OF THE HEARTLAND

Muslims of the Heartland

*How Syrian Immigrants Made a Home
in the American Midwest*

Edward E. Curtis IV

NEW YORK UNIVERSITY PRESS

New York

NEW YORK UNIVERSITY PRESS
New York
www.nyupress.org

© 2022 by New York University
Paperback edition published 2023
All rights reserved

Library of Congress Cataloging-in-Publication Data
Names: Curtis, Edward E., IV, 1970–   author.
Title: Muslims of the heartland : how Syrian immigrants made a home in the American Midwest / Edward E. Curtis IV.
Other titles: How Syrian immigrants made a home in the American Midwest
Description: New York : New York University Press, [2021] | Includes bibliographical references and index.
Identifiers: LCCN 2021014002 | ISBN 9781479812561 (hardback) | ISBN 9781479827220 (paperback) | ISBN 9781479812608 (ebook) | ISBN 9781479812578 (ebook other)
Subjects: LCSH: Syrian Americans—Middle West—History—20th century. | Muslims—Middle West—History—20th century. | Muslim families—Middle West—Social conditions. | Middle West—Race relations—History—20th century.
Classification: LCC F358.2.S98 C87 2021 | DDC 977/.0049275691—dc23
LC record available at https://lccn.loc.gov/2021014002

This book is printed on acid-free paper, and its binding materials are chosen for strength and durability. We strive to use environmentally responsible suppliers and materials to the greatest extent possible in publishing our books.

Manufactured in the United States of America

10 9 8 7 6 5 4 3 2

Also available as an ebook

To the memory of Cassie Moses Saffa Caffery,

my maternal grandmother

CONTENTS

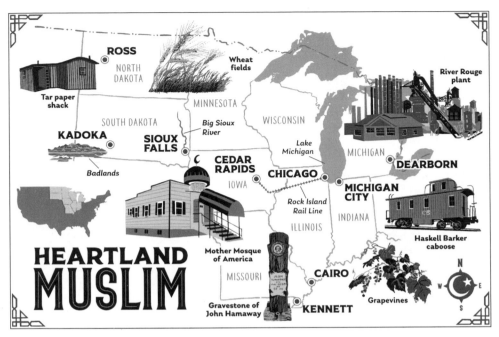

Heartland Muslim Map. Created by Scott Schiller.

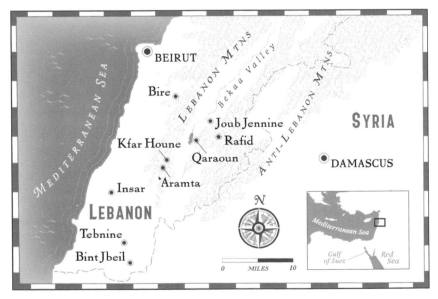

Places of Origin Map. Created by Scott Schiller.

LIST OF MAJOR CHARACTERS

Mike Ahmid Abdallah (1887–1974), farmer from Rafid in the Bekaa Valley, located in contemporary Lebanon. Farmers Union member. Raised sheep. Second husband of Lila Abdallah.

Hasibe Aossey (1903–1996), co-founder of Rose of Fraternity Lodge in Cedar Rapids. Grocer. From the village of Insar, located today in the south of Lebanon. Moved to Cedar Rapids in 1927. Daughter of a Shi'a Muslim shaykh, or religious teacher.

Mike Muhammad Aossey (c. 1900–1995), immigrated from Insar. Brother of Abdoo, Sam, and David, who also went to Iowa. Peddler. Quaker Oats employee. Grocer.

Hussien Ayad (1890–1983), immigrant to Michigan City, Indiana. Railroad track layer and factory employee.

Joe Hassan Chamie (1887–1918), immigrated to Sioux Falls, South Dakota. Served in Company I, 361st Infantry, 91st Division of the US Army. Died 1918 during the Meuse-Argonne offensive.

Boaley Farhat (1884–1964), immigrant from Rafid, originally went to Costa Rica. Owned 160 acres in Ross, North Dakota, by 1911. Pacifist. Progressive. Husband of Rosanna Lynch. Father of ten kids.

Aliya Ogdie Hassen (1910–1991), born in Sioux Falls, South Dakota, in 1910. Daughter of Fatima Juma Hajj and Alex Ogdie. Grew up in Sioux Falls, South Dakota. Moved to Detroit in 1925. Poet. Lover of dance. Collector of family lore.

Fatima Hamed Igram (1916–2008), born in Fayette County, Iowa. Cedar Rapids Muslim community leader. Wife of Hassan Igram. Stepmother to Abdullah Igram, World War II veteran.

Hassan Igram (1898–1980), peddler, utility worker, and grocer in Cedar Rapids, Iowa. Immigrated from Joub Jennine in the Bekaa Valley. Husband first of Goldie Gregg, then of Fatima Hamed. Father of Abdullah.

Mary Juma (1864–1947), immigrant from Bire (Bee-reh) in the Bekaa Valley. Peddler. Sodbuster. Arrived in North Dakota with husband, Hassen, in 1902. Gave birth to Charles in 1903 in town of Ross.

Sam Omar (1882–1956), homesteader in Ross, North Dakota. Immigrated from Bire. Wheat farmer.

Allie Joseph Said (1914–1943) from Michigan City, Indiana. Moved to Dearborn, Michigan. Died while serving with the US Army Air Forces in World War II.

Mary Shamey (1913–1995), also known as Mary Allie, Mary Terraine, and Mary Unis. Born 1913 in Michigan City, Indiana. Moved to Dearborn, Michigan. Married Sam Hussein Unis, veteran of World War I.

Hassen Sheronick (c. 1881–1934), immigrant from Joub Jennine. US citizen by 1903. Dry goods store owner and operator in Cedar Rapids, Iowa.

Negebe Sheronick (1907–1989), daughter of Hassen. Educated in Joub Jennine. Immigrated first to Toledo, then to Cedar Rapids. Major fundraiser for local mosque.

Introduction

My Syrian Muslim Heartland

When I was little, the Syrian Lebanese maternal grandmother who taught me to be a proud Arab mentioned something about our family that I never quite understood. The men in her mother's family would "never set foot in a church." She uttered this fact as if she felt compelled to tell me, but I was also sworn to keep it a secret.

I didn't think too much about it. Perhaps I wouldn't let myself. As a brown-skinned boy, the son of an Arab mother and a white father, I didn't need another reason to think of myself as out of place. I already experienced colorism and racism. One of the most repeated and painful questions I faced during my youth was: "*What* are you?" Sometimes, to be polite, people would ask me about my "nationality." It was perfectly clear to everyone that I was a kid from Southern Illinois. This was actually just another way to ask about my race. I already felt like an outcast, and the idea that some of my family members were not Christian would have been yet another obstacle to overcome. Mt. Vernon, the crossroads of Southern Illinois, was in the Bible Belt. In the 1970s and early 1980s, Gideons passed out copies of the New Testament after school, strangers came to your door to ask you whether you were saved, and accusations of occult associations flew in many directions. I wasn't the only kid worried about their salvation. I also knew and sometimes visited with one of the few Jewish families in town—their daughter was my teacher—and the stereotypical anti-Semitic comments that I heard about them would make anyone think twice about voluntarily embracing a non-Christian religious identity. I don't think I was worried that my ancestors were Muslim—I believe it was the possibility that they were atheists that terrified me.

My grandmother, who moved into my neighborhood when I was eight years old, did more than anyone, except perhaps my Black nationalist fourth-grade teacher, to help me fight my sense of weirdness and inadequacy. She knew, deeply and maybe more painfully than I ever guessed, what it was like when someone questioned whether you belonged to your native land. If the question of my existence was "What are you?" my grandmother's answer was that you are an Arab, a Syrian, a Lebanese, and when I asked what the difference was, she told me, "Oh, honey, there is no difference." Today and back then, people might find that to be a silly answer, but it turns out that Granny wasn't the only person who believed that Syrian, Lebanese, and Arab identities were or should be one and the same. Granny shared the politics of many of the people discussed in this book.

Granny was the proud daughter of Ottoman Syrian immigrants who thought that the Syrians were responsible for most of the good things in the world and very few of the bad. She directed my education as an Arab American. Since then, I have read countless stories of other Arab Americans whose grandmothers did the same for them. I learned about the gold bracelets put around her wrists in Damascus's Souq Al-Hamidiya and the many wonders of the Levant, stories that were shared with me as she tossed our daily dose of parsley-laden salad. The generous amounts of olive oil she used in her cooking made those old gold bracelets glisten as she spun her tales. Her memories would be strengthened when shipments of candied chickpeas or dried apricot paste would arrive from one of my aunts or uncles. Spending time with Granny in the kitchen was a magical, sensuous experience as the smells of tabbouli, freshly baked pita, chicken and rice, and baked kibbi filled the air. That yellow linoleum-floored kitchen in Southern Illinois was the womb where my Arab identity was born and nurtured through constant feeding of my belly and my mind and my heart. Even though she drank Nescafé, she remembered the strong Turkish coffee she drank during summer trips to Lebanon. There were equally strong opinions and harsh words about the occupation of Palestine, the Lebanese civil war, and the Jewish lobby.

Granny was born Cassie Moses on May 14, 1917, in Mounds, Illinois, just north of Cairo, the southernmost point of a part of Illinois nicknamed Little Egypt. Her father, my great-grandfather, was George Moses, who, according to the 1920 census, immigrated to the United States in 1899 as a very young boy. Granny told me that the family name was actually Samaha, but that it was changed by immigration officials. According to the 1904 Cairo city directory, George Moses's father went by the name of Samaha Moses. No doubt he knew the biblical story of Moses, and I often wonder whether he chuckled a little that he was a Moses living in a town called Cairo. Granny told me that he was originally from Bteghrine, a mountain village located in contemporary Lebanon. She said that when she visited their village, the priests all spoke Greek. It must have sounded like Greek to her because what she actually witnessed, it seemed, was a Melkite liturgy, performed largely in classical Arabic. By the time I began to formally study Arabic in 1990, she had lost much of her proficiency in colloquial Arabic, and she found my modern standard Arabic to be ridiculous, but her accent was still fantastic.

Like so many others, Granny's Syrian family got their start as peddlers. Cairo was an ideal spot for that profession. It was located at the confluence of the Ohio and Mississippi rivers, the point at which Huck and Jim of Mark Twain's *Huckleberry Finn* were supposed to disembark and make their way to freedom. The town provided the peddler with a chance to sell not only to Cairo's sixteen thousand or so residents, but, more importantly, to the railroad passengers and bargemen. By 1915, several Syrian families and individuals were living there, and just like in Sioux Falls and Cedar Rapids, they became major players in the town's grocery business. Proprietors included the Elias Brothers, A. Feisel, A. A. Hanna, Koury and Semmon, S. G. Malouf, A. Malouf, and Albert Tenoos. Others, like Michael Saliba, worked as clerks in some of the stores. Samaha Moses and his son, George, went a different way. They became farmers. According to Mrs. Adeby Coury, who was interviewed in 1980, Samaha Moses was "an old man" when she arrived in Cairo. He "peddled all his life," she said, spending "the night at a particular farm" near Mounds, Illinois. "He made up his mind that he was going to save enough money to buy that farm, which he finally did. It was a big farm. He was helped by his one son, George, and they became very wealthy, working the land and raising livestock."[1]

In 1916, George Moses married Mary Hamaway, my great-grandmother. She was also born in Ottoman Syria. In 1913 she was living in Kennett, Missouri, a town about ninety miles or so from Cairo, Illinois. She could neither read nor write, and she never went to school. Her father was John Hamaway. Her mother was Nazira Abdalla Hamod (sometimes Hamor). As I did the research for this book, decades after my grandmother told me that at least some members of the Hamaway family were not churchgoing people, I began to wonder whether my great-grandmother's family was Muslim. The first clue I found was a catalogue of the family names in Sioux Falls provided by Aliya Ogdie Hassen. She said that the Hamaways (spelled a variety of ways, including Hamwi) and the Hamods were part of the Muslim community there. And these families kept coming up in my research on the Muslim Midwest, especially in Michigan City. Later, I also saw an allusion to John Hamaway's brother, who once "worshipped at the shrine of Mohammed." I will likely never know for sure. Shortly before I finished this book, one of my distant cousins told me that someone in the family was Armenian Orthodox. Maybe that was my grandmother's secret. What was important to me as I was researching and writing this book was the deeper connection I felt as I understood how Arabic-speaking Christian and Muslim Midwesterners had built a world of shared networks, friendships, and political interests before World War II.

Whatever their religious backgrounds, both sides of my mother's family were part of a mass migration of half a million people from Ottoman Syria, which at the time included Syria, Lebanon, Palestine, and Jordan. By 1914, one-fifth of all Syrians lived abroad. The majority of those who came to the New World arrived in Argentina, Brazil, and the United States. The victims of a weak economy in the eastern Mediterranean, they were drawn to the New World by opportunities in both agriculture and industry. Those who settled in the United States worked as part of a foreign-born labor force of tens of millions of people who made it possible to triple imports, quadruple exports, and quintuple foreign investments between 1870 and 1914.[2] Many hoped to make money and return home. Some of them did. Some went back and forth across the Atlantic many times. Others were stranded in the Americas, at least temporarily, because of World War I. They were citizens of the Ottoman Empire, which had controlled Greater Syria, also called the Levant, since the sixteenth century, but in the wake of the defeat of the Ottomans, their situation changed. The British and French victors of World War I divided up the area into four mandates, including Lebanon, Syria, Palestine, and Transjordan. The Great War became a turning point, and many Syrians decided that they would stay in the United States permanently.

Though Syria America's "mother colony" was in New York City, tens of thousands were attracted to the US Midwest, where the development of railroads and waterways linked the booming business of agriculture to heavy industry around the Great Lakes. In this period of US history, America's progressive self-image was symbolized by the nation's premier railroad town, Chicago, which also hosted the country's most important world's fair, the Columbian Exposition of 1893.[3] Stretching from the prairies of the Dakotas to Ohio's coal-fired factories aside Lake Erie, this twelve-state area came to be called the Midwest, "the nation's brawny, broad-shouldered industrial and agrarian heartland."[4] From the 1890s until today, the region has been defined, not without argument, as including the states of Illinois, Indiana, Iowa, Kansas, Michigan, Minnesota, Missouri, Nebraska, North Dakota, Ohio, South Dakota, and Wisconsin.[5] It may seem strange to group together the shortgrass prairies of the western Dakotas with the Great Lakes, but the Midwest was a human geography, not a natural one. Human history rather than natural history forged this region.

The history of its Syrian Muslim inhabitants is important. Their comings and goings, their networks, and their everyday lives reveal how the American Midwest worked as an interconnected region. The steam-powered locomotive and then the automobile were part of that story, but it was even more entangled than the means of transportation that connected them all. The Midwest's growing towns, new factories, and new farms provided opportunities for Syrians in America to make a new home. Though the majority of Syrians who came to the Americas were Christian, a sizeable minority of those who settled in the American Midwest were Muslim. Most of the first mosques built in the United States were in the Midwest, which became America's Arab Muslim heartland. This book charts the history of their settlement before World War I, when the Midwest was really booming economically, and then follows the stories of their children through World War II, by which time the immigrants and their kids rooted themselves, their culture, and their religion in the Midwest.

If some of my ancestors were part of that story, it is also clear that they stopped identifying as Muslim. But these relatives didn't necessarily become enthusiastic Catholics either. As I was writing this book, my mother remembered that Mary Hamaway would go to church on special occasions, but she was not religious about attending weekly mass like her husband. No one would talk about this openly, which is perhaps why a half century later my grandmother shared the information as if it were something to keep quiet. Their situation was not unique. During World War I, when Mary and George were married, Syrians in small Midwestern towns were sometimes unable to find marriage partners from the same religious community. It was impossible at times to be choosy. Plus, Mary Hamaway could not speak English very well. In 1916, this limited her potential marriage partners in the boot hill of Missouri. She became proficient in English later, but she always spoke her native colloquial Arabic, too. In the old country, it was highly unusual for a Muslim woman to marry a Christian man; this violated most interpretations of Islamic law. But in the Syrian Muslim Midwest, it was not so strange. What were Mary's parents to do?

In addition, George Moses may have shared their politics. It is not clear to me if they thought of themselves at the time as Ottoman subjects or as Syrian or Arab nationalists before World War I, but George Moses was certainly a strong supporter of Arab causes at a later point. Cairo had an active Syrian-American Club in the 1930s and 1940s, and by the 1950s, he was hosting anti-Zionist Palestinian students from Southern Illinois University, Carbondale, to give speeches not only to the Arabs of Cairo but also to the English-speaking white fraternal organizations. My grandmother's Arab nationalism and pro-Palestinian politics were inspired by her father, whose voice she respected more than any other person's in the world. Perhaps it was his voice she echoed when she told me that there was no inherent conflict between Muslims and Christians, that we cared about each other back in Syria, and if left to solve our own problems, Arabs could get along with one another just fine.

Most of the Syrian Midwestern Muslims in this book expressed the same point of view. Syrian and Arab nationalism, which dreamed of a future in which European colonialism would be overcome and the Arab people would be able to form their own independent nation(s), was very popular among Syrian American Muslims in the 1920s. My grandmother, like others of her generation, may have downplayed the real conflicts among Muslims and Christians. But she was typical in her desire for unity, a longing so deep that it reordered people's memories such that all they could remember of the past, all that was important, was Muslim-Christian cooperation, not conflict. I never heard my grandmother say an ill word about Arab Muslims. She told me that we were one people. Perhaps her God, like that of some Muslims featured in this book, was a universal deity who did not distinguish among Christians and Muslims.

From the beginning, writing this history of the Syrian Muslim Midwest was deeply personal, and my emotions were never far from the page. When I was doing research in the Naff Collection at the National Museum of American History in Washington, DC, I noticed an interview of someone from Cairo, Illinois. It was about one of my grandmother's family friends, the Coury family. I opened it up, and began to read. I never knew that the Courys, who were Christians, were from the same small village of Bteghrine. As I started getting into it and read the descriptions of the village, my mind immediately wandered to foggy mornings in green mountains that gave way in the middle of the day to huge, sunlit vistas. Tears started coming down my face, and I worried about ruining the archival documents. I put it away for later viewing.

When I traveled to the History Center at Cedar Rapids, I also visited the National Muslim Cemetery and saw for the first time the graves of the people whose oral history interviews I had been reading. Being there made me feel like I was meeting them in a way that I could not in the archive. The cemetery felt like the sacred ground not of strangers but of friends, of distant uncles and aunts. I had a similar feeling when I stopped by Kennett, Missouri, to visit the grave of my great-great-grandfather John Hamaway.

My grandmother gave me more than an emotional link to the Syrian Muslim Midwest; her stories about Syrians gave me ideas about what to look for as I was doing research. She was not an academic specialist, but her experience became a lens that I used to identify major themes in this book. For example, she told me about all of her visits to other Syrians across the region. She liked visiting our cousins in Iowa; she befriended Syrian families in St. Louis; she went to parties and conventions (*haflis* and *mahrajans*) in Terre Haute, Indiana; and she met her husband when she was attending college in South Bend. Because of those stories, I already knew deep in my bones that there was a Syrian Midwest—that this was more than just a bunch of disconnected small towns and cities. It was a real regional community of people that had fun together, did business together, married one another, and shared many of the same experiences. This book shows (rather than tells) how their regional network of friendship, business, religion, and culture paralleled the railroads, rivers, and roads of the Midwest.

Similarly, it was not a shock to find out that many Syrian fathers were devoted to the education of their daughters. My great-grandfather paid for my grandmother to attend St. Mary's College. This was perhaps not

FIGURE 1.1. The author's great-great-grandfather was buried in Kennett, Missouri. His selection of gravestone was a popular choice among holders of Woodmen of the World burial insurance policies. Credit: Edward Curtis.

so much an act of feminist liberation as a commitment to the family's aspirations for middle- and upper-class social status. It was also an opportunity for my grandmother to meet the right husband—namely, an educated Arab American Roman Catholic.

At St. Mary's, my grandmother became engaged to my grandfather, William Paul Saffa, who left Drumwright, Oklahoma, to play football for Knute Rockne at Notre Dame. A knee injury kept him from playing on the football team, but he did compete in gymnastics. Physical prowess and strength were important to Grandpa Bill Saffa, who invited all his grandkids to feel his biceps and to punch him in the stomach. He had those steely abdominal muscles until the day he died. So when I discovered how important male athletic skill and strength were among Syrian Muslims, it did not surprise me. When I saw the photograph of the Adonis-like professional wrestler Yussif Hussane for the first time, it was like I was looking at my grandfather.

I admit that my family's romantic views of the rural Midwest—its fields, forests, creeks, and hills—and of the natural world more generally influenced my approach to the research, as well. My great-grandmother, Mary Hamaway Moses, nurtured a wide variety of fruit trees, vegetables, and flowering plants, everything from loofahs and Syrian cucumbers (whose seeds, I was told, were smuggled out of the old country) to plum, apple, and pear trees. Her little yard in Mounds, Illinois, even had potted lemon, orange, and banana trees, which were brought inside during the winter. She was looking back to Syria, and she rooted something of the old country in her new land. All those Syrian plants competed for space in town, where she moved later in life, but they had ample room to grow in the modern farmhouse where she spent most of her years as a young mother. When Mary Hamaway moved to the Moses farm, the family first lived in a stucco log house said to be a hundred years old. In 1942, they built what was described in the *Mounds Independent* as a modern home located on a "knoll which overlooks 300 acres of their farmland." The house included three porches, one of which was a south-facing "glassed-in conservatory," providing lots of space for Mary's plants to flourish. This farm became the site where my great-grandfather, the patriarch, oversaw the weekly meetings of the extended family.

Even though Granny was trained to be a proper lady, the country life was always a part of her. Granny made me tolerate ticks and cuts as we foraged along tarred-and-graveled roads in her old Ford LTD for wild berries and young, tender grape leaves, which would be stuffed with cinnamon- and allspice-seasoned meat and rice, and then slowly simmered in a broth with onions, tomatoes, and lemon juice. I was introduced at an early age to gardening by my granny's second husband, James Caffery. My Curtis grandparents were also from Southern Illinois, and they loved the land just as much. It was generous to us, and I was taught to appreciate and love it right back.

I wondered whether other Syrian Midwesterners had the same experience. In this book I provide a lot of details about the places that were part of their lives so that you can see, hear, feel, and even smell what it was like to be one of the book's major characters. I found out that they had a variety of feelings about the land, its flora, and its fauna. For example, Muslim kids were just as excited to win 4-H competitions for the best farm animals as non-Muslim kids were, and Muslim boys loved hunting upland game like pheasants and ducks as much as the next person. Iowa's farmers were often blessed with excellent farmland and generous yields on corn, soybeans, oats, and other crops. But the wheat farmers of North Dakota struggled with constant drought, over time discovering that the prairies taken from Lakota Sioux and other Indigenous people were best used for grazing, not for planting crops. Syrian Muslim city folk felt at home in neighborhoods where there were many other Arabic speakers right next door, and they enjoyed the burgeoning number of public parks and beaches when they were allowed to use them, but they also lived near some of the most noxious-smelling factories the Midwest had to offer. Perhaps they were a little less smitten with Midwestern landscapes than my family was.

Syrian Muslims were ordinary Midwesterners in other ways, too. Though some of their religious beliefs and rituals were different, their religious congregations worked in the same ways others did. Whether we are talking about the German, Bohemian, Polish, Irish, or Italian Roman Catholic parish, the Sephardic or Ashkenazi synagogue, or the Scandinavian congregation of Holiness Christians, Midwesterners often made the ethnic-religious congregation the most important public institution of their collective life, a place where they could preserve their traditions.[6] But the congregation also became a vehicle of assimilation. It was essential to their roles as patriots, parents, and community members. In cities such as Detroit as well as in towns such as Cedar Rapids, Iowa; Ross, North Dakota; and Michigan City, Indiana, Arabic-speaking Muslim congregations were centers of community-making among Muslims themselves and with non-Muslims too. The Sunni and Shi'a Muslims, representing the two main groups or sects in Islamic religion, worshipped together in these places and proudly publicized them in both Arabic- and English-language newspapers. Up, down, and all around the Midwest, they passed by and through fields, forests, rivers, lakes, and hills in trains and in automobiles as they went out of their way to visit one another's communities and mourn each other's dead. They were not planting themselves as a foreign element inside America; they were building their Syrian Muslim communities as an expression of their American and Arab identities, both of which they treasured. Attachment to the old country did not detract from love of the new country. It did not stop Syrian Muslims from embracing their lives as Americans. They grew roots, like my granny's wild grape leaves, in the Midwest.

This book tells the tales of only a few people and a few communities to bring the Syrian Muslim Midwest of the first half of the twentieth century to life. It is not what historians describe as a comprehensive narrative. I have not tried to narrate the stories of all Syrians nor of all Muslims, many of whom were African American and South Asian. I have also avoided, as much as possible, the academic language that makes it hard for people who are not professors to read history books.

But like most historians, I do try to explain how larger historical forces affected the lives of the book's major characters. At times, all people are swept up into historical whirlwinds that inevitably influence what they do and who they become. For example, many Americans, of various racial and ethnic backgrounds, opposed the US fighting in World War I. The federal and state governments responded by making it illegal to speak out against the war, accusing pacifists and others of sedition. Many Syrian Muslims were happy to support this war since they thought it might lead to independence for their native lands and provide them with a chance to earn their US citizenship through military service. But there was also tremendous pressure on them to be supportive. They knew, like most Americans, that they would pay a heavy price if they took a public stance against the war.

Syrian Muslims, like everyone else, were also affected by the larger racial politics of the United States. From the moment they arrived, many Syrian leaders worked to be on the white side of the stark American "color line." Many—not all—embraced the idea that they were white, a belief that exists among many contemporary Arab Americans. Certainly, I was raised to believe this even though I saw a brown face staring back at me in the mirror every day. In any case, it is easy to understand why they wanted to be white. Their immigration in the late 1800s coincided with the country's move away from its own constitutional guarantees of equal protection under the law without regard to race (the 14th Amendment) and voting rights for all men (the 15th Amendment). By the 1890s, racial segregation became legal again.

At that time, Syrians were not yet legally white in the eyes of federal law. They fought their classification as "Orientals" or Asians. Before World War I, they succeeded, more or less, in convincing US courts that they were racially white. But after World War I, things got worse. In the 1920s, the rebirth of the Ku Klux Klan as well as federal anti-immigration policies threatened the gains that Syrians had made toward achieving the commonly held goal of being accepted as white people. The 1924 National Origins Act effectively cut off immigration from Syria, stigmatizing Syrians as non-white.[7] How they fared in such times depended not only on the law and their individual circumstances, but sometimes on the particular town in which they lived. Life was easier in Cedar Rapids, for example. By the 1930s, there were leaders and opinion makers there who unabashedly embraced Muslims as fellow community members.

During the years after World War I, there were other cultural and social practices that linked Syrian Muslims to their Midwestern neighbors. Like other Americans in the Roaring Twenties, they found pleasure in Sunday drives on newly constructed roads. Some embraced jazz and flapper fashions; a few engaged in rum-running and the numbers racket. The Great Depression hit most Americans hard, and Syrian Muslims were no exception. Farmers went broke, sometimes losing their livestock and their land. Autoworkers in Detroit were laid off. I document one Syrian Muslim who became a homeless rail rider. But in Cedar Rapids, Michigan City, and Dearborn, the Syrian community's grocers prospered. The number of mosques actually expanded in this era. Kids still attended school and sang in the choir or played in the band. They went to Sunday school at the mosque and sometimes at the church with their Christian friends.

The book reveals how ordinary Syrian Muslim Midwestern life often was. In doing that, it fights back against the bleaching of Midwestern history. This is my most important and personally meaningful contribution. I grew up assuming that my brown skin was a foreign intervention in a white land. But my family's history was far more typical than some would like to suggest. We Midwesterners are a more diverse, cosmopolitan bunch than many people outside our region suppose. Some of us in the Midwest have also forgotten who we are. Perhaps we wanted to. I hear a lot of stories about how diverse populations—Latinx agricultural workers, Black migrants from Chicago, immigrants from India, Pakistan, and Bangladesh—are new to the rural Midwest. Of course, these particular people may be new, but it is incorrect to assume that there have never been Asian, African, and Latin American immigrants in the rural Midwest before now. Even when the Midwest was at its "whitest," many non-white people were present, living in the next state, the next town, or maybe down the road. The truth is that the Midwest has never been all white and all Christian. Never. We have always spoken different languages and practiced different religions. Indigenous peoples who lived here before and after Africans and Eurasians arrived in the region were and are culturally diverse. Those of us who trace our lineage to other parts of the world are also racially, ethnically, and religiously plural. Some of us have had to fight harder than others for our dignity and opportunities, and it is way past time to fix that problem. Getting to know the stories of Syrian Muslims is an important step forward for those of us who want to cultivate the Midwest we desire—a heartland that loves all its people and loves us abundantly.

PART I

1900 to World War I

1

Muslim South Dakota from Kadoka to Sioux Falls

The rattlesnake was the final straw.

Aliya Ogdie Hassen, born in Sioux Falls, South Dakota, in 1910, used to tell a story about her mother, Fatima, who endured harsh winters and howling coyotes on her 120-acre homestead in South Dakota. One day, as she was hanging the wash, a rattlesnake bit the farm dog that was guarding her infant twins. She killed the snake, and issued her husband an ultimatum. She was either moving into town or she was returning to her home in the Bekaa Valley, currently located in Lebanon but then part of Greater Syria, part of the Ottoman Empire. Her husband obliged, finding someone else to run the farm. They moved to Sioux Falls.[1]

Aliya Hassen's mother, Fatima Juma Hajj, was born in 1873 in Syria, and was buried next to her husband, Alex, in 1957 in Mount Pleasant Cemetery, located in Sioux Falls, South Dakota. Their names are rendered on their tombstone in both Arabic and English. Aliya's father, Alex, was known as 'Ali in Arabic. This shared marker also records the words of the Islamic profession of faith: There is no god but God; Muhammad is the Messenger of God. It features the Islamic crescent and the Seal of Solomon, which was an Islamic talisman dating from medieval times. Fatima and Alex may have come from Syria, and they were always proud of their Arab and Muslim roots, but they made a real home in Sioux Falls. South Dakota became home to them, even as they lived on land that was the property only decades before of America's First Nations.[2]

According to his daughter, Alex Ogdie traveled both to the United States and to Argentina in the 1870s. She heard that he had to get out of town. The family was in the tobacco smuggling business and ran into some trouble with the Ottoman authorities. "A soldier was killed," she

FIGURE 1.1. Alex and Fatima Ogdie with two of their kids. Source: Arab American National Museum.

said. At some point, Alex Ogdie returned and married Fatima. He then left again for the United States, heading to Omaha, Nebraska, and then Sioux Falls.

The names of Muslims such as Alex Ogdie are not well-known in US history, even among US historians, but Ogdie and thousands like him deserve a place in any story about America's heartland. He got his start as a peddler. He also claimed a homestead in western South Dakota. He was listed in the 1900 US census under the name Alack Ogda and lived as a boarder at 204 Phillips Avenue North with thirty-six other male Syrian peddlers and one female housekeeper.[3] That was a lot of people for one house, but all of them would not have been there at the same time. They made their living as traveling salespeople. The boardinghouse, which backed up to the Big Sioux River, was located at the foot of an iron bridge. When he was in town, Alex Ogdie could find nearly anything he might want right outside his door. Next to the boardinghouse was a telegraph office. Across the street there was a fruit store, a barber, a billiards hall, a furniture store, a hotel, and a laundry.[4]

In 1905, Fatima joined her husband, and they decided to homestead in western South Dakota. They lived about nine miles northeast of Kadoka, which was not officially incorporated as a town until 1906. The Ogdies were part of a population boom of almost one hundred thousand people who crossed the Missouri River to settle the western, semiarid part of South Dakota. In this area, the population rose from 43,782 in 1900 to 137,687 in 1910. Some of this land was offered to settlers for free; other parts were sold for the low price of $2.50 to $6 an acre. The Ogdie homestead was located on the Missouri Plateau on the Great Plains; the elevation of nearby Kadoka was 2,500 feet. This gently rolling, sometimes green, sometimes brown shortgrass prairie sat beneath wide-open skies. The horizon went on and on. But just southwest of Kadoka was the beginning of the Badlands, "a labyrinth of ravines and narrow ridges with buttes, domes, and spires . . . laid bare by erosion and weathering." Today, Kadoka refers to itself as the gateway to the Badlands. The area's spectacularly red, orange, brown, and gray rock formations draw almost one million visitors a year.[5] A little farther west of Kadoka are the Black Hills, a mountain range of 3,500 to 7,242 feet. Rainfall in the western part of the state was not as generous as that in the long-grass prairies of eastern South Dakota. The years of plentiful rain yielded a fine wheat crop, but years of drought brought disaster.[6] Summer temperatures were warm, but winter weather was often frigid. The *average* winter temperature when the Ogdies arrived was 18 degrees Fahrenheit (almost −8 degrees Celsius).[7] There would have been many days when the family was caught in subzero temperatures; in 1905, for example, the temperature dipped to −28 degrees Fahrenheit at one of the state's weather stations.[8]

By June 24, 1909, Alex Ogdie was granted the land patent to his 120-acre homestead; President William Howard Taft's stamped signature was affixed to the bottom of the document. Ogdie's section was located north of the Pine Ridge Indian Reservation. Only decades before, the US Congress had recognized that the very ground to which Ogdie was given title belonged to Indigenous peoples. The 1868 Treaty of Fort Laramie, signed with leaders such as Red Cloud of the Oglala, ushered in a short period of peace between the United States and the Lakota (Sioux). It created the Great Sioux Reservation in the Dakotas as the "perpetual home" of the Lakota people. In 1887, however, the General Allotment Act, also called the Dawes Act, began the process of severing Native peoples from their collectively owned lands; it sought to allot that land to both settlers and Indigenous people for the purpose of farming. The Great Sioux Reservation was coveted not only by yeoman farmers, but also by railroad companies, ranchers, and land speculators. As a result, the US Congress passed a March 2, 1889, law "to divide a portion of the reservation of the Sioux Nations of Indians in Dakota into separate reservations and to secure the relinquishment of the Indian title to the remainder." Alex Ogdie's land was part of that remainder. It was made available for homesteading, and it was surveyed for that purpose in 1890.[9] The disruptions to the lives of Native people were felt and heard around the world that year when the US Army massacred hundreds of

Lakota people in a failed attempt to disarm them at Wounded Knee, located about sixty-five miles from Kadoka.

Whether Alex Ogdie knew about the history of his land is unknown, and his daughter's recollections of Native peoples reflected only warm, if romantic feelings. Aliya said that her father sold his wares to Indian customers.[10] She liked to remember that as a girl she slept "under buffalo robes and Indian blankets."[11] Evoking the mythic narrative of the American pioneer, Aliya Ogdie Hassen laid claim to a story of homemaking shared by many of the white colonists who saw themselves as inhabiting America's heartland. Other settlers told the same stories about the dangers they overcame—the bad weather, the coyotes, the rattlesnakes. Before Native Americans had been removed from these lands, before the prairies were fenced and plowed, such stories talked of the "savage" ways of the Indigenous people. But by the time Syrians made it to the Dakotas in the late nineteenth and early twentieth centuries, Native peoples no longer posed a threat to white sovereignty. Syrian tales of sacrifice did not include details about battles with Indians, but, like other settler myths, their pioneer stories established how hard they worked to put down roots in America, to become native to America by participating in that most American of things, the settlement and cultivation of Indigenous peoples' land.[12] Syrians such as Alex Ogdie did not set out to do this intentionally. They, too, were the victims of uncontrollable forces that had taken away local political control of their villages and limited their abilities to resist their absorption into an international labor market. Their goal was simple—a better life for themselves and their families. But their "homesteading was predicated on Indian dispossession."[13]

The homesteader's life was no life at all for Aliya's mother, but Sioux Falls was different. Indigenous people had been living or traveling through the area for more than two millennia, but in 1876 it was incorporated as a city by the Dakota Territory assembly. The Big Sioux River's promise of water power was attractive to millers, but the town benefited even more from the coming of the railroad in 1878. Sioux Falls was the first town in South Dakota to light its streets at night using electricity, and, by the time Fatima Ogdie arrived there, electricity was also powering street trolleys. The John Morrell meat processing plant, established in 1909, transported its products using the refrigerated railroad car, a technology that allowed consumers to purchase fresh rather than salted meat. By 1911, Morrell was processing "500 cattle, 6,000 hogs, and 1,000 sheep" a day.[14] The growth of industry and agriculture provided the opportunities that Syrian and other immigrants needed to establish themselves in Sioux Falls. By 1915, about a dozen out of fifty-two grocery stores in town were owned by Syrians. The city directory featured the names of grocers such as Hassan Ballas, Aly Hanshie, Alex Serhan, and Mehmd Swiden.[15]

In South Dakota as a whole, 234 of the 670 self-identifying Syrians in the South Dakota state census of 1915 were Muslim; that was 35 percent of the reported Syrian population.[16] Unlike the federal census, the state census at the time asked people about their religion—Muslims were classified as Mohammedans, a label referring to the idea that Muslims were followers of the Prophet Muhammad, the Messenger of God. Many historians have rightly emphasized that many more Christians than Muslims emigrated from Syria to the Americas before World War I, but in both North and South Dakota—which represented a small part of the overall Syrian diaspora—the percentage of Muslims was much higher. To young Aliya, there seemed to be more Muslims than Christians.

Among the many Muslim families in Sioux Falls were the Hamways, Swaydens (Swidens), Badhees, Asads (Assids), Hamods, and Haymoons. The Christian families included the Haggars, Haddads, and Solomons. As Aliya remembered, the Muslims and Christians frequently socialized, especially in winter, and enjoyed self-catered Arab feasts. On the weekends, they would gather "to read poetry" and to recite "epic tales" that included the ancient histories of their clans, *A Thousand and One Nights*, and the story of the Persian hero Rostam. On long winter nights, a storyteller would go on for hours about Majnun, whose love for Layla drove him mad; about 'Antar, the pre-Islamic poet, and his great love for 'Abla; about Jayda, who cried and cried when her great love, Khalid, was slain. Arabic-language newspapers from New York and Detroit were read aloud to all since many Syrian Americans could speak but not read or write Arabic.[17]

The Muslims, both Sunni and Shi'a, would sometimes pray together in people's homes and Syrian-owned stores. They also buried their dead with Islamic funeral prayers in Mt. Pleasant Cemetery.[18] There is good reason to believe that both Sunni and Shi'a cooperated with one another in Sioux Falls. On this frontier, ethnic solidarity sometimes overrode religious conflicts. But moments of tension were not unknown. A Syrian Christian wrote to the local paper to say that Syrian Muslims were not as civilized as Syrian Christians—he put distance between himself and a Syrian Muslim accused of arson by calling the Muslim a "Turk."[19] On another occasion, a Christian Syrian starting teasing Muslims by "making up little songs" about them. One Muslim, a Shi'a man, responded with a song of his own: "I am a Shi'a / I don't hide it / Not like you who blaspheme God / by giving him a wife, child, and partner" (referring to Mary, Jesus, and the Trinity, the Christian belief that God is three persons, Father, Son, and Holy Spirit). Her father, Aliya said, put a stop to the back and forth.[20]

Aliya's father did his part to keep the Syrian community unified. Aliya recalled that he was a leader and she described him in heroic terms: "the wisest, strongest [man] in town [who] could lift the heaviest weight in contests held regularly between his travels. Best wrestler, shot, and swordsman." Aliya said that at first he could neither read nor write in Arabic or English, a fact also recorded in the 1920 federal census. But his lack of English fluency did not impede his success as a salesman. "The farmers in that area were Germans, Norwegians, and Swedes," said Aliya, "and their English was not much better." Alex Ogdie was a hard worker, but he drew a line when it came to driving a sleigh in the sub-zero temperatures. He avoided the snow-covered roads and the snow drifts in the deep midwinter. Instead, he used a horse-driven wagon as soon as the roads were passable in the spring and then would stay on the roads until late fall. Away for months a time, he would visit the family for a fortnight, restock his wagon with merchandise, and then go back out on the road.[21]

All that time away also led, at one point, to Alex fathering a child with a Norwegian woman. By 1900, there were about twenty thousand Norwegians in South Dakota, most of whom had come to establish farms. Norwegian women provided labor that was essential to their families' success. Some single women and girls came to the state as hired hands. Women milked cows and maintained vegetable gardens. They also worked in the fields, gathering hay for livestock or tying and stacking bundles of wheat. They washed clothes and cleaned houses.[22] Though it is not clear how Alex Ogdie met his son's mother, there would have been plenty of opportunities for peddlers to interact with Norwegian women while traveling throughout the state. Their South Dakota–born son would sometimes visit his father's house in Sioux Falls. Aliya found him "fascinating." He was tragically killed in World War I, she said, and "her father grieved."[23] It is not clear what his wife, Fatima, thought about her husband's son, but she remained married to Alex for the rest of his life. She was determined to make a go of it in South Dakota even when life was rough.

Some Syrian women, like Marie Corie, came to the country without their husbands, and their stories of intrepidity rival those of any other woman pioneers. Corie made her living as business partner to fruit seller Alex Ainshley in Sioux Falls. But when she decided to marry another Syrian man, named Abdou Hamway or Abde Hamit, her business partner got upset and accused both of them of adultery and bigamy.[24] The saga, which played out in the courts, became quite the item of gossip. At first, the couple said that they had obtained divorces from their spouses in Syria. But, in one instance, the new husband said that he was "Mohammedan and consequently entitled to take as many wives as he sees fit." Perhaps the man was just joking. Traditional interpretations of the various schools of Islamic law limit a male to a maximum of four wives. Or maybe he was referring to the Shi'a Muslim practice of "temporary marriage" in which one legally marries for a short period of time and provides for a woman in case she becomes pregnant. It is also possible that the reporter just made the comment up. The important point is that Syrian women who arrived in South Dakota, like many other woman pioneers, were often strong, independent figures who, as much as they could, set their own course.

Whether it was her own father's dalliance with a Norwegian woman or talk of other people's escapades, Aliya Hassen did not grow up in a sheltered environment. She enjoyed the warm community forged by Syrians in Sioux Falls, but she was also exposed from an early age to people of different ethnic backgrounds and different ways of life. She did not live in a fancy house or a fancy neighborhood. At first, they resided at 229 West Sixth. But, by 1914, they had moved into a one-and-a-half-story wood-framed family home at 522 Weber Avenue. There were newlyweds next door: Bert Dowd, twenty-four, an Irish Catholic, was married to Norwegian Mabel Gunderson, eighteen. Mabel made her living on Weber Avenue as a mangler, that is, as a washerwoman who would hand-crank clothes through a washing machine consisting of two rollers and a tub. The Chiles, Hatwick, and Anderson families lived on the same block, and the Swidens, a Syrian family, were just a block away.[25] There were other Syrians in the neighborhood, too: Alex Sirhan ran a confectionary, and the Haggars had both a grocery and a dry goods store.

Across the street from the Ogdies' house was Illinois Central Railroad's Sioux Falls roundhouse, where steam engines would stop, undergo repairs, and turn around.[26] Built out of brick, which protected against the threat of fire, the semicircular roundhouse featured four different stalls. A locomotive was guided from its track onto a turntable, which was "a large platform mounted on a rotating pivot and resting in a circular pit." Then the locomotive was rotated until it was aligned with the right stall. It was then propelled into the stall and serviced by the yard's employees, who stayed in two bunkhouses on the premises. Perhaps they patronized the Syrian confectionary and dry goods stores across the street. There was also a separate car repair shop on the premises. It would have been a noisy place, abuzz with the squeaking of trains and the sounds of heavy repair work.[27]

Looking back on her youth, Aliya did not remember much discrimination against her people. But there is no doubt that Syrian Muslims in Sioux Falls, as elsewhere, were the victims of racial, ethnic, and religious harassment. They were classified in the South Dakota census as white, yet they were not always treated that way. First, there was the issue of their Arabic names. A 1912 article in the *Sioux Falls Argus-Leader* said that "you could not pronounce them even if they were spelled for you." The article, which discussed an assault and battery court case involving a Syrian husband and wife, stated that the foreign names caused the city attorney to stumble "in reading the complaint." The paper did not print the names of the parties involved, and instead declared, tongue in cheek, that they should be "nameless here forevermore."[28]

Second, Syrian Muslims did not practice Christianity, which was the majority religion. Despite the First Amendment's protection of religious liberty, not all government institutions—not to mention the country's citizens—respected religious difference. In 1911, for example, a judge in Deadwood, located in western South Dakota, refused to allow a Muslim plaintiff and a Muslim defendant to swear "by the Koran and with Mohammedan oaths." In the case of *Khan v. Khan*, both parties said that they "would believe each other only by swearing on the Koran." They even brought a Muslim religious leader, to whom the newspaper incorrectly referred as a "priest," from Aberdeen, over three hundred miles away, to witness their oaths. But South Dakota circuit court judge W. G. Rice, Deadwood's former city attorney and a former South Dakota state senator, ruled that "only American oaths would be accepted in his court and that foreigners must comply with the accepted customs in this country."[29] Even though the Qur'an and Islamic oaths had been part of the country decades before the United States gained its independence— even though there were hundreds of Syrians in South Dakota—the judge still considered them to be foreign to America.

Then there was the issue of how Syrians looked. The husband involved in the assault and battery case, the paper said, was a "typical Bedouin in appearance." Though it is not exactly clear what the paper meant, the reference to a Bedouin appearance played on a whole host of stereotypes from American literature, drama, and circus culture that depicted Arabs as nomadic, robe-wearing, camel-driving, tent-dwelling people of the desert. There were actually very few Bedouins in the parts of Ottoman Syria from which Syrian South Dakotans emigrated. Most of them had lived in or around small towns in what today is Lebanon; their villages had more sheep and goats than camels. But most Americans in 1912 had never met a Bedouin, much less an Arabic-speaking person. Stereotypes of Arabs loomed much larger in the US culture than actual Arab people did. And Arabs themselves were employed to play stereotyped Arab caricatures in circuses and fairs, including the 1893 Columbian Exposition in Chicago, which featured an Egyptian tableau vivant. In dramatic performances, novels, and travelogues, what was called the Muslim Orient was often depicted as a place of sexual fantasy where men kept their women in harems, protected their honor at all costs, and otherwise spent the day smoking tobacco through a water pipe. The Muslim Orient was also seen as a land of despotism, religious fervor, and personal vendettas.[30]

This stereotyping, sometimes called orientalism, was a significant aspect of intellectual, religious, and cultural life in Sioux Falls. As in other cities, there were various orientalist entertainments. One was silent movies. In 1914 the Olympic Theater played *The Mohammedan's Conspiracy*.[31] Starring James Cruze and Flo La Badie, the Thanhouser-produced film brought to screen a version of the magazine serial "Adventures of a Diplomatic Free Lance" by Clarence Herbert New. The plot revolved around an Egyptian conspiracy to poison the food supply of the country's British occupiers by putting deadly germs in their water supply. The female English heroine poses as a young male Egyptian fruit seller to investigate the plot but is found out. Fortunately, she is saved by her faithful Indian Muslim servant, Abdul.[32] As with contemporary Hollywood films about Muslim terrorists in the late twentieth and early twenty-first centuries, *The Mohammedan's Conspiracy* valorized a saviorlike Muslim figure who helped to save white people from the threat posed by other Muslims. There was also plenty of laughter to be had at the natives' expense. Overall the film taught its audiences that their fears of the Muslim mob—or hordes, as the *Argus-Leader* referred to them—were justifiable. They were not to be trusted.

The *Sioux Falls Argus-Leader* also regularly reported on Muslim affairs abroad, expressing concern about Muslim violence and women's oppression.[33] This topic had a ready audience among Christians in Sioux Falls who felt called to bring the gospel to Muslims and to convert them. "Women's societies that supported Christian missions were extremely popular at this time," according to Modupe Labode. "Christian magazines and slide shows fueled popular knowledge of the Balkans and Western Asia."[34] These media reproduced the stereotypes about Islam and Muslims with which many in Sioux Falls were already familiar. Other press coverage of Muslims was fairly sophisticated; Muslim politics in Turkey, India, China, Morocco, Russia, Malaya, and other countries were analyzed in ways that paid attention to local, national, and international contexts. When Theodore Roosevelt visited Egypt in 1910, the newspaper printed the spirited criticism of Egypt's Constitutional Reform League directed at Roosevelt's paternalistic attitudes toward Egyptians, whom he argued were better off being colonized by Europeans.[35] One article also recognized Muslim attempts to preserve various cultural practices against the onslaught of European colonialism, as when it compared the case of Gambian Muslims resisting trousers to Scottish people holding fast to the kilt.[36] But even as news coverage explained how European colonialism had affected Muslims in Africa and Asia, Muslim violence or "fanaticism" was persistently presented as an expression of Islamic belief, that is, as a natural outcome of practicing Islamic religion. Such lazy thinking made it seem as if Muslims were somehow under the spell of their religion when, in truth, Muslims were like other religious people. They used their religion as a resource for responding to their needs, which often had little to do with political violence.[37]

The most quoted Sioux Falls Christian pastor on all things Islamic was First Congregational Church's Dr. Frank Fox, a graduate of Valparaiso University and Chicago Theological Seminary who was also active in a number of Masonic lodges. He brought hundreds of new members to his church and oversaw the construction of a new church building. In 1910, his congregation sent him to the "Holy Land" for a sabbatical. Relying on his ethnographic observations and history books, Dr. Fox sought to show the superiority of his faith over all others.[38] One of his sermon series, entitled "The Mohammedan in History," shared basic facts from Islamic history while also repeating many well-worn stereotypes about Islam. According to Fox, Muslims were pleasure-seeking "hordes" who relied on the sword to spread their religion.[39] Islam was a "menacing" and potent presence.[40] Over and over again, he faulted Islam for assigning "a degraded place to womanhood," which evidenced how much the religion was "a failure and a curse to the human race."[41] He claimed that "Mohammed let loose the beast in man; and all the cruelties of the battlefield cannot equal those of the Mohammedan harems."[42]

Such negative views of Muslims likely shaped the way that other South Dakotans, many of whom were also born in a foreign country, treated their Syrian "Mohammedan" neighbors. At the least, they didn't help. And young Syrian men sometimes fought back against both verbal and physical attacks. When Joe Chamie (also spelled Shammie), a Syrian Muslim youth, was arrested in 1912 for fighting, it exposed what the *Argus-Leader* characterized as persistent "friction" between "young Americans" and "young Syrians." Chamie had come to the United States with a number of other family members from the village of Qaraoun, located today in Lebanon's Bekaa Valley. A lot of the Syrian Muslims who came to the Midwest were from the Bekaa Valley, and, like many others, they sometimes emigrated in small groups of family members or friends. It was like that for the Chamies. In 1907, Joe lived with Samuel Chamie and Hassan Chamie at Mahomet and Sadie Chamie's dry goods store on 219 West Sixth Street.[43] When he appeared in court five years later, Chamie told the judge that a group of Americans had "pitched onto him." His choice was "to fight or be terribly beaten up." He chose to "protect himself, which was every man's right." But the paper noted that, despite his efforts, young Chamie, who would later serve in Company I, 361st Infantry, 91st Division of the American Expeditionary Forces (AEF) in World War I, "looked as if he had been considerably beaten." An unnamed Syrian elder accompanied young Joe to court and told the judge that the "time had come when it must be decided whether or not a Syrian has any rights in this city." This man said that "life here had become too much of burden for his people." The community had the "money to back a fight to a finish, and the matter must be settled some way or another." The newspaper was sympathetic, hoping that "some degree of understanding may be reached where the disgraceful occurrences of the past may be stopped."[44]

It was not the only time that an important institution of the Sioux Falls establishment would side with Syrians against anti-Syrian violence. In 1914, Syrian storekeeper Hasson Bolles (also spelled Hassan Ballas) was attacked in his own grocery store on 723 North Main by a "small boy" and his "slightly larger brother." Bolles was charged in the altercation. In municipal court, the judge heard testimony that the small boy had "called Bolles out." The boy threatened to "show him [Bolles] how the white hopes to do it." Such a comment revealed the extent to which Syrians were not always accepted as white people. The judge let Bolles go and demanded the white youth, who was unnamed in the article, appear in juvenile court.[45]

Some leaders in Sioux Falls advocated including Syrians and other foreign-born people in their definition of American national identity. During World War I, as xenophobia and anti-immigrant violence were on the rise, the *Sioux Falls Argus-Leader* endorsed a definition of "true Americanism" that included many of the ethnic groups that had colonized South Dakota. Commenting on a speech delivered by Rev. A. P. James at a meeting of a powerful veterans' group, the Grand Army of the Republic, the paper called it "one of the best addresses ever given on a patriotic theme in this state." In his talk, James said that the unity of different races and regions of the country would allow the country to face any challenge. America was "one people, one flag, one country, one constitution, one destiny." The nation's strength came from people of different ancestries, including "Englishmen, Germans, Swedes, Holland-ers, Syrians, Italians," Jews, and Slavs.[46] It is telling that the Reverend James named neither Native nor Black people in his litany of American racial or ancestral groups. His notion of unity was still basically white— whiteness was just expanded to include Syrians and Jews.

Assimilation into the American mainstream is often associated with the disappearance of ethnic particulars—the language, the dress, the food, the religion, and other aspects of culture that might set a group apart from the shared English-language popular culture of the United States. One need only tune in to certain contemporary media channels or drop into a Facebook conversation to see the potency of this "com-mon sense." But this conventional wisdom does not explain how Syrian Muslims assimilated to US culture. Something else was going on in the upper Midwest and other parts of the United States, too. Syrians, like Norwegians, Swedes, Germans, Poles, Bohemians, Jews, and many oth-ers, often publicly celebrated their ethnic and religious heritage as a way to participate in American life.[47] Syrian ethnicity and Islamic religion became pathways to becoming American, and being an American was not necessarily seen as antithetical to maintaining one's ethnic and reli-gious ties to people outside the United States.[48]

Alex and Fatima Ogdie's household demonstrated how one could be both Syrian and American at the same time and how these identities were often complementary. The Ogdies consciously preserved various elements of Arab culture. For example, according to Aliya, there were no chairs in the house. The family made its own pillows and divans, which sat close to the floor. Everyone was required to take off their shoes in the living room. Aliya's father also emphasized the values of Arab hospital-ity. Once she let someone from a rival Arab family come into the house and offered him food and drink. When her father came home, he told the startled man, "Don't fear. You have eaten our bread and salt. You are safe." After taking the man into town, her father told Aliya, "You have done right. Never forget you are Arab. Never will an Arab refuse to help a person in need, even an enemy. You could not with honor have refused." Fatima, who covered her head with a lace cap, was generally in charge since Alex was on the road so much. The children were told not to "talk back to adults or contradict a parent." When an Arab guest arrived, they were directed to "kiss the back of their hand and say, 'Ahlan wa Sahlan [welcome].'" But many of the lessons were indistinguishable from other Americans' notions of etiquette, child discipline, and gender norms. Her brothers were instructed to remove or tip their cap when passing a lady on the street. It was a "yes, ma'am" and "no, ma'am" house, and "children stood when an adult entered a room" and remained standing until the adult sat. Corporal punishment helped to enforce such rules. "The strap was always handy," she said. The children had a long list of chores to complete. Aliya's mother taught her to sew, cook, and can foods. Aliya also walked to school. But Syrian children, like all children, negotiated with their parents. Aliya's mother was strict. Her father was the easy one. He would let Aliya go to dances, which would make her mother angry. Her mother made her cover her hair when she went out in public, but Aliya would just take the cover off after leaving the house.[49]

No doubt some Syrian Muslims resisted elements of US culture, but many others did not. For most, there was no war between the old ways and the new ways. Yes, the American-born children of Syrian-born parents sometimes found their mothers and fathers to be hopelessly devoted to the past, but this is hardly a Syrian thing—children of many backgrounds thought their parents were too old-fashioned. The identities of Syrians, both young and old, were complex and multiple. Like the Irish and the Germans, Syrians developed an ethnic identity and a sense of group solidarity in the United States that gave them the power they needed to exercise their rights as Americans.

The incorporation of self-consciously ethnic and religious practices in daily life was not confined to the privacy of the family home, either. In the early twentieth-century United States, there was no better way of performing and displaying your ethnic and religious identity in public than joining a parade. On July 4, 1916, the Muslim community of Sioux Falls "staged what was probably the most novel parade and celebration ever seen on the streets of Sioux Falls," according to the *Sioux Falls Argus-Leader*. Approximately sixty "Mohammedan Syrians" hoisted both Syrian and US flags into the air as they "marched through the business district of the city under the leadership of Deeb Hossine and [Mo] hammed Yusif, who, as gladiators, gave a remarkable exhibition of sword fighting." Sword fighting was a martial art popular in many parts of the Ottoman Empire—and one in which Alex Ogdie was said to have been trained. Describing it as more complicated than regular fencing, one reporter marveled at how, on another occasion, "the contestants struck savagely at each other from all directions, but each thrust, no matter whether aimed at the head or the feet, in front or behind, was skillfully parried in regular order."[50] The citizens of Sioux Falls were impressed not only with the swordsmanship display, but also with the group's music and dancing. Carrying musical instruments and drums, other Syrian Muslims accompanied the swordsmen as they paraded toward the Minnehaha County Courthouse. They stopped at the imposing edifice, a large, three-story Romanesque building with too many arched windows to count and a six-story clock tower built of quartzite stone. That year, Norwegian American artist Ole Running was busy painting sixteen large murals inside the building, which also contained "slate stairs, granite pillars, stained glass windows, and tiled fireplaces."[51] Once in front of the courthouse, the Syrian Muslims played more music, and performed "old country dances." According to the newspaper, there was a large crowd on hand to cheer.[52]

The organization responsible for the parade was a Syrian lodge called Bedr-El-Moneer, or "The Full Moon."[53] Its leader was Hossine Abu-Deeb (Assin Bo Deeb), who went by Charles H. Deeb in the 1916 Sioux Falls city directory; Abu-Deeb was a crusher employed by Wisconsin Granite Company and lived on 431 Weber Avenue, the same street on which the Ogdie family lived.[54] The vice president was Alec

Sarhan and Sam Hesham was its secretary. Just a few months before it staged the parade, the organization submitted an application to the state government in Pierre for a charter. It claimed to be the first lodge for Syrians in the state and in the paper was named "Hajeryt Ahan Buoder Almaner of Sioux Falls." Its members were asked to "wear an emblem showing the clasped hands of fraternity surmounted by the crossed flags of the Syrian and American people." The largely Muslim religious identity of its membership was known, as the article from the *Argus-Leader* made clear, but its primary purpose, at least in its article of incorporation, was not explicitly religious. This was, instead, an organization designed to integrate Syrians and Syrian identity into American culture. It would "promote acts of charity and benevolence" and, just as importantly, help Syrian immigrants become "desirable, intelligent and law-abiding citizens of the United States of America." In order to do so, the lodge would educate them "in American ways" and make them "competent to exercise the right of ballot." It would also instruct "the children of our countrymen to attend the public schools, to the end that they may be educated as American children are educated, in order that they may become intelligent and useful citizens of our adopted country."[55] The Syrian Muslims of Sioux Falls wanted to make it perfectly clear to the state government that they would not be forming their own schools like Roman Catholics often did. They would join the Protestants instead.

There was a fear among many Americans in 1916, as in the post-9/11 era, that the cultures of Muslims, like those of Catholic and Jewish immigrants, were incompatible with American culture. Some believed, wrongly, that Syrians would refuse to integrate. In 1916, the Muslim enemy of America was "the Turk," specifically the Ottoman Empire, which was allied to the Central Powers of Germany and Austria-Hungary. Syrian Muslims in South Dakota, as elsewhere in the United States, were rightfully afraid that they would be seen as "Turks." For example, one letter to the editor about the founding of the lodge complained that the paper was wrong to identify the "Mohammedan" community as Syrian. "I see in Tuesday evening's Argus-Leader that a lodge of Syrians has been formed in this city," the writer stated. "To tell the truth, this is not a Syrian, but a Turkish Mohammedan lodge."[56]

But by 1917, there was awareness, at least on the part of some in Sioux Falls, that Arabs had joined the British in the Great Arab Revolt against the Ottoman Empire and the German "Kaiser." Reprinted from the *Kansas City Star*, "Why the Holy War Failed" offered analysis of why Arabs had joined the British in the revolt rather than support the Ottoman government's call for "jihad" against the Allies.[57] The paper attributed such Arab feelings to the superior colonial rule of the British, but in reality, Arabs were casting their lot with the Allies because they thought it was their best chance to establish independent Arab nation-states. Aliya Ogdie Hassen said that "the Syrians thought that World War I would get rid of the Turks from Syria."[58] As the war raged on, American philanthropists called desperately for aid to Armenian and Syrian refugees, who were seen as sympathetic victims. Just a dollar "would keep a Syrian or Armenian alive for one week," said the *Argus-Leader*.[59]

There was surely some danger in bringing attention to oneself and one's community as Syrian and Muslim. But whatever fear there was, some Syrian Muslim South Dakotans decided to face it by seeking public recognition of their identities. For them, this was no time to hide; it was a time to assert themselves as Americans. In addition to claiming their religious identity on the 1915 state census and parading in front of the courthouse, Muslims reported their religious identity when they were admitted to the local McKennan Hospital. In 1916, the hospital had 1,070 admits. Fourteen of them said that they had been born in Syria; thirteen were classified as "Mohammedan."[60]

In 1917, everyone in Sioux Falls became painfully aware of what could happen if you opposed the war or just tried to avoid it. That year, the US Congress passed the Espionage Act, which did much more than punish spies. It also made it possible for the federal government to prosecute and imprison people for up to twenty years if they made any statement that encouraged Americans to refuse military service, otherwise "obstructed" the enlistment of soldiers, or made any statement that interfered with the success of the US military.[61] The next year, the US Congress passed a set of even more draconian amendments to the law referred to as the Sedition Act, which punished "any disloyal, profane, scurrilous, or abusive language about the form of government of the United States, or the Constitution of the United States, or the flag of the United States."[62] Despite the fact that the law clearly violated the First Amendment's guarantee of free speech, it was upheld as constitutional by the Supreme Court in *Schenck v. United States* (1919). The prosecution of the law had a grave impact on all German Americans, who were the "nation's largest foreign group and nearly half of South Dakota's white population."[63] In Sioux Falls, newspaper editor Conrad Kornmann was convicted by a jury of his peers for writing personal letters that were critical of US government propaganda. The government relied on the propaganda since many Americans were not yet ready to support the US entering the Great War on the side of the Entente, which included Great Britain, France, and Russia. Kornmann's letters were written before the passage of the Espionage Act, leading the Supreme Court to throw out the conviction. But the damage to his reputation was irreparable. His newspaper failed, he was forced to sell his farm, and he left the state.[64] German Americans who were members of pacifist Christian communities such as the Amish and Hutterites were also prosecuted for refusing to serve in the armed forces; some them died while imprisoned in Fort Leavenworth, Kansas.[65]

The smaller Syrian community of Sioux Falls had a different point of view on the whole. In addition to freeing the land of their birth from what they called Turkish rule, supporting the US war effort provided a path toward citizenship and political status in the United States. There was enthusiasm for joining the war. The "Syrian Colony is very patriotic," declared the *Argus-Leader* on June 21, 1918. The colony "contributed liberally of its men to help swell Uncle Sam's army." At least eighteen

Syrian youths joined the AEF. Aliya Ogdie Hassen remembered that "everyone talked about the war, the mustard gas, the massacres, the Russian revolution. The young boys would say that they would soon be old enough to fight."[66] Hammas Swiden, one of the Ogdies' neighbors, was one of them. The Haggar family, who had at least four boys in service, feted recent recruits with a picnic supper at Lien Park and entertained their families on other occasions. The Syrian colony's contributions to the war efforts also included their purchase of war bonds and support of thrift stamps. The *Argus-Leader* made a point that the community was both Christian and Muslim; it referred to Muslims as "Mohammed religionists" in the article on Syrian American patriotism.[67] Eighty-six members of the community, including Alex Ogdie, donated $539.50 to the Red Cross.[68]

Joe Chamie, the Syrian Muslim who was beaten up by a couple of white kids when he was twelve, made the ultimate sacrifice for his adopted homeland. Chamie was in his late twenties and working as a farmhand when he registered for the draft.[69] He declared his intention to become a US citizen, and a 1918 change in US law meant that, by serving in the military, his wish would be granted. On July 2, 1918, Chamie was made a US citizen at Camp Merritt in Bergen, New Jersey.[70] On July 6, just a few days later, Private Chamie shipped out on the *Scotian* from New York as part of the AEF.[71] As his next of kin, Chamie listed his uncle Mehmed Chamie, who lived a block away from the Ogdies.[72] According to the Red Cross, Private Chamie was wounded in battle on September 29. Just three days earlier, the 91st Division had begun its assault on the German army as part of the Meuse-Argonne offensive, one of the deadliest campaigns in US military history. General John J. Pershing commanded over one million US troops in the campaign. More than twenty-six thousand of them lost their lives. The 361st Infantry, like other units, was charged with trying to take German trenches. The problem was that, to do so, soldiers had to traverse "several hundred yards of mud, debris, shell holes, tangle foot and concertina wire" as they charged German machine gun nests.[73] Private Chamie was hit in the leg. He received care at an American hospital, but it may have taken some time before he was given medical attention. Because of a German artillery barrage, it was impossible to evacuate all of the wounded until September 30.[74]

Chamie did not recover. According to his grave marker, he died on October 17, 1918. He was "buried with full military honors," wrote Genevieve Swezey, Red Cross casualty researcher. "The coffin was covered with the American flag and flowers given by the American Red Cross were placed on the grave. After the chaplain had read the prayers the firing squad fired three volleys and the bugler sounded the last 'taps' while all the soldiers present stood at salute." His burial place, she said, was "located on a lovely hillside, overlooking a quiet French village." This was the Meuse-Argonne American Cemetery, located near Romagne-sous-Montfaucon, about sixty miles from the northeast French border with Luxembourg. "The spot seems an ideal one for our American boys, who have fought so bravely in this world war for democracy," Swezey wrote. "He was laid to rest with others, who also had made the supreme sacrifice."[75] Such memorialization, a common rhetorical trope since President Abraham Lincoln's Gettysburg Address, placed a Syrian Muslim at the heart of the American story, interpreting the spilling of his blood as a sacrifice that made the life of the nation possible. Even as his body was laid to rest in foreign soil, his memory was repatriated in his new nation. The public recognition of this Syrian Muslim's sacrifice for America was not seen in Sioux Falls as the act of an outsider. Joe Chamie was one of "our boys."

Except for one thing. As the dead were buried, all service members except for Jews received a Christian cross as their grave marker. To this day, Joe Chamie's body is buried underneath a cross.[76] Joe Chamie was a Muslim. He grew up in a Muslim family, and as an adult he remained Muslim—the 1915 South Dakota state census said so. But the US Army did not allow service members to identity as Muslims. The fact that Joe Chamie's body lies under this Christian symbol erases the embodied sacrifice of this Muslim killed in action for America. No one passing by his grave today would know that he was Muslim.

FIGURE 1.2. Joe Hassan Chamie was a Muslim who fought and died for the United States, but he is buried underneath a cross. Credit: FindAGrave.com.

This is why it is so important to unearth this buried past. We Midwesterners have become invisible to ourselves. To rediscover the diversity of our origins, we must adopt the mindset of an archaeologist. Instead of seeking adventure abroad like the fictional Indiana Jones, however, we must assume that the evidence of our shared past is hidden in plain sight, right beneath our feet, in the heartland.

2

Homesteading Western North Dakota

It could get cold in Bire (pronounced "Bee-reh"), located about twenty-five miles west of Damascus, Syria. In January, the average temperature was a little above 45 degrees Fahrenheit (8 degrees Celsius). At night the mercury might sometimes go below freezing. January was also the rainy month, and the town's nine inches (230 mm) of precipitation could get in your bones and stay there until the spring warmup. But that kind of cold was nothing compared to the winters of Ross, North Dakota, located in the northwestern part of the state. In 1903, the year after Sam Omar filed his claim on a 160-acre homestead, there were three days in February, February 14, 15, and 16, when the low temperatures were −35 Fahrenheit (−37 Celsius), −46 Fahrenheit (−43 Celsius), and −42 Fahrenheit (−41 Celsius). The average high temperature that month would have been something like 22 Fahrenheit (−6 Celsius), while the average low was about 0 Fahrenheit (−18 Celsius).[1] Snowstorms could be dangerous, as one Syrian immigrant learned in January 1911, when he went out to fetch a pail of water and lost his way. The man wandered for hours, and had he not stumbled his way to someone else's shack, "no doubt [he] would have frozen to death."[2]

Growing up in Bire, located in the temperate Bekaa Valley now part of the Republic of Lebanon, Sam Omar helped his father on what Sam remembered was a 120-acre farm. They grew wheat, much of which was made into flour and sold at market; barley, which was used to feed farm animals and also sold at market; and "lentils, which were raised for home use." Cows or oxen would haul the wooden plow that split the ground. "Seeding was done by hand," said Sam, and "we harvested with a scythe." It was then time for threshing, separating the grain from the rest of the plant. This was also done without any machine, sometimes by "trampling the straw." When Sam was old enough, he went out on his own, and rented some land to farm. He spent a few years as a tenant farmer before deciding to come the United States.[3]

"I came to America because I received letters from friends that were in Michigan, North Dakota, and New York," Sam later remembered. "They all said that America was the land of opportunity. They said that land was free and plentiful." So, in the spring of 1902, friends and family in Bire gave a "big farewell party in honor of those leaving." Sam, who was twenty years old, joined Muhammad Taha and Husayn Yousef and boarded a ship in Beirut, the port from which so many Syrians would leave for the Americas. "We took a French boat to France," said Sam, "and crossed the Atlantic on a German boat." Sam said that "the food was good on these boats but the sleeping quarters were close." He recalled that "twenty to thirty men slept in one room which was equipped with double deck beds." His ship for the transatlantic journey was the *Pennsylvania*, a Hamburg America Line steam-powered ocean liner launched from Belfast, Ireland, in 1896. It could carry more than twenty-five hundred passengers, though most of those, as Sam noted, were sardined together in third class. Sam endured the journey from Boulogne-Sur-Mer in France without getting sick, and arrived in New York on May 22, 1902.[4]

New York was impressive—"everything looked so new," Sam remarked. But the young men from Bire had a plan, and they soon departed. "We took a train to Grand Rapids, Michigan, and visited with Syrian friends for about ten days," said Sam, and "then came to North Dakota." Sam, who was described on his immigration papers as a brown-eyed, black-haired, and dark-skinned white man about five feet, six inches tall, 160 pounds, first worked around Fessenden, near the middle of the state. He immediately declared his intention to become a US citizen, renouncing his allegiance to the Ottoman sultan, Abdul Hamid II. He also declared, as required, that he was not an anarchist or a polygamist. The important thing to Sam was to get to work. Farm laborers were paid good wages, he said, for haying, threshing, and shocking, which involved harvesting grains such as wheat, tying the crop in bundles, and then stacking the bundles next to one another so that they could dry.[5]

Sam Omar joined 250,000 other pioneers who came to North Dakota from 1898 to 1915. During those years, railroad mileage in the state increased from 2,662 to 5,226 miles.[6] The Great Northern Railway, which ran through Ross, was responsible for bringing tens of thousands of settlers like Sam to the western part of state.[7] Having invested tens of millions in their infrastructure, the railroads engaged in nationwide advertising that helped to create a frenzy, news of which reached Syrians through their social and business networks. The number of people and farms in western North Dakota quadrupled from 1900 to 1910 with little regard to whether the land could actually sustain that many people. Homesteaders were told by agricultural experts, often supported by the railroads, that if they used what was called "dry farming" techniques they could unlock the potential of the earth and raise bountiful crops. The secret, it was said, was in plowing deep enough to release moisture in the subsoil. The theory was incorrect, but the promise was enough to bring people west.[8]

There were four daily trains—two eastbound and two westbound—in and out of Ross.[9] By 1910, there were 298 people living in Ross Township proper, and 22 of them were either born in Syria or were the children of those who were; these families included names like Farhat, Bahnes, Alley, Caled, Ally, Abdallah, Salem, Abdalla, and Sadeen. Other Syrian families, like the Omars, lived in adjacent townships.[10] Across western North Dakota, Syrians, both Christians and Muslims, filed hundreds of homestead claims, especially in Pierce, Williams, and Mountrail counties. For a ten-dollar filing fee, a homesteader could stake a claim to 160 acres of land; by 1912, they could obtain 320 acres.[11] In order to keep it, that is, to gain a deed to the land, the claimant had to "prove up," generally meaning that he or she would have to spend five years on the homestead, build a house of some kind, and farm it in some way. Not every Syrian wanted to be a farmer, but if you proved up, you could then sell your land for hundreds, even thousands of dollars.[12] That is exactly how

Hassyn Alla Juma saw it: "What I wanted to do was get rich in a hurry and return to Syria," he said. "I hired a man to break and sow the land for me, and also hired someone to harvest and thresh. I have never done any of my own farm work."[13] But Sam Omar, who had farming in his blood, was different. Sam was allotted two 80-acre tracts that were perpendicular to one another. Just two decades before, Sam's land had been in the legal possession of the Mandan, Gros Ventre, and Arikara nations. But on July 13, 1880, President Rutherford B. Hayes issued an executive order that cancelled their titles to the land. In 1891, the US Congress legalized this cession, and then the land was surveyed and parceled into homesteads the very same year that Sam arrived in the United States.[14]

Sam was one of at least seventy-one Syrians who eventually applied for a homestead in Mountrail County.[15] Most of them were Muslim. In fact, the Mountrail County town of Ross would come to be called North Dakota's "Muslim colony." As in South Dakota, the majority of the thousand or more Syrian-born people who came to North Dakota before World War I were Christians, but hundreds of Muslims also arrived in the state. Perhaps 30 percent of all Syrians in North Dakota were Muslims, a proportion similar to that reflected in the 1915 South Dakota state census.[16] Among those who, like Sam Omar, filed a homestead claim in the early 1900s were: "Mose Hamid, Albert Mustafa, Joseph Forbite, Hassin Juma, Abdul Rahmen, Hassin Farhart, Gosman Omar, Mahmed Sadden, Albert Salem, Charles Salem, Abdula Mosfa, Hamid Hassin, Hassen Merrik, Hasian Dorosq, Side Abdallah, Abdella Adray, Faya Iish, Abdel Allie, Amid Assem Juha, [and] Jaja Allie Juha."[17]

Sam Omar's original homestead claim, filed in Minot, North Dakota, on March 24, 1903, was issued under the name Hcsien Aomar. To make things even more confusing, Sam actually began to farm the wrong land—it was sometimes hard to figure out exactly which part of the prairie belonged to you. Your closest neighbor was often so far away that you did not know where your land stopped and that person's land started. So, in 1904, Sam filed paperwork with the US Land Office to amend the name under which the claim had been filed and to clarify exactly which tracts of land he was farming. He pointed out that he did not write or speak enough English to understand or make himself understood when he filed the original claim. In 1905, his claim was amended.[18]

In the meantime, Sam got to work. He erected a simple, ten-by-twelve-foot lumber-framed house on his land, which was located about two miles south of town. It had one door, one window, and a floor made of tar-papered boards.[19] During this period, the majority of homesteaders in North Dakota, many of whom were claiming land in the western part of the state, were building their first homes out of lumber. Side Abdallah, for example, said that his "first home was a one-room, 12 x 14 [feet], frame shack." This type of house construction represented an important change in how most settlers in North Dakota lived. In 1870, most new houses built on homesteads were built with logs. As the number of immigrants, especially from Russia and Scandinavia, increased in the 1880s, however, more homes were built out of sod—these earthen homes were often most effective for keeping out the unbearably cold winds on the Great Plains. Plus, sod was cheap and abundant on the prairie. But as lumber became increasingly available, more and more settlers decided to build simple frame houses. "Cheap lumber from the pine forests of Wisconsin and Minnesota, milled in St. Louis and shipped west by rail, could be had in every hamlet that was served by a railroad," wrote Norman Risjord. "A settler could purchase an assortment of 2x4 studs, 2x6 rafters, 1x6 boards, a few rolls of tar paper, and some nails; haul these materials to his claim; and erect a shack in a few days, often using wood or even tarred paper to build their walls."[20] They could choose different colors of tar paper—black, red, or blue, which was the most expensive. The space between the outside walls and tar paper was the house's only insulation. These structures, which were meant to be temporary housing, were freezing in the winter, and on Sam Omar's land there were few natural barriers to block the winds and the snow blowing across the plain. But the advantage of such dwellings was that they could be easily dismantled and their lumber used for building a house elsewhere. Many of them looked like covered wagons, since their roofs were arched rather than gabled.[21]

Sitting about twenty-four hundred feet above sea level, Sam Omar's homestead was part of the Missouri Plateau, "a rugged, open country stretching away to the Rocky Mountains." It was in the semiarid part of the state that could suffer from long periods of drought.[22] The Missouri River formed the southwestern boundary of Sam Omar's county. His 160 acres were grasslands. A little over a hundred years after Sam moved there, this area of North Dakota rose to national attention because of an oil boom made possible by the hydraulic fracturing of shale that was formed millions of years ago in the Williston Basin.

But Sam would not be lucky enough to strike oil. He would earn his living in a more arduous fashion. "I soon bought a team of horses, a walking plow, and a drill," which is the farm implement used to make a slot in the ground for seeds.[23] Sometimes, homesteaders like Hassyn Alla Juma would hire others to bust the sod—that is, to remove the thick layer of prairie grass and other vegetation on the land. But not Sam: "I broke the land myself, and put in my first crop with the plow and drill." Since he did not own the all the equipment he needed, however, he "hired someone to cut the crop for me and thresh it."[24]

By 1906, Sam Omar was cultivating forty-five acres. In the autumn of that year, he filed his intention with the federal Land Office to make "final proof in support of his claim." Rather than waiting the full five years, homesteaders like Sam were allowed to apply for the commutation of their full term. In order to do so, two witnesses would testify that the claimant was living on his or her homestead and was actually using the land for agricultural purposes. Sam paid $1.50 per acre for each of his 160 acres. The next year, on August 13, 1907, the acting recorder of the US General Land Office issued land patents for two eighty-acre tracts to Sam Omar. President Theodore Roosevelt's stamped signature was appended at the bottom of the document.[25]

Like others in his area, Sam farmed wheat. It was the king crop of North Dakota: "From 1898 to 1915 the acreage planted to wheat doubled, going from 4,300,000 acres to 9,400,000; and production rose from 69,000,000 bushels to 159,000,000." This made North Dakota the leading producer of wheat in the United States at the time.[26] Farmers generally planted Red Fife or Scotch Fife, a glutinous, hard-grained spring wheat, but by the time Syrians began to farm there, durum wheat was also sown. Thought to be less susceptible to drought and disease than Red Fife, varieties of durum wheat also produced better yields. The only problem with durum wheat was that it was less glutinous, better suited for making noodles than bread.[27] Though wheat accounted for more than 60 percent of all agricultural wealth in North Dakota, farmers also grew significant amounts of flax, barley, hay, and oats, which were sometimes fed to the horses.[28]

In addition to using a plow and drill, some Syrians purchased a drag, an implement with iron teeth that would cultivate the ground after it was plowed; it would smooth and level the seedbed. They also used a disc harrow that would loosen the ground, break up chunks, or plow under weeds or the remains of a harvest, and a binder, an implement that cut and then tied together stalks of wheat.[29] This is how Boaley (Abu 'Ali) Farhat farmed his land.[30] Like others in Ross, Farhat came from Rafid (pronounced "Rah-feed"), which was located just south of Sam Omar's hometown, Bire. Both Rafid and Bire were located on the eastern side of the Anti-Lebanon Mountains, also known as the Eastern Mountains. Farhat's father was a farmer, and back in Rafid, they "seeded about twenty acres of wheat, ten acres of oats, and ten acres of snova [perhaps, snobar, or pine nuts] and beans." They also raised livestock. As a young boy, Farhat "herded goats and sheep" for his family. "We had five or six cows, two or three oxen, one horse, one hundred and fifty goats and sheep, fifty or sixty chickens, and one donkey." The donkey was used, he said, to carry "cheese, butter, and leben [yogurt]." Farhat came to America for economic opportunity. "I had thoughts of becoming rich and returning to Syria to live in luxury for the rest of my life," he remembered. His mother paid for his trip, and like hundreds of thousands of Syrian emigrants, he headed first for Latin America, not the United States. "I stayed for two years and went broke," Farhat said. But his brother helped him out, sending him seventy dollars so that Farhat could join him in North Dakota. The trip from Costa Rica to New York took sixteen days, and then Farhat headed for Ross. He filed a homestead claim for 160 acres, which he would own by 1911, and built a "10 x 12 feet frame shack." Farhat raised cattle and sheep, and he purchased five horses and tilled the ground with a sulky plow, which looks a little like the cart used in harness racing. Pulled by a horse, the farmer sits above the single-blade plow, turning up perhaps fourteen to sixteen inches of soil at a time.[31] The use of such equipment meant that Syrian farmers were adjusting to different ways of raising wheat and other crops in western North Dakota. Whatever language barriers were present, they learned how to farm the grasslands.

Another homesteader from Rafid who mastered the new farming techniques was Mike Abdallah—who for much of his life also went by the first name of Ahmid and sometimes Amid. He, too, adjusted to the demands of farming in North Dakota. In Syria, he worked for his father until "I was full grown man" before setting out on his own. "For seven years, I farmed for myself in the Old Country." He planted crops on "about forty acres, with a team of oxen" that pulled a "wooden plow equipped with an iron lay." He would plant his winter wheat in August and then put in a spring crop in April. When it came to the "seeding, reaping, and threshing, I had to do [that] by hand," Abdallah said. It was "very hard to make a living." Farmers living in Syria had little control over the international agricultural markets. In addition to the economic uncertainty, Abdallah worried about being forced to serve in the Ottoman army. So, in 1907, he joined other young men from the village, including Hassyn Alla Juma, and left for America. After arriving in Fargo, North Dakota, he "tried to peddle for about three months, but I couldn't make a living at that." He then went to Ashley, over 130 miles away. For three years, he worked as a farmhand "making from twenty-five to thirty dollars a month." Then, in 1911, Mike Abdallah came to Ross, and for four years, continued to work as a farm laborer. During harvest season, he made $1.25 per day threshing, separating seed from chaff. In 1915, he filed a homestead claim, and the next year he became a naturalized citizen of the United States. In 1917, he made his final proof and became owner of 240 acres outside of Ross. Even if the weather was much worse in North Dakota, the farming was much easier, he said. In the old country, "the work was very hard as everything had to be done by hand, while in this country the work was really very easy as most of it was done by machinery," he remarked, referring to the additional farm implements available to him in the United States.[32]

In addition to adopting novel agricultural technologies, some Syrians who had been farmers in the old country attempted to apply what they already knew about farming to their new environment. They had a knack for dry farming, it was said. For example, one newspaper article approved of how the Old World "Syrian peasant makes use of the moist subsoil" in raising watermelons, tomatoes, and cucumbers in a place where there was no rain during the growing season.[33] Another article, reprinted from the South Dakota papers in 1911, declared that Syrians had introduced a new crop to the region. This novelty was none other than the so-called Syrian pea, which the paper said was known as "hamus"—that is, *hummus*, the Arabic word for chickpea or garbanzo bean. Elias Rizk of South Dakota was said to have raised "forty bushels to the acre last year when it was so dry that his other crops were practically a failure." This "dry weather crop" was comparable, the paper said, to "the ordinary navy bean" and its foliage could be fed to livestock.[34] The *Argus-Leader* in Sioux Falls declared that this was a "new kind of pea grown for the first time in this country."[35]

In the second decade of the twentieth century, North Dakota sponsored a "Better Farming" campaign that sent field agents into each county, stressing the importance of crop rotation and advising farmers to raise livestock as an additional income stream.[36] This practice was adopted by some of the Syrian farmers, such as Mike Abdallah, who credited his "steadiest income" to the raising of cattle and sheep.[37] Boaley Farhat said the same thing.[38] The planting of cash crops in western North Dakota as a steady source of income depended on a range of factors over which the farmer had little control. Different tracts of lands produced very different yields even when the same techniques were applied, and there was always the possibility of drought.

But perhaps the most frustrating challenge was human-made. It was the same challenge for every small farmer of whatever ethnic background. Even if you managed to harvest a lot of wheat, you did not always get the price that you deserved. The elevators, the businesses that would purchase and store your grain, colluded with one another, often using a set purchase price that was determined not so much by the open market but by terminal operators in Minneapolis. To make matters worse, inspectors would grade your crop unfairly, often giving it a lower score and a lower price than it deserved. But when it was time for the elevator to resell that same wheat, the inspector might determine it to be of higher quality and thus fetch a higher price. And still there was more corruption. When the dust was removed from your crop, the suction draft method that was used to do so sucked away some of your grain, so, you weren't paid for everything you delivered. The elevator profited from such "waste." According to Elwyn Robinson, "in ten years the elevators at the head of Lake Superior shipped out 26,868,000 bushels more than they had received." That was grain they never paid for, taken right out of the hands of farmers. The farmers fought back. They looked for reform-minded politicians, and found one in 1906. Pro-reform Democrat John Burke won his campaign for governor by running against the railroads and other moneyed interests. Even more importantly, farmers banded together to purchase their own elevators. The privately owned elevators tried to put these cooperatives out of business by offering farmers a higher price for their crops, but most of the farmers policed themselves and were loyal to the cause. The majority of North Dakota's grain elevators remained in the hands of private owners, but by 1920, cooperatives owned one-fourth of all elevators in the state.[39]

White settlers often had no idea they would face such challenges when they arrived. What they knew was that the government was offering free homesteads. And Syrian men and women, who counted as white for this purpose, came for that land. In the next county over, Williams County, fourteen of eighty Syrian homestead claimants were women.[40] In Mountrail County, there was at least one Syrian Muslim women, Aisha Mostafa, who staked a claim.[41] Mostafa arrived in El Paso, Texas, in 1907, crossing the border with many other Syrian migrants.[42] Born around 1872, she was about thirty-five years old when she arrived in the United States. In 1909, she acquired her first sixty acres in Mountrail County.[43] On October 17, 1913, she became a naturalized US citizen there.[44] And then a year later, in 1914, she was granted an eighty-acre homestead in Cottonwood Township located immediately northwest of White Lake, a little less than seven miles from Ross.[45] Her neighbors included Mostfa Osman, Hassan Munry, Mary and Hassan Farij, and Gottlieb Biert.[46] In 1918, her son, US Army Private Raymond Hassen, would sail on the *Carpathia* as a member of North Dakota's 138th Infantry.[47]

Other women whose names were not listed on the land patents were present at the creation of the community. Before Aisha Mostafa, for example, there was Mary Juma, who traveled to the United States with her husband. Like Sam Omar, she was from Bire. She kept hearing about the "riches in America." Even though her husband, Hassan, owned a farm in Bire, it was "very small" and provided only a subsistence living. Like so many others from Bire, they decided to take a risk and joined a dozen others from the village to prepare for the journey to a new world. "We sold all our possessions," Mary Juma said later through a translator, "and borrowed two hundred dollars from a man, giving our land as collateral." Like Sam Omar, they were feted before they left. "We feasted, danced, and played games at the party." But "it was a sad farewell." Mary and Hassan were leaving behind two daughters with a maternal aunt.[48] They did not know what life would be like in America and they likely couldn't afford the passage for the whole family. They hoped to make some "awful simple" money, and return home as soon as they could. It was not unusual for family members to be cared for by relatives as Syrian migrants set out for America. That doesn't mean it wasn't hard to leave them behind.[49]

Like most others, the Jumas sailed from Beirut to France. But instead of arriving in New York, they disembarked in Montreal, Canada, around 1900. They peddled their way across Canada with "a horse and cart," but after a few months, they crossed the border and went to Nebraska in 1901. "We traveled through the entire state in a year," Mary remembered. "In 1902, we came to western North Dakota where we started to peddle."[50] The first historians of the early Arab American experience often saw peddling as the quintessential labor of Arabic-speaking immigrants. In reality, Syrian immigrants worked as unskilled laborers in a variety of places, especially in factories. The symbolism of the peddler was important to future generations, however, as Syrian and Lebanese families passed on stories of their humble beginnings, which some saw as the foundation of later entrepreneurial success. And there is no doubt that peddling was a cornerstone of Arab American economic activity. Many of the first peddlers hawked religious objects such as "rosaries, crosses, and icons" said to be blessed in the Holy Land. But as peddlers developed a rural clientele in the Midwest, clients told them that what they really needed were items such as "underwear, shorts, socks, garters, suspenders, and working gloves and hats." Female customers would ask for "powder, combs, needles, [and] thread" in addition to "jewelry, perfume, fancy scarves, picture frames, mirrors and other bric-a-brac." The peddlers also sold "hand-embroidered and crocheted linen tablecloths and covered, delicately tatted doilies and dress collars, lace-trimmed pillow cases and sheets, and ribboned dusting caps that some asserted were made in the old country."[51] Peddler packs could weigh as much as two hundred pounds, but people who could afford to do so used a horse and cart, as Mary Juma and her husband did. The horse-drawn cart allowed peddlers to offer heavier items, including Oriental rugs.

It was typical for female Syrian immigrants to peddle at one point or another; historian Alixa Naff thought that perhaps 75 to 80 percent of them did so.[52] But many middle-class Americans did not view peddling as respectable work, especially for a lady. Social workers largely opposed women's peddling, which they said was a threat to the integrity of the

Syrian immigrant family. Arab woman peddlers were deemed dangerous to themselves and to US society—their mobile lifestyle allowed
them too much sexual freedom and they were too vulnerable to sexual
violence, according to reformers.[53] It is ironic that Arab culture is often
blamed for limiting the freedom of Arab women when in the United
States it was white social workers at the turn of the century who tried
to put the Arab woman back in the home. Some opinion makers complained about the cheap stuff that female peddlers offered for sale, too.
"Who has not felt sympathy for them even while being bored by their
tedious array of miscellaneous goods?" asked the *St. Paul Globe* (Minnesota). "These little women who gather a pittance by vending showy
and insubstantial items, articles [that] have a peculiar place in the world
of commerce," the paper said. Among their wares were "a bunch of pins,
a pair of garters, a glaring red bandana, a string of beads, a pair of arm
rings or a pair of suspenders, a little red celluloid button rose, or a yard
or two of flimsy lace." It was one thing, the writer said, if the peddler was
"dark-haired, slender, pretty, and graceful." Whether walking or "squat-
ting in a charming pose," a beautiful peddler rewarded your purchase
with a "sweet smile." But if the peddler was "ugly enough," it was only
her persistence that made you "accept of their wares."[54]

Whatever prejudices there were against female peddlers in this era,
it was not enough to stop Mary Juma from hitting the road with her
husband. She was a hard worker and willing to pound the pavement,
the dusty trails, and snow-covered fields to make a living. As she was
on the road, she and her husband ran into other Syrian peddlers, and
taking a break from work, they would arrange to share a meal and talk
about their experiences. During cold winters and hot summers far away
from home, it must have brought them comfort. When Mary Juma arrived in North Dakota, however, she realized that homesteading offered
a different path. It seemed like all the Syrians were staking claims to
free or inexpensive land there. "We decided to try homesteading, too,"
she said. They obtained the services of a person called a land locator in
Minot, North Dakota, and walked along the tracks of the Great North-

ern Railway to pick out their new homestead. They paid fourteen dollars to make their claim.

Hassen and Mary invested both time and money in their homestead, eventually taking the patent, or deed, to their land on July 29, 1907. They dug a well, erected a barn, and planted some trees. They built a fourteen-by-twenty-four-foot double-boarded, wood-frame house with a shingled roof. The house was built bigger and better than your average homesteader's tar-paper shack. They borrowed money in Minot to purchase a horse, plow, drag, and a disc, and they eventually cleared and planted one hundred acres of land. Mary Juma helped to bust the sod. She helped to pull up the rocks. Then once the land was ready, they used a seed drill to plant their crop like Sam Omar did. They also kept chickens and some cattle on the farm. "We were always able to make a very good living by farming and raising livestock," she said. Like other women who lived on farms in North Dakota, Mary's labor was as much about maintaining the farm as it was about making a home. When there was a little less to do on the farm, her husband would leave to go peddling in eastern North Dakota and Minnesota. Somebody had to feed and care for the livestock and keep things going.[55]

In 1903, Mary gave birth to Charles. She called him "the first Syrian born in western North Dakota."[56] Charles grew up in Ross. Even as a young boy, he was expected to help on the farm. He plowed with a team of six horses and used the drag with a team of four horses. But he also went to school. When he was twelve, he was one of 1,454 children who attended school in Mountrail County. When Charles enrolled, he could not speak English and the other children made fun of him. "They called me all the dirty names you could think of," he still remembered in the 1970s. It took some time for him to learn English, but he kept at it. More than two-thirds of children under twenty-one years of age attended school in Ross in 1915.[57]

The school was housed in an elegant two-story building with a large basement, high ceilings, tall, rectangular windows, and a hip roof. Its façade, which included the school's main entrance, rose three stories above the ground; it featured arched windows and friezes, and was topped off by a six-arched belvedere and cupola. The *Ross Valley News* called it a "well-built, cheerful, and commodious structure."[58] The school included primary, intermediate, and high school up to the second year. In January 1915, Miss McPherson offered a primary school curriculum that, in addition to reading, writing, and arithmetic, explored the "life of the Eskimo." The irony of teaching about the lifeways of the Inuit and Yupik in the middle of the western North Dakota winter was surely not lost on some of the children. Students were also offered a manual training class. Their January 1915 assignments were to produce a dictionary stand and sand tables. The fifth graders were learning about Christopher Columbus. Seventh graders studied the history and geography of North Dakota in addition to memorizing James Russell Lowell's "The Present Crisis," a 1,005-word nineteenth-century poem about American slavery and the struggle for freedom. Physical geography final examinations were also administered that month.[59] It was partly because of this education that Charles Juma came to identify strongly as an American. But he was also Arab.

In 1917, Charles had to quit school. His father, Hassen, died and was buried with Islamic funeral prayers at the local Rose Hill Cemetery. The family was in debt. Mary and Hassen had yet to pay off the high-interest loans that they took out to purchase farm equipment and supplies. Charles and Mary asked the Citizens State Bank of Stanley to refinance the debt, but the bank advised them to take out a loan from the Federal Land Bank, which had been established in 1916 to offer cheaper credit to farmers and ranchers. With his father gone, Charles had to take over the farm. He was unable to finish the eighth grade. Mary Juma would live the rest of her life with her son, and her presence kept Charles connected to Arabic, since it was the only language she spoke.[60]

Their house was a meeting place where Syrian Muslim neighbors would stop by and socialize with one another. Many of them were from Bire or Rafid. They shared ties of memory and experience. Back in Syria, many of them had planted wheat, the same staple crop that was also planted in western North Dakota. Just like Sam Omar, they used oxen and a wooden plow, often "seeding, reaping, and threshing" by hand. In the Bekaa Valley, they had lived in houses that were not built out of lumber and tar paper, but out of stone. Their floors were made of wood poles. "A mixture of wet clay and lime was spread over the poles and branches, packed in hard, and smoothed by running a heavy roller over the floor," explained Mary Juma. "This was allowed to dry and the result was a hard floor looking like cement." The roofs were made in a similar fashion. Their memories of home included the natural environment, the mountains that surrounded the Bekaa Valley, the smooth patches of land and the rocky hills. "There were fig, plum, peach, apple, and pear trees. Grapes were in abundance, too," said another person who settled in Ross.[61] Many decades later, everyone interviewed from Rafid wistfully remembered how much better the weather was in Syria. Perhaps the memory was intensified by the passage of time and a settler's mentality that emphasized the hardships endured to make it in America. Even the snow back in Rafid felt better. "It sometimes snows a foot or more over there," said Mike Abdallah, "but still the people go bare-footed and the water under the snow feels warm as though it had been warmed on the stove for about fifteen minutes. The water on top of the ground is always warm to drink and good."[62]

In addition to the memories of sweet water and warm weather, these settlers from the Bekaa Valley shared a common language that bound them one to another. They would speak Levantine colloquial Arabic with one another, and those educated in Syria could also read and write in formal Arabic, the Arabic used in books and newspapers. Mary Juma did not know how to read or write—in Arabic or in English—but others would read to her, and she stayed informed about national and international news.

Some residents, like Boaley Farhat, subscribed to Arabic language newspapers such as *Al-Bayan*, which began publication in 1910. *Al-Bayan* was established by Druze editor Suleiman Baddur, but the newspaper included both Druze and Sunni Muslim writers. Arabic-speaking

Syrians across the Americas were linked by dozens of Arabic-language newspapers in addition to business directories and books of poetry published mainly by Christians of various sects but also by Muslims and Druze. These publications nurtured a shared identity among Syrians living in the Western hemisphere, describing news back home but also events in the New World.[63] The coverage of political events in Syria and the feelings of exile expressed in the newspapers created a sense of community and sometimes fueled conflicts among Syrian Americans. But nostalgia and concern for the old country also, perhaps ironically, nurtured the solidarity needed to survive and prosper in a new land. Ethnic identity in the United States, almost always connected to an imagined homeland overseas, is never just about one's country of origin; it is a bond of consent that builds community in the new world, too. Arabic was alive on the prairie, so much so that Charles Juma, Mary's son, who was born in North Dakota and grew up there, not only developed fluency in spoken Arabic, but spoke Arabic for the rest of his life. By the time he was eleven or twelve, he would serve as an English-Arabic interpreter, sometimes in court.[64]

These Syrian Muslims shared the bonds not only of homeland, but also of religion and food. The Juma family would join other Muslims to pray together in people's homes. Men such as Boaley Farhat, Hassyn Alla Juma, and Mike Abdallah had been tutored in reading the Qur'an and knew how to perform the Friday congregational prayers. Hassyn Alla Juma remembered that, once a year, likely during the Prophet Muhammad's birthday, he would sing a hymn of praise, or *nasheed*, to the Prophet. In both Syria and North Dakota, these Muslims also celebrated Ramadan, the month of fasting, and Eid al-Fitr, the Islamic holiday that marks the end of the sacred month. "There was a lot of feasting," Mary Juma said. For decades, they continued to make the staples of a Levantine diet, especially flatbread or pita, which many Norwegians in North Dakota thought of as a kind of lefse. When a non-Syrian woman would marry a Syrian man, it was not unusual for her to learn how to cook Levantine food.[65]

This sense of community was one reason Syrians in North Dakota managed to settle down in this place. Like Syrians in South Dakota, they were sometimes the object of racial discrimination or ethnic prejudice. It wasn't that most people were mean to them—many people were in fact helpful or sympathetic. Norwegians and Swedes, for example, were often invoked as "the most friendly people" toward Syrians. As Aliya Hassen had pointed out in South Dakota, Scandinavians were new to the country and were struggling to learn English, too. But even if most people were personally pleasant, there were still ample examples of prejudice. Mike Abdallah, who emigrated from Rafid, said that one time a crowd of people "wanted to know what nationality I was." One man asked "if I was Jewish." Mike said that he nodded no. Then, the same man asked if he was a "sheeny," an archaic epithet for Jews. Mike thought that he said "Syrian," and so he nodded yes. "Everyone laughed very hard," he said. In 1904, the *Ward County Independent* referred to the two Syrians from Ross who were accused of stealing a horse as "dusky gentlemen." Sometimes, the Syrians were called "Blackie."[66]

Syrians were immigrating to the United States during the era when systems of racial segregation were being perfected across the country. In the South, this meant a system of racial segregation that formally discriminated against Black people in all realms of life. In other parts of the country, racial segregation was sustained through a number of different strategies, including discrimination in the courts, housing, the workplace, and schools. Sometimes called the "Progressive Era" of US history, a term associated with more scientific and forward-looking government, this era was also what historian Rayford Logan dubbed the "nadir" in race relations.[67] The supremacy of white people, over and against Black people but also Asians, Indigenous, and Latinx people, was not achieved simply because some white individuals were mean to non-white individuals, but also because white people created laws, policies, and institutions that enforced their racial supremacy.[68] Among the many foundations of white supremacy was immigration policy, which was based on race. According to a 1790 law, only "free, white persons" were eligible to become naturalized US citizens. US law explicitly banned Asian people from becoming US citizens. Immigrants from East Asia, South Asia, and West Asia fought this discrimination.

The question facing Syrians was this: Were they white and thus eligible for US citizenship? Some Syrian-born people, both Christians and Muslims, had already become naturalized US citizens. And their children, by virtue of having been born in the United States, were citizens. But in 1909, as popular outcry against immigrants increased in many quarters, the US Department of Commerce and Labor said that Syrian-born people were not white, but Asiatic (that is, Asian or Oriental). From a geographic perspective, Syria was indeed located in Asia. But determining the racial identity of Syrians as Asian had far more to do with politics than with the arbitrary line that falsely separated the European peninsula from the Asian landmass (now called Eurasia). It was also about more than the skin color of Syrians—Syrians had no one skin color. Though stereotyped as olive-skinned, Syrians could also be perceived by others and themselves as porcelain white or black. The battle over the race of Syrians was instead about who would or would not be included in the ruling racial class of the United States, and various factors from geography and biology to culture and religion were used and abused at various points to litigate their whiteness.

Syrian Americans forcefully defended their white identity, which became an issue that drew together the entire Syrian diaspora in the Americas. The *Williston Graphic*, a newspaper published in a town fifty miles west of Ross, captured the martial response of Syrian American leaders in an October 14, 1909, headline: "Syrian War for Citizenship." The article reported that Syrian religious leader Rev. B. Bellama, or Father Benedict, of Minneapolis, Minnesota, was planning on bringing an immediate test case in Hennepin County Court to challenge the idea that Syrians were Asian, not white. After giving mass, the priest called on other Syrians to join the United Syrian Society of New York, which was cooperating with Ottoman Pasha Joseph Zia to defend the rights of Syrians in the United States.[69] North Dakota's *Grand Forks Evening Times* reported on November 5 that a Los Angeles Superior Court had overruled the government's contention about the race of Syrians in a naturalization case there: "The court ruled that a Syrian was not a Mongolian, but of the Aryan race and hence could not be barred from citizenship."[70] One North Dakota Syrian Christian leader garnered attention just a couple weeks later for making the same argument, adding that it was shameful that the government was banning those who came from the same land as Jesus. "If the Lord Jesus Christ . . . applied for citizenship in this country . . . would you . . . refuse him?" he asked.[71]

The timing of the decision to bar Syrians from US citizenship could not have been worse for Syrian homesteaders. In 1909, many of them had staked claims on homesteads but did not yet have the chance to "prove up." Now that they were ineligible for citizenship, they feared they would also become ineligible to take title to their land. Sam Omar had received his land patent in 1907, but many others had not. At least one person's case was now tied up. Various North Dakota officials who disagreed with the ruling were looking for ways around the problem, the newspaper made clear: "No oath or affidavit of citizenship is necessary" if officials granted "the right to commute," that is, to reduce the residency requirement from five years to fourteen months.[72] By paying $1.25 to $2.50 an acre after fourteen months' residency, it would be possible to obtain title to the land.[73]

In 1915, a federal judge ruled in *Dow v. United States* that Syrians were indeed white, and thus eligible for naturalized citizenship.[74] This decision overturned some previous court decisions, but also confirmed the racial categorization used by North Dakota on census, marriage, and death records. Still, the legal declaration that Syrians were white did not then mean that they were always treated as such. They might be singled out in US society as well as in courtrooms and other institutions as a class of people who were different, exotic, untrustworthy, violent, or criminal—a group that deserved to be carefully watched. There were literally hundreds of articles in North Dakota newspapers about Syrian North Dakotans before World War I, and many, if not most, of them associated Syrians with something negative.[75]

Syrian Muslims from Ross challenged the idea that they were disloyal to the United States through their willingness to shed their blood and the blood of their children by fighting for the country in World War I. Many knew that they were now stuck in the United States for a long time, perhaps for good. The 1915 sinking of the *Lusitania* by a German U-boat made international news. Passenger travel across the Atlantic was unsafe. Plus, these Syrians were no friend of Kaiser Wilhelm and his alliance with the Ottoman Empire. Many of the young Syrian men had come to the Americas to flee conscription into the Ottoman armed forces. Though some had hoped for a different kind of Ottoman Empire, the alliance of the Ottomans with Germany and the Ottoman centralization of power largely dashed such hopes. Syrian Americans cared about what was happening in their old homelands, and many hoped that their service would result in freedom for Greater Syria, or an independent Lebanon and Syria, or a unified state referred to as the Arab Nation.[76] Joining Americans from across the United States, they also supported the unprecedented international relief campaign to assist Syrian and Armenian war refugees. On June 4, 1916, Syrians from all parts of North Dakota met in the town of Williston "to discuss the ways and means by which to relieve and save the starving people in their old country, Syria and Lebanon in Turkey." They formed the Syrian Relief Committee and set out to raise funds.[77]

But there was another meaning, another outcome from North Dakotan Syrian participation in the war. Putting on the uniform of the American Expeditionary Forces meant fighting, side by side, with people from a variety of ethnic and national backgrounds, creating a sense of solidarity and community that had not existed before. Over thirty thousand North Dakotans, including Native peoples, served in the war. "Twenty percent of all North Dakota nurses served—a higher percentage than from any other state," according to Joseph Stuart. Dressed in white uniforms, the nurses sometimes paraded on horse-drawn floats though the streets of towns like Bismarck before shipping off to Europe. Around 270 women volunteered to go abroad, although far more women were devoted to wartime activities at home. In Minot, fifty-four young women formed the "Girls Military Squad," which met at the local armory. They raised money for the Red Cross and conducted military drills. "Khaki suits of the regulation military style have been ordered and a capable military instructor from the regiment will drill the squad," said the *War County Independent.* "The young women will use regular army guns for drilling," the newspaper added.[78]

As tens of thousands of men and women left the state, those who stayed at home followed the progress of their troops. Hundreds of service members sent letters home.[79] Articles in the newspapers were discussed in people's homes, in diners, and during stop-and-chats on the streets. Town squares and people's homes were decorated with huge gold star flags; the Stars and Stripes was everywhere. Political cartoons published in newspapers made fun of the German kaiser and made clear to the state's many ethnic Germans that it was now time to repress or shed their cultural affinities with their homeland. The federal government in addition to state newspapers, civic organizations, churches, and charitable groups generated powerful prowar propaganda depicting the enemy as an existential threat to Western civilization. We were fighting for democracy and freedom, it was said. Such propaganda, like all government propaganda, was criticized by some. But it is also clear that the propaganda, working in tandem with federal laws that outlawed pro-German speech and jailed antiwar dissenters, was effective. Most Americans either acquiesced to the idea or genuinely believed that the US had no choice but to come to the aid of the Allies, to stand up for human decency itself.[80]

There were Syrians who did not want to go to war. "I didn't favor America's entering the World War," remarked Boaley Farhat, "because I believe that war is evil and disputes can be settled without fighting."[81] Side Abdallah said the same thing. But Hassyn Alla Juma had a different view: "[I] favored America's entering the World War because I believed we were right and I was glad to fight for the United States." A homesteader, Hassyn Alla Juma first filed his intention to become a US citizen in 1910. Though he was denied citizenship in 1913, it was granted the year after. Juma was thus obligated to serve in the armed forces. He was inducted into the US Army on July 23, 1918, in Fargo, North Dakota, and was sent to Camp Custer in Michigan. Private Juma served in the 160th Depot Brigade. He was discharged on March 6, 1919.[82]

Kassam Rameden, who lived about an hour's drive north of Ross near the Canadian border, later told a Works Progress Administration (WPA) interviewer that he, too, was happy to fight for the United States. "We were told it was to 'make the world safe for democracy,'" he remembered. Unlike Hassyn Alla Juma, Rameden was not yet a US citizen when he registered for the draft in Valley, Montana, on June 5, 1917. In 1918, he formally declared his intention to become a citizen when he was stationed at San Diego's Camp Kearny as part of the 157th Infantry. His military service meant that, barring any extraordinary circumstances, he was entitled to become a US citizen. And he certainly earned it. That same year, Private Rameden left Boston as part of the 157th Infantry's Camp Funston Detachment. The 157th Infantry participated in the American Expeditionary Forces' most brutal campaign, the Meuse-Argonne, and also fought in the Champagne-Marne, Aisne-Marne, St. Mihiel, and Champagne 1918 campaigns. Over three hundred thousand Americans, including Private Joe Chamie of South Dakota, lost their lives. But Kassam Rameden survived, and he departed Bordeaux, France, to come back to his new home—to the United States—on March 28, 1919.[83]

A little while after Rameden returned, the Midwest became stereotyped throughout the United States by writers such as novelist Sinclair Lewis as both isolated and isolationist. Some of its people were anything but that. Kassem Rameden and other Syrian Muslims, living in hamlets in western North Dakota, were as connected as one could be to the rest of the world—the multiethnic Great Plains, a newly colonized Middle East, and war-torn Europe. After World War I, those Syrians would plant a little more of themselves on the prairie, establishing a Muslim legacy that still resonates today.

Peddling in Cedar Rapids, Iowa, a Town of Ethnic Tradition

On September 22, 1903, the Superior Court of Cedar Rapids, Iowa, declared Hassen Sheronick a naturalized US citizen. According to court records, he had been in the United States for eight years.[1] He had become an American, but he still missed the town where he was born. Resting on the foothills of the Anti-Lebanon Mountains, Joub Jennine looks west toward the flat farm lands of the Bekaa Valley, which are walled in by the dramatic snow-capped Mount Lebanon range, over a mile high. The Litani River runs close to the historic village center. Weather in the Bekaa Valley is temperate—January temperatures averaging in the 40s (6–9 degrees Celsius) and August in the 70s (23–25 degrees Celsius). Cedar Rapids was colder.[2]

Whatever the challenges, Hassen Sheronick was determined to make Cedar Rapids his second home. News of his citizenship was important enough to warrant coverage in the *Cedar Rapids Gazette*: "Hasson Sheronick and his nephew, Mahod Sheronick, natives of Syria, Turkey, took out naturalization papers today in the city's recorder's office and became full-fledged citizens of the United States." In addition to noting that the elder Sheronick was a merchant, the paper said, tongue in cheek, that his young nephew "had tempting offers from Abdul Hamid, the sultan, to enlist in the Turkish army" but that he "prefers to remain in this country."[3] That same year, Sheronick was listed in the *Gazette's Cedar Rapids Directory* as proprietor with brother Ahmed Sheronick of Sheronick Brothers, a grocery store at 1220 South Third Street. The directory spelled his first name as "Hessong," and his relatives would later write his name as Hussien. The Sheronicks' grocery store was located in a narrow two-story wood-framed building about seventy-five feet long and thirty feet wide on an ethnically and religiously diverse street just a couple blocks from the Cedar River. Their neighbors included people named G. D. Schoonmaker, Jacob Rosenbloom, and J. H. Nemecek. Right next door was Mrs. Mary Rudick, a widow who had been born in Bohemia.[4]

Syrians like Hassen Sheronick came to Cedar Rapids, Iowa, for the same reasons other immigrants did. It was a boom town. Though its population in 1860 was only 1,830, by 1900 the town had 25,656 residents. Half of them were either immigrants or the children of immigrants. The largest immigrant community was Bohemian—which is why Cedar Rapids now houses the National Czech and Slovak Museum—but there were others from Southern and Eastern Europe, including Jews, Italians, and Greeks. Located on the Cedar River, Cedar Rapids' success exemplified a formula for Midwestern and US economic growth in the era of industrialization and immigration. Its river provided a transportation route and powered the city's mills. The surrounding farm lands yielded crops such as oats, which immigrants would then process and package at the American Cereal Company, which eventually became Quaker Oats. During this period of US history, most people did not live in huge cities such as New York. They lived in towns like Cedar Rapids, places that had a population of fewer than seventy-five thousand residents. Despite the persistence of the color line—that is, the forced separation of Black people from non-Black people—and the existence of anti-immigrant discrimination, there was plenty of piecemeal work and wage labor for both male and female migrants from other parts of the United States and from Europe and the Mediterranean.[5]

Cedar Rapids was abuzz with economic opportunity when Hassen and Ahmed Sheronick established their store. The Sheronicks' store was located eight blocks away from Union Station, finished in 1897, from which hundreds of trains arrived and departed each day, carrying goods and people to "Chicago, Minneapolis, Omaha, Kansas City, and St. Louis" and beyond. Stretching the length of two city blocks, the brick station featured an impressive four-sided clock tower topped by a cupola and a tall flagpole. In front of the station was Greene Square Park, which provided a tranquil, green space of respite beyond the incredible noise and smell of hundreds of coal-burning, steam-powered engines squeaking along six train tracks. The passenger terminal similarly projected a sense of calm and refinement. Passengers sat on polished, dark wood benches, waiting for their trains as they gazed across the large open floor or looked up toward a high ceiling accented by impressive wood beams. In the winter, they were warmed by seven-foot-tall red sandstone fireplaces. Brass rails were affixed to the terminal walls. The freight depot located just past the terminal was different and more utilitarian. Horse-drawn wagons, which were parked side by side along the street, delivered goods for transport and then carried other things away.[6]

Evoking the symbol of the rapids that ran through the downtown and raced around a little island that squatters had once called home, Cedar Rapids projected an image of civic progress. By 1899, the town erected a large civic auditorium for public lectures and conventions. The public library, located a little past Union Station, about ten blocks away from the Sheronicks' store, was made of Indiana limestone and large, Roman-style brick and was built in the Italian Renaissance style. Completed in 1905, the gray-colored library signaled how the leaders of Cedar Rapids saw themselves not only as people out to make money, but also as sober cultivators of civilization. Women often led philanthropic campaigns, and it was Ada Van Vechten who convinced steel magnate Andrew Carnegie's foundation to fund the building of Cedar Rapids' library.[7]

At the turn of the century, setbacks in Cedar Rapids were temporary. When the downtown Clifton Hotel in front of the Fourth Street railroad tracks burned down in 1903, the elegant Allison Hotel took its place by 1905. That year, the massive, six-story Third Avenue Hotel was erected, as was the Palmer Building, home of the Palmer method of penmanship. When the Quaker Oats mill went up in flames in 1905, the company built a much grander thirteen-story plant that included seven "gigantic concrete elevators." The downtown was full of people going here and there. Horse-drawn carriages tried to stay out of the way of the electric-powered street cars. Bicycles and automobiles, like the 1903 Oldsmobile, shared the same road space. With four train tracks on Fourth Street alone, there were constant delays in getting from one part of downtown to another. Streets would become even more congested on parade days. In 1905, for example, one could see elephants walking down First Avenue as the circus came to town. The next year, as Cedar Rapids celebrated the fiftieth anniversary of its incorporation as a city, horse-drawn floats paraded down Second Avenue. High above the paved streets on which the floats moved were strings of lights and too many power lines to count. Wooden utility poles reached the top of tall three-story buildings whose neoclassical architecture featured arched windows, decorated friezes, and cornices. There were taller buildings, too, and one of them had a spectacular mansard roof and lots of Victorian brick chimneys.[8]

Sports, recreation, and entertainment were also considered important to establishing a proper city. The Young Men's Christian Association building, erected in 1888, "had a swimming pool, gymnasium, auditorium, library, lounge, rented rooms." The Young Women's Christian Association (YWCA), started a little over a decade later, "provided exercise facilities promoting the physical fitness of women." In 1911, the YWCA was built on Fifth Street right across the street from Greene Square Park.[9] For families seeking a little more fun and frolic, there was the Alamo, opened in 1906 as a permanent amusement park. Its figure-eight roller coaster was "fifty feet high and 1,550 feet long." The park also offered "a roller-skating rink with a hard maple wood floor, an elaborate dance pavilion, a 100-foot Ferris wheel, and live vaudeville performances." Until the motion picture industry revolutionized popular entertainment, Cedar Rapids had an impressive opera house where vaudeville, melodrama, music, and plays were enjoyed by countless residents. Away from all this hustle and bustle, those who could afford to socialize with the upper crust could do so at the Cedar Rapids Country Club and Dance Pavilion, which began operations just a few years later.[10]

The Cedar Rapids economy depended on white ethnic labor, and so long as Bohemian, Jewish, Italian, Greek, and Syrian men and women did not make trouble or introduce radical ideas to Cedar Rapids, their ethnic difference was celebrated in ways that modern advocates of cultural diversity would recognize. When these groups could afford to do so, they erected buildings that took up physical space to signal their belonging to Cedar Rapids. Beginning in the 1870s, for example, Czech and Slovak children were offered instruction in the native language of their parents. In 1901, the community built a school for formal Czech language instruction. Then, in 1908, they built the handsome three-story Sokol (Sokolovna) Gymnasium, named after a Bohemian movement to train both the mind and the body. Chiseled into its façade were the names of important national figures such as the writer and poet Svatopluk Čech, philosopher and Iowa immigrant František Klácel, and Miroslav Tyrš and Jindřich Fügner, the founders of the Sokol movement. Syrians quickly established themselves as part of Cedar Rapids' public life, taking obvious cues from the Bohemians. Though the Syrian community did not yet have their own building, they had begun to claim public attention for their identities as far back as 1890, when some Syrians staged a traditional wedding at the YMCA to raise funds for the education of a Syrian boy and girl. Admission was fifteen cents.[11] By 1897, the local newspaper reported on an actual Syrian Christian wedding, which it explained was really an engagement party. The elaborate affair, overseen by a Bohemian Presbyterian minister, included Syrian music, dance, costumes, and a sword dance performed with broomsticks.[12]

Some opinion makers in Cedar Rapids thought that the retention of such ethnic traditions was to be embraced rather than criticized. In 1908, the *Cedar Rapids Evening Gazette* advised its readers to "never forget native dishes." The paper proclaimed that "Jews, Syrian and Italian residents have special dainties which no American food can replace." Yes, this ethnic cooking involved "strange names and methods of making," but the newspaper urged its targeted readership—literate, white, middle-class readers—to consider the matter from the perspective of the immigrants. Take a ham and egg breakfast with coffee, for example: "Did you ever stop to think what a strange dish it would be to some of the people who make up the cosmopolitan population of the city—imported

Americans who pass you every day on the street?" Greeks, the paper said, preferred "salt fish" with cognac. Jews had their own kosher version of "ham and eggs"; the "ham" was actually pastrami, a beef brisket that was dried, smoked, and spiced.[13] Syrians, according to the *Gazette*, loved mutton, and they generously used mutton tallow as seasoning. In addition, Syrians cooked a great deal of "brhol," meaning bulgur, or cracked wheat. Sometimes, they would stew the mutton and bulgur together, and for the holidays, they would prepare a dish of "chopped mutton, rice, and spices rolled in grape leaves and steamed like hot tamales." (Not much has changed in this regard; stuffed grape leaves remain a holiday favorite among people from Syria and Lebanon.) The drink of choice among Syrians was "aruig," that is, 'araq, "a kind of white whiskey made from grapes, but always dr[u]nk in moderation. The Syrians import the liquor in considerable quantities from their native land."[14]

The *Cedar Rapids Gazette* did not advocate the view that one had to abandon ethnic tradition in order to become an American. Instead, the paper asserted that many foreign dishes eventually became part of the American palate: "The Bohemian, the Germans, and the French we have known so long are no longer strange." German sauerkraut and frankfurters and Bohemian "poppy seed and prune 'kolaches' are also familiar delicacies to most Americans." In fact, kolaches were probably not well-known in places where there were no Czech and Slovak immigrants, but their inclusion as "normal" food indicated just how much this ethnic pastry was considered part and parcel of mainstream Cedar Rapids culture. It was the same with French cuisine: "Every little lunch stand that has as much as two stools and a coffee pot . . . calls itself a café," and their menus used terms such as "au jus," "a la cassarole," and "a la mode, which appetizing phrases are occasionally but not frequently spelled correctly," including by the newspaper itself, which misspelled the word casserole.[15]

The tenor of the newspaper's coverage of Syrians in Cedar Rapids was at times different than that in some other Midwestern newspapers, including those in North Dakota, in that even when Syrians were involved in criminal or civil disputes, their ethnicity was not automatically used to explain their behavior. To be sure, there was a fair share of articles that perpetuated stereotypes about Syrians, especially when they just started arriving in Cedar Rapids. In the 1890s, the *Gazette* advised its readers to watch out for the shrewd, "oriental" Syrian peddlers, "to keep them under surveillance" when they were "about your premises."[16] But by the first decade of the 1900s, such explicitly racist comments were less frequent. The remaining element of racism in these stories was the labeling of a person as a Syrian. When white, Christian people were the subject of news stories, their racial and religious identities were generally omitted in news coverage; they were treated as individuals. But people who were racial, religious, and ethnic minorities were generally labeled and identified as such even when the news story had nothing to do with their group identity. For example, when Hassen Sheronick's brother, Ahmed, served as a translator for a woman in a divorce case, the woman's brother got into a fight with Ahmed and was arrested. The headline of the news item was "Assyrian Mixup"—many Americans at this point confused Assyrians, who are an ancient, Christian Middle Eastern group, with people from the land of Syria. There was little newsworthy about the role of ethnicity in this story, but it was still narrated as an ethnic story. Nevertheless, this news coverage was markedly better than that found in many other newspapers as evidenced by the fact that there was no concern expressed about the troublesome nature of the community or its lack of integration.[17] The same was true when Sheronick became embroiled in a number of business disputes that made their way to civil court. No aspersions were cast on his character or the character of his ethnic community at a time when many other newspapers did not hesitate to use news stories to stoke anti-immigrant bias.[18]

Sometimes, outright sympathy for Syrian immigrants was expressed. For instance, when a federal official attempted to take away the citizenship of Syrian Americans in 1909, a situation described above, local attorneys and the *Gazette* came to their defense. The Syrians, argued the *Gazette*, were Caucasians and thus eligible for US citizenship. Further, the paper said, it was unconstitutional to deprive someone of "life, liberty, or property without due process of law," and "taking the rights of citizenship away" deprives a person of their liberty.[19] This was neither the first nor the last time that the federal government, rather than local or state officials, would be responsible for questioning the citizenship of Syrians in Cedar Rapids.[20] Echoing other periods of US history, including the twenty-first century, the federal government was deeply concerned at this time with illegal immigration. Some Syrians were clearly smuggled across the US border, and thus guilty of violating US immigration law.[21] Federal law enforcement officials put the entire community under surveillance and as a result the paper began to cast aspersions on Syrians as a bunch of illegals. In 1910, for example, a federal immigration investigation by the US Secret Service led to the arrest of a prominent figure in the Cedar Rapids Syrian community; he was charged with using the immigration papers of a deceased man in order to vote. The man pled guilty and was fined $500 The *Gazette* saw the arrest as part of a larger pattern of immigration fraud among Syrian immigrants—according to the paper, maybe "half" of all Syrian Americans were recycling the immigration papers of community members who had either died or moved back to Syria. Unlike some of the other coverage of Syrians in Cedar Rapids, this story presented Syrians as secretive and their community as impenetrable, making it seem as if the government had no choice but to conduct a "quiet investigation" of Syrians—stealthy surveillance was advocated to keep track of the whole community and protect the America homeland from their illegality.[22]

Though all Syrians were made out to be suspicious by such anti-immigrant sentiment, Syrian Muslims had special burdens to overcome as a result of their religious identity. Here again, however, there was a difference between the newspaper's extensive coverage of Muslims abroad and the coverage of Muslims of Cedar Rapids, who were acknowledged in articles on the local Syrian community. Hundreds of articles about Mohammedans and Moslems abroad had appeared in the pages of the *Cedar Rapids Gazette* by 1917. The paper included detailed international news of Muslim political activity in Russia, the Caucasus, Crete, China, Philippines, British India, Egypt, and the Ottoman Empire. Muslims were sometimes portrayed as victims, but they were more often than not associated in this period with propagating or threatening political violence, particularly directed at Christians.[23] In the 1890s, concerns about the Ottoman Empire sparked discussion of "universal war" with the "bloody Turk" and "Mohammedan barbarism."[24] One 1902 anti-Muslim headline laid bare the bias of some Americans as plainly as possible: "Mohammedans No Good." In this case, the US-based Odd Fellows, a white fraternal organization, would not authorize a lodge in Turkey due to Turkish people's "national inhumanity." It was said that "a man could not be a loyal Turk and a loyal Odd Fellow at the same time," echoing a commonly held stereotype that Islamic and Western cultures had inherently contradictory values, and that one could not be loyal to both.[25] Low opinions of Muslims and Arabs had staying power. At Cedar Rapids' First Presbyterian Church, a guest lecturer spoke in 1910 about how the Arabic Islamic civilization of Iraq and Spain reached its spectacular zenith in the Middle Ages, but now "the modern people of the desert are little more than savages."[26]

By the time the Great War was raging in Europe, the coverage of foreign Muslims softened a bit and became more nuanced. Even as articles about Muslim fanaticism continued to be published, there was an acknowledgement that Muslims held different, sometimes opposing political goals. "While the sultan of Turkey is recognized as the temporal head of the Mohammedan faith," said the *Gazette*, "the Mohammedans who actually represent his supremacy are about as a drop in the bucket."[27] Only one-twelfth of the world's Muslims actually lived under Ottoman rule, the paper said. Another sign of more humanizing coverage of Muslims was the way in which Ramadan was described. Though Ashura, which marks the martyrdom of the Prophet's grandson, Husayn, was said to be a "ghostly spectacle," Ramadan was called the "Muslim Lent," referring to the period in the Christian calendar from Ash Wednesday to the day before Easter. It was treated with respect and reverence.[28] The Islamic calendar and the ritual observances of the holy month of fasting were explained in great detail to readers.[29] No Cedar Rapids Muslims were mentioned in connection to the story.

Whatever prejudices the Syrian community faced, the years before World War I (1914–1918) were years of growth. Hassen Sheronick's story illustrates that success. After 1903, when Sheronick became a naturalized US citizen, he returned to Joub Jennine in the Bekaa Valley to build a house, get married, and start a family. The year was 1904. His daughter, Negebe (Najibe) was born in 1907.[30] In 1911, he returned to Cedar Rapids to open another store. He steamed from Cherbourg, France, on the SS *Adriatic*, arriving in New York on May 31.[31] By 1912, he was selling dry goods at 329 Ninth Avenue, where he would stay until 1919.[32]

It must have been one noisy dry goods store. Trains on the Chicago, Rock Island, and Pacific Railroad passed fewer than forty feet away from Sheronick's two-story wood-framed business. One wonders if items sometimes fell from the shelves. The railroad was known informally as the Rock Island Line, which a couple decades later would be enshrined in US musical history through the recording of the folk song by the same name. At the time, it also operated the luxurious *Golden State Limited* from Chicago to Los Angeles. The early 1900s purchase of the Burlington, Cedar Rapids, and Northern Railroad by Rock Island added 1,310 miles of track through Iowa and Minnesota, including a direct line from Cedar Rapids to Sioux Falls, South Dakota.[33] No doubt the Rock Island's "mighty good" trains could be felt and heard in Sheronick's store as they squeaked along the tracks. And it wasn't the only railroad in the neighborhood. Just beyond the Rock Island line, about eighty feet, was the Chicago and Northwestern Railroad. Located past all those tracks, catty-corner, was a twenty-eight-foot-tall brick building that housed the Blue Valley Creamery Company, and next door to that was a farm implement and thresher supply store.[34] This was an industrial section of Cedar Rapids but people also lived in the neighborhood, sometimes on the second story of a commercial building.

Hassen Sheronick was one of several Syrians to operate a dry goods store. In fact, Syrian business directories of 1908 and 1909 showed that among the 3,162 Syrian-owned businesses in the United States, the dry goods store was the most popular.[35] In addition to clothes and linens, the dry goods store might offer canned goods, coffee, and spices—it depended on the locale. Though more Syrians were beginning to open groceries and fruit stands, a dry goods store in a place such as Cedar Rapids still played a key role. Not only did it offer goods for sale to local residents, it also supplied many of the peddlers who would set off from Cedar Rapids to the many small towns and farmsteads in Iowa. According to his daughter, Negebe Sheronick, Hassen Sheronick's store offered credit to dozens of Syrian peddlers who would stock their packs with goods and go out on the road for months at a time. "When they returned," she said, "they paid him, purchased more, and went out again."[36] Hassen was more than a supplier. He was a business coach and would give them useful phrases in English to use on the road: "Ma'am, could I sleep here tonight? Ma'am, would you give me something to eat? Ma'am would need something?" He was a surrogate father, too. If they misbehaved, he would "give them a licking . . . he felt it was his responsibility and they looked to him. He was their anchor."[37] Hussein Ahmed Sheronick, who later researched his family's history, wrote that "the peddlers would eat, sleep, and socialize together in the living quarters of Sheronick's store, a haven of refuge where peddlers could freely converse in Arabic."[38] Except when the trains passed by.

One of Hassen Sheronick's clients was 'Abdu Aossey, known at various points in his life known as Abdo or Abdoo. Born around 1887, Abdo first immigrated to Brazil, where he became a horseback peddler. This was not unusual. The top three New World destinations of Syrian emigrants, Argentina, Brazil, and the United States, were formerly slaveholding countries in need of labor to fuel economic booms. In all three countries, Syrians worked farms, performed industrial labor, and became known for their prowess as peddlers. They formed national business networks in each of these countries, and expanded their individual and communal wealth by cooperating with one another and extending assistance to newcomers.[39] Abdo benefited from those networks in both Brazil and the United States. Leaving for Brazil in 1905 and then arriving in the United States in 1907 or 1908, Abdo went to Cedar Rapids.[40]

Abdo obtained goods from Sheronick's store and also worked with Syrian Christian Tom Beshara, who was called the "chief" of the Cedar Rapids Syrian colony by the local newspaper.[41] He then set out on foot. There must have been hard times along the way, since Abdo worked as a farmhand. The 1910 US census lists Abdo and his brother, Sam, as wage earners on a farm (rather than as self-employed peddlers). They were lodging with twelve other Syrians at a boardinghouse owned by dry goods retailer Abraham Dabakey in Webster, Iowa, about sixty miles from Cedar Rapids.[42] Many Syrians, both Christians and Muslims, worked on farms in Iowa, and some owned or rented their own farms, too. But they were not, generally speaking, among Iowa's homesteaders as in the Dakotas; they arrived too late for that.

Abdo was a hard worker, and he eventually earned enough money to buy a horse and buggy. "Being out on the road," remembered his brother Muhammad, Abdo "learned more about business, saved money, made friends, and then bought a general store in Urbana, Iowa," a town of three hundred people a little more than twenty miles outside Cedar Rapids.[43] Abdo also sent for his brothers to join him in America.[44]

Brother Muhammad Aossey, known in Iowa as Mike, was born in 1900 or perhaps as late as 1904 just miles away from the Mediterranean in what today is Southern Lebanon. The Aossey (or 'Asi) clan lived in the Shi'a Muslim village of Insar, then a part of Ottoman Syria. As a seventy-five-year-old, Mike Aossey remembered that, back in the old country, his family owned land, but some of their plots were larger than others. Some family members were sharecroppers; other members of the family had just enough to "take care of themselves." Both men and women worked in the fields. As a boy, Mike ate from his family's fig trees. The Aossey family also owned olive groves and grew wheat. His family did not own goats, but the village was full of them. Their milk was used to make yogurt. Mike attended Qur'an school, learning to read and write as he learned about the Word of God.[45]

Mike, who had six brothers and one sister, was the youngest of a large family. When he was very young, perhaps two, his father passed away. The family lands generated food and income for the family, and his older brother, Abdo, stepped in to fill the role of father. Abdo was very strict, and when he got in trouble, Mike would fly to his mother for comfort. Shouldering a lot of responsibility as a young man, Abdo joined the wave of Syrian emigrants to seek better economic opportunities in the Americas. Like so many others, Abdo would also pave the way for members of his family to join him.[46]

First came Sam and David, and then, in 1913, Mike—no more than thirteen years old—set out on the journey. Sailing from Syria to Marseille, France, the port from which so many Syrians would leave for the Americas, Mike was detained by the authorities on account of his young age. Brother Sam met him in Marseille, coming all the way from Urbana, Iowa, to retrieve him. While he waited, Mike stayed in a hotel with other Syrians, working in the kitchen in exchange for food and lodging. He bought produce and peeled vegetables. Marseilles may have been in France, but with so many Syrians living, working, or waiting there, Mike said it was "just like Beirut." He spoke mostly Arabic in his daily life, though he also learned a little French in the hotel.[47]

From Marseille, Mike then traveled to Cherbourg, where he and other Syrian migrants underwent physical examinations. If found to have an ailment—especially an eye disease called trachoma—migrants were turned back. Mike passed his physical inspection, and crossed the Atlantic, where he underwent yet another medical exam at Ellis Island in New York. After only three hours there, he was free to enter the United States. He spent his first night in America at an Arab-operated hotel, and then traveled to the new family home in Iowa. It was good that Mike had learned to take care of himself in Marseille because he would soon be on his own in America.[48]

Abdo was too busy taking care of his own business to take care of Mike—in Mike's words, Abdo "was moving around too much." Mike attended school for only a few weeks. The family did not pray together on Fridays and they did not observe Islamic holidays. Instead, Mike would go to church with some Christian (non-Syrian) boys from Iowa. The church became a place to connect socially, but Mike also saw it as a spiritual experience. Reflecting the attitudes of other Syrian Muslims living in sparsely populated Midwestern states before World War I, Mike did not see attending church as some sort of betrayal of his Muslim heritage. "Worship is worship no matter where you do it," he later said. Mike seemed to believe in a universal God, one that was as present for Christians as for Muslims. After the church service, Mike and his friends would go fishing at a nearby creek.[49]

One time, the boys caught soft-shell turtles, "cut them up," and ate them raw. Decades later, he still remembered. It was the first time he had seen something like that, and it stuck with him. Mike Aossey must have viewed raw turtle eating as strange, even foreign. But by being there to witness it, it made him less foreign to his new land. He was making new memories in a new place. Going to church with the boys and fishing with them connected Mike Aossey to people outside his own ethnic group, to new sounds, new places, and a creek. Those experiences became a part of him.[50]

During his first year in the United States, Mike Aossey's older brother was on the move and on the make. In 1913, Abdo sold the store in Urbana, and Mike moved with him to nearby Quasqueton (pop. 394), where Abdo purchased another store. After trying to make a go of it for about a year, Abdo decided to move back to Urbana to buy a store with an older man named Thomas Allbones.[51] He also continued to peddle.

Mike went out on his own for a while. Sometime after 1913, he moved to Cedar Rapids, where he already knew a number of other Syrian emigrants. He had little education—some Arabic-language schooling in Ottoman Syria and less than three months spent in Iowa classrooms. But there was opportunity in Cedar Rapids for unskilled laborers. Mike took

FIGURE 3.1. The Aossey brothers used a horse-drawn cart, like many other peddlers, before World War I. Credit: Faris and Yamna Naff Arab American Collection, National Museum of American History.

a job for eighteen cents an hour with the Quaker Oats company. Quaker Oats was not only one of the biggest employers in town; it was also a behemoth of America's quickly growing breakfast cereals industry. The company was sued by the US Department of Justice in 1915 for violations of the Sherman Anti-Trust Act. Essentially, the government alleged that the company had "attained supremacy in the oatmeal industry"— its oatmeal monopoly—through unfair business practices. The suit was ultimately unsuccessful, and Quaker Oats remained dominant.[52]

Mike took a job sweeping floors and cleaning machines in the ever-expanding plant. There were lots of machines to clean, starting with the Richardson Grain Unloaders, which would lift the railroad cars of oats that arrived on the Northwestern, Rock Island, Milwaukee, or Illinois Central railroads from the states of Iowa, Nebraska, South Dakota, and Minnesota. Belts and hoppers would then carry the oats through the milling process, which included removing all the extra material such as chaff, separating the oats by using discs and screens, drying the oats in the drying house, sending them through the milling stones, rolling the oats in steel cylinders, and packaging the oats using the Stokes and Smith Semi-Automatic Wrapping Machine, which was invented in 1917.[53] Unfortunately, Mike Aossey worked the night shift at Quaker Oats. One night, he fell asleep on the job and was fired.[54]

In 1918, he decided to try his luck elsewhere, moving to one of the fastest-growing cities in the United States. He had heard that Henry Ford's company was paying five dollars a day; "there was lots of money in Detroit. Ford was hiring and it was a good place to work." So Mike appeared at Ford wearing his best suit and asked if he could apply for a job. "Come back with work clothes on," he was told. The next day, he was hired for a "knock-out job," a term that refers to a dirty, dusty, noisy set of tasks sometimes performed in dangerous working conditions with heavy equipment. Mike tried the job for four days, and then told his employer that he would have to quit. The company offered him a job working an elevator, but it was too boring. So he applied for Henry Ford's Trade School. It was free, and he was accepted. He had finally found his place. For two years, he would spend the mornings studying to become an electrician. He worked in Ford's Power House, which was equipped with eight turbo generators that supplied electricity to Ford's enormous River Rouge plant and the town of Highland Park.[55] As a foreign national, Mike was excused from conscription during World War I. Mike was checkmarked as an "alien" on his World War I draft registration card; the recorder marked his race as "oriental" rather than white.[56]

During the war years, Syrian Christian and Muslim immigrants hoped that the lands of their birth would become free. They sometimes found themselves on opposite sides of the question of what should happen to Syria. Some Christians, especially Maronites, wanted an independent, Christian-led Lebanese state that would be separate from Syria, while Muslims often supported an independent Syria or what they called the Arab Nation, which would bring Arabic-speaking West Asia or at least Greater Syria together as one country. Syrian American newspapers, literature, political organizations, and civic groups fiercely debated the question across the country, including in the Midwest. Syrian Muslims and Christians were generally united in their opposition to the Ottoman Empire and their hope that US involvement in World War I would lead to independence of some sort. But they disagreed about how the lines on the map should be drawn and who would rule.

Such concerns with the political fate of their native lands did not prevent Syrians in Cedar Rapids from investing fully in their new homeland. Indeed, the community was anxious to demonstrate its loyalty to the United States. "Members [of the] Syrian Colony [are] Loyal" read a 1917 headline in the newspaper, which reported that Deputy US Marshal Healy, a federal law enforcement officer, had investigated whether there were treasonous elements in the Syrian community. Rumors of such had been spreading, perhaps born from false accusations made by one member or faction of the community against another. Christians and Muslims sometimes disagreed with one another, and those disagreements occasionally spilled over into violence. In 1914, for instance, a friendly game of billiards at a local establishment led to a religious disagreement, "a theological discussion in which billiard cues instead of quotations were used to drive home arguments." A Syrian Muslim was playing pool with a Syrian Christian at 226 South First Street, a narrow twenty-eight-foot tall brick building downtown next to the Cedar River.[57] They argued about who should pay for the game. Words were exchanged. Religious insults flew. The owner kicked them out, but they took their pool cues with them to fight in the street. A duel ensued—using pool cues rather than swords. A police officer arrived on the scene just in time to prevent "a call for the coroner." Both men were taken into custody instead.[58]

Whatever disputes and tensions remained among Syrian Muslims and Christians in 1917, Deputy Marshal Healy found no evidence of political dissent among them. On the contrary, "sixty to seventy-five percent of the Syrians possessed Liberty loan bonds," which were savings bonds issued by the federal government to finance US military activities in World War I. In addition to purchasing these bonds, which paid a low rate of interest, Syrians were making donations of one to ten dollars to the Red Cross. Members of the community marched into Healy's office with their receipts. "It is a pretty good sign of loyalty if a person will buy Liberty bonds and support our Red Cross," he told the *Gazette*. "If there is anything the pro-German hates to do, it is to buy Liberty bonds."

Pro-German rather than pro-Turkish sentiment was the real concern of law enforcement officials in Iowa. German Americans were the state's largest ethnic group, and officials worried about their pro-German sympathies. There was also concern among the state leaders about whether, in counties with especially high numbers of German-descended people, there would be enough men to fight in the war. Of the "216,299 men subject to conscription" in Iowa, according to Nancy Derr, about 60,000 were born in the countries that represented the Central Powers of Germany, Austria, Bohemia, Hungary, and Turkey—the "enemy." There were far more German-born Iowans than Turks, including the Arabic-speaking Syrians of Cedar Rapids: there were 48,662 Germans of conscription age versus 307 men born in the Ottoman Empire. It turned out that such xenophobic anxieties were overblown. Among all those men who were born in the countries of the Central Powers, "only 1,822 were designated 'alien enemies' and thus made ineligible for military service." The rest were eligible and many served.[59]

It was nearly impossible not to support the war. Federal and state governments and key institutions, including the press, schools, and many philanthropic organizations, moved quickly to mobilize for war, and the citizenry responded. It all happened in a matter of months. In April 1917, when President Woodrow Wilson made a formal request that the US Congress declare war against Germany, many people in Iowa and across the United States were still opposed to US participation. Some wanted to remain neutral. Some draft-eligible men did not want to fight in a brutal, long-lasting conflict. Others, including Amish and Mennonites as well as Iowa's Amana colonies, were pacifist Christians. But even peaceful dissent against war became impossible. Anything less than full-throated prowar sentiment was seen as potential treason. Deputy Marshal Healy attended antiwar rallies around the state to warn those in attendance against their seditious talk. As more and more Iowans joined the military, their families, friends, and neighbors lashed out in public and in private against those who refused to do their part in supporting the war effort. They were angry about bearing an unfair burden, and some of them turned to vigilante violence, threatening Iowans who organized against the war. Using the Espionage and Sedition Acts, federal officials arrested and prosecuted antiwar activists who were given long prison sentences for making antiwar speeches or publishing less than enthusiastic editorials. The "Hun," an epithet for Germans, was depicted as a ghastly beast, sometimes an apelike creature on prowar posters. And on May 23, 1918, Gov. William L. Harding issued the Babel Proclamation, which forbade the speaking of all languages in public save English. Speaking foreign languages, he said, represented an "opportunity [for] the enemy to scatter propaganda." Some Bohemians and Scandinavians protested, pointing out that they were different from Germans, but to no avail. Some telephone operators reported party line conversations in other languages to authorities.[60]

The entire town of Cedar Rapids and its many ethnic communities had mobilized for war. The *Cedar Rapids Evening Gazette* brought news of each battle, each negotiation, each wave of enlistments to its fifteen thousand or so subscribers. Syrian Muslims and Christians were both expected and willing to do their part. Cedar Rapids' civic leaders boasted that their plan to support the war effort was superior to that of many other small cities; they said towns across the United States could learn from their model. Rather than using one centralized and autocratic bureaucracy to direct the purchase of Liberty bonds or organize donations for the Red Cross, Cedar Rapids built a voluntary association called the War Activities Bureau. Headquartered on the main floor of the Hotel Montrose, which offered to rent space to the organization at a reduced rate, it was led by Mrs. C. C. Loomis, county chair of the Woman's Committee of the National Council of Defense. The Bureau coordinated the activities of volunteers as they went door-to-door raising money or educating the public about the need to conserve food during wartime.[61] The Syrian community took part in these campaigns, including one to aid the Armenian and Syrian refugees who had been expelled or displaced by the Ottoman government. On June 11, 1918, "the Syrian committee working for Armenian and Syrian relief in Cedar Rapids today turned in the results of their campaign at the headquarters in the Hotel Montrose." The *Cedar Rapids Evening Gazette* explained that the local Syrian community was modest in size but it "gave freely," donating $130.50 to the effort.[62]

This philanthropic engagement was a civic ritual and a public performance that wedded Syrians to the nation and to their town—not only the idea of the nation and the town, but its people and places. To be sure, such socialization, like all socialization, was coercive, perhaps even for those who most enthusiastically supported the war. But no matter what the intent and complicated feelings of those who participated in giving money, knocking on doors, and hand-delivering donations to Bureau headquarters, their actions were placing them, quite physically, at the heart of US nation-making during World War I. There was no place more committed to the nation's war effort than the community in which they lived: "Iowa won the contest among the forty-eight states in 1918 for the fastest collection of its multi-million-dollar quotas in the third and fourth Liberty Loan bond drives."[63]

What people do with their money—and their bodies—matters. As in Sioux Falls, South Dakota, Muslims from Cedar Rapids registered for the draft and served in the US Army, ready to sacrifice for their new country. On June 5, 1918, Hassan Igram registered. Still a citizen of the Ottoman Empire, he said that he had declared his intention to become an American citizen. He did so, it seems, in Detroit, Michigan, on March 26, 1917 (and would again declare his intention December 15, 1924, in Cedar Rapids, perhaps because he did not have a copy of nor could he find the original declaration.)[64] On both declarations, he said that he arrived in New York City in late 1914.

Like the Sheronicks, Hassan Igram grew up in Joub Jennine in the Bekaa Valley of what today is Lebanon. According to his son, Abdullah, Hassan Igram's family in Joub Jannine were farmers. Hassan Igram learned to read and write in Arabic as a young boy. Fearful that he would be conscripted into the Ottoman military, he left town as a teenager and followed in the footsteps of others from his village. Stopping in Danbury, Connecticut, for a short while, he landed in Cedar Rapids and then set out, like so many young Syrian boys, as a peddler.[65] By 1918, Igram was employed by the Cedar Rapids Gas Company. It is not clear what Hassan Igram's job was at the plant, but no matter what it was, it was quite a change from farming in Joub Jennine. The kind of gas distributed by the Cedar Rapids Gas Company was different from the natural gas that most people use today. This was manufactured or "town gas." The plant steamed, combusted, or otherwise processed coal, coke, and oil; various flammable gases as well as poisonous tars and other by-products were the result. Some of the tar and other undesirable by-products were discharged into rivers or simply dumped into landfills, creating environmental damage still poisoning American waterways and other sites today. In 1918, the Cedar Rapids Gas Company served 8,862 homes, businesses, and other consumers, producing about "320,000,000 cubic yards of natural gas at a cost of $278,268 plus."[66]

After the war, Syrian Muslims in Cedar Rapids would continue to work for companies like Cedar Rapids Gas, but they became better known as entrepreneurs, especially in the grocery business. The city's population grew in the 1920s. There weren't many peddlers. In order to be successful at door-to-door sales, you needed a truck or a converted sedan. The corner grocery offered many an even better opportunity. People like Hassan Igram came to own their own businesses, and Syrian Muslim men and women invested just as heavily in their ethnic and religious communities.

4

Michigan City, Indiana, and Syrian Muslim Industrial Workers

Even if it sometimes smelled of fish a little too strongly, it was a beautiful lakeside setting for one of the most important Syrian Muslim communities in the Midwest. It could get cold in the winter—the average daytime temperature in January was just above freezing and at night the mercury dipped to 20 degrees Fahrenheit (almost -7 Celsius). But in July the daytime temperature hovered around 83 degrees Fahrenheit (28 Celsius) and a breeze from the lake often made it feel cooler; at night it was around 64 degrees Fahrenheit (18 Celsius). Sitting on the south shore of Lake Michigan in the state of Indiana, Michigan City was a gateway to the world's largest freshwater sand dunes, produced over thousands of years by the winds and waves of the United States' largest body of water (at least in terms of area). Over one hundred miles wide and three hundred miles long, Lake Michigan is one of the five glacial Great Lakes that account for one fifth or more of the world's supply of fresh water. Its shores had been settled at least two thousand years ago by the Hopewell people, but as white settlers arrived it was the Potawatomi who "fished, trapped, and hunted, and picked the wild cranberries and blueberries that sprinkled the marsh" just south of the lake. In the summer, they left the "mosquito-plagued marshes and moved to higher ground or to the dune country along Lake Michigan," which is exactly what many white people would do to beat the summer heat in the late 1800s. Many Potawatomi were expelled from their homes in the 1830s; Michigan City was incorporated in 1836.[1]

Indiana controlled only forty-five of Lake Michigan's 1,638 miles of shoreline, and Michigan City became its most important nineteenth-century port, shipping lumber and grain that made its way to international markets via the Erie Canal and St. Lawrence River. The town's sand dunes were used in the production of glass jars for the Ball Brothers and sometimes as fill along Chicago's shore, about sixty miles away. By the late 1800s, the dunes were a tourist destination. Visitors also came to tour the Indiana state prison located in Michigan City. The town boasted about its modern amenities such as street cars and wooden-planked streets. By 1886, its roads were lighted by electricity rather than gas. It had numerous bands and orchestras, fraternal organizations, and social clubs. In the early 1900s, when Syrians arrived in meaningful numbers, the summers were particularly busy with "chautauquas," which involved lectures by renowned speakers, "circuses, dog and pony shows, and vaudeville acts." Interurban trolleys connected Michigan City to nearby towns in Indiana and to Chicago.[2]

Some Syrian Muslims such as Hussien Ayad helped to build or maintain the tracks on which those electric trains ran. He was born around 1890 in a village near the Bekaa Valley's largest river, the Litani. His father passed away shortly before his birth and his mother died shortly afterward. Hussien left for America as a very young man, as young as eleven or twelve as he remembered it later—but it was also possible that his date of birth on his Ottoman records was incorrect. Whatever his age, he decided to follow in the footsteps of others from the Bekaa Valley who were already in Michigan City. "The ticket sellers placed me with four other immigrants from Lebanon in a fishing boat just as if we were part of its cargo," he later wrote, "and the boat stopped at every village, emptying its cargo and taking on cargo." It was so "slow, comparable to the crawl of a lizard." Finally, they arrived in Beirut, where they "squeezed into" an Italian ship on which they "greeted the new year, 1902," with "spaghetti and macaroni and grape juice."[3] It seems from there he may have made his way to Liverpool, England, and then across the Atlantic on the American Line's SS *Haverford* to Philadelphia.

After his arrival in Michigan City, Ayad boarded with a "man whose village was not far from my village." His first job was laying tracks for an electric train, perhaps on the South Shore Line. But then he went to work for the biggest employer in town, Haskell and Barker, which produced railroad cars. "By 1903," according to historian Elisabeth Marsh, "2,200 workers were producing 10,667 cars a year (roughly 29 cars per day). And by 1907 it was the largest manufacturer in Indiana, employing 3,500 men and covering 100 acres to produce 15,000 cars a year." During the first decade of the twentieth century, Michigan City experienced steady population growth, going from 14,850 residents in 1900 to 19,207 in 1910. The city's booming economy, which also produced sitting chairs, hosiery, boots, shoes, copper barrels, and copper casks, relied on immigrant labor.[4]

In 1900, a little more than two-thirds of all residents were either first- or second-generation Americans. Industrialists such as John H. Barker, who headed Haskell and Barker in this era, recruited Syrians to join this burgeoning immigrant labor force. Barker believed that the more ethnically diverse the local labor force was, the easier it would be for him to prevent labor organizing.[5] Many workers came from Chicago, where Arabic-speaking immigrants had been present for a couple decades; some of them had traveled to America for the 1893 Columbian Exposition, the world's fair. This population included Christians and Muslims not only from the parts of Greater Syria that would become Lebanon and Syria but also from the Palestinian cities of Jerusalem and Ramallah.[6] In addition to employing some of these Chicagoans, Barker recruited people from as far away as Springfield, Illinois. The industrialist purchased land where the Syrians could live together in Michigan City. Local historian Elizabeth Munger estimated that there were as many as seven hundred Syrians on Barker's payroll—if correct, that was even more than the number employed at the time by Henry Ford.[7]

The town had a vision of itself as progressive, establishing a large, lovely city park in the 1890s. Mayor Martin Krueger, a German immigrant, convinced Barker and others to support the repurposing of an abandoned lumberyard where some poor residents had erected temporary housing. Located east of the city center on the lakeshore, the new Washington Park featured a bandstand and, by the first decade of the 1900s, a theater, merry-go-round, roller coaster, and bathhouse. Trees were planted, and people picnicked, strolled, and gazed at pictures and paintings exhibited in the park's peristyle, whose long colonnade and domed center was modeled on a building from the 1893 Columbian Exposition.[8] The park's paths crossed manicured lawns ornamented with both round and rectangular gardens. There were long benches where gentlemen in their suits and ties and ladies with long dresses and large hats could rest and chat.[9] Hussien Ayad remembered that "boats from Chicago carrying hundreds of visitors" came to the "park on the shores of Lake Michigan." Some of them would visit the Hoosier Slide, the two-hundred-foot high sand dune that was Indiana's most popular tourist destination at the time. "There used to be a hill where the Electricity Plant now stands, a sand hill which when climbed, gave you a view of all of Michigan City located in and among verdant trees and foliage," Hussien Ayad wrote. Tourists also came for the Fourth of July celebrations. During the day, they would enjoy the parade and "then after dark came the thrilling display of fireworks, lighting the holiday scene," he recalled.[10]

The town did not treat all visitors the same, however, and the Michigan City police force made sure that only the right kind of people used Washington Park.[11] Like other "progressive" towns, Michigan City sought to protect the life and liberty of white, Christian, and respectable middle-class people. African Americans were not welcome, and during the first decade of the 1900s, Syrians were also seen as a danger to white people and their pursuit of happiness. In 1907, for example, a Syrian was arrested "after he insulted a woman who was working at a concession stand in Washington Park." The *Michigan City Evening Dispatch* reported that, as a result, the "Turks" would not be allowed around amusement concessions, and "the police have decided to give them strict attention in the future. They will not be permitted to lounge about on the grass or benches or congregate in groups on the walks where ladies are compelled to pass them." The next year, a Syrian man was arrested for picking flowers in the park, although the court determined that he was only carrying flowers through the park, not picking the park's flow-crs.[12] As in Sioux Falls and other places, non-Syrian residents of the lakeside sometimes harassed Syrians. In 1908, three white boys followed three Syrian boys home and hurled stones at their house. After windows were broken, a fight between the boys broke out. One Syrian's tooth was lost. The police came, and the instigators agreed to pay five dollars to the homeowner in restitution. When the fine went unpaid, the non-Syrian troublemakers were sent to a probation officer.[13] Syrians were also seen at times as potential carriers of eye disease: "Trachoma Feared in Michigan City: Syrian, with Disease, Eludes Inspectors," proclaimed a headline in the *South Bend Tribune*, which expressed relief that this man who allegedly had trachoma was eventually arrested.[14]

Syrian Christians in town also clashed with Syrian Muslims during the first decade of the 1900s. One dispute was big enough to make the newswires, appearing in papers throughout the country, including in the *Cedar Rapids Gazette*. William Hipp, identified as a "Turk," which is what a Syrian Muslim man was still called, was "fatally stabbed." Twenty or so people "of both factions were seriously injured." Hipp left behind his wife, Theresa, who lived on 205 East Michigan. The causes of the conflict were several, according to the story. The men were arguing about "religious, racial and political matters," but liquor played a big role. Both the Muslims and Christians had been supplied with free liquor by political candidates. (Indiana later banned the sale of liquor on election days, a law that stayed on the books until 2012). "Knives, clubs, stones and guns were used freely" during the fight, which led to the arrest of twenty-two people and the investigation of many others. The *Gazette* headline called the dispute a "race riot," which revealed the thinking of many white, Protestant Americans toward Syrians. The term "race riot" was generally used to describe the public violence of non-white people.

There was another racial component coloring the interreligious violence. Some Syrian Christians held to the view that they were a different "race" than Syrian Muslims—they said that they were white and the Muslims were not. The Syrian Muslims defended what they believed to be their whiteness, which led to ongoing disputes. Liquor was almost always involved. An early July 1907 altercation involved fifty fighters, and one police officer was "beaten and stabbed" when the fire department and police tried to take control of the Syrian neighborhood. "Ordinarily," reported the *Michigan City Evening Dispatch*, "they manage to get along pretty well, but it is said that both factions had indulged freely in the use of intoxicants yesterday, this fact precipitating the row." In 1908, thirty-four Syrian Christians signed a letter to the *Evening Dispatch* identifying the "riotous Turk" as the cause of their emigration from Syria, but the letter was as much about their disputes in the United States as in the old country. "The civilized world knows that the Turks are barbarians," they said.[15] In truth, intra-Syrian disputes were not the product of ancient enmities between people from two different religions but between people engaged in a contemporary struggle for economic resources, social status, and political rights.

Both Syrians and non-Syrians sometimes exploited these tensions for personal gain. Haskell and Barker foreman Thomas Walsh was accused of extorting money from would-be employees at the railroad car factory, for example. When jobs for some but not others materialized, it led to another violent conflict between those whom Walsh "weeded out" and those whom he retained. Over 150 people were involved. "Intense feeling exists in the city against these foreigners," concluded the *Brazil Daily Times*.[16] In another instance, Mohamed Debaja lost his job when two Syrians falsely accused Debaja of demanding money before he would hire them. A local court fined the two men five dollars.[17]

Indiana newspapers were sometimes overtly racist in their coverage of the US Department of Commerce and Labor decision to deny citizenship to Syrians based on the idea that they were Asiatic, not white. The two things were linked: when the government denied citizenship to Syrians based on the idea that they were not white people, it made it more likely that the press would also talk about them as non-whites. As the newspapers reported, George Crutchfield, chief examiner of the government's naturalization office in Chicago, provided the LaPorte County clerk and superior court judge with memoranda supporting the govern-

ment's position and sent representatives to oppose Syrians at their naturalization hearings. Instead of denouncing the racism, the *Indianapolis
News* blamed local Michigan City politicians for "coddling" Syrians to
obtain their votes. Syrians had been rising in Michigan City society, but
"owing to riots, fights and their habits of living," the town's politicians
had now become "a little shy about handling the 'guinea' vote," as the
newspaper put it, using a slur generally used to question the whiteness of
Italians.[18] The treatment of Syrians as foreigners continued in Michigan
City, as the government attempted to deport hundreds of the town's residents until the US courts declared Syrians to be white and thus eligible
for citizenship in 1915.[19]

So it was in spite of both legal and social discrimination that by the
second decade of the twentieth century Syrians were able to establish a
vibrant community in Michigan City. One commercial hub of the Syrian
community, both Muslim and Christian, was close to the lake, near the
intersection of Michigan, Pine, and Franklin streets. Among those who
lived or worked in this area, according to the 1905, 1913, and 1916 city
directories, were Syrian confectioners and grocers, including Samuel
Aboud, Naman Koury, Abraham Semaha, and Assad Shikany. It was a
bustling area where "the sidewalks" were "filled with people in a lovely
sight that pleased the heart," wrote Hussien Ayad. Downtown Michigan City was home to all manner of businesses from barbers and bakers
to cobblers and haberdashers. There were also cigar shops, dry goods
stores, boardinghouses, furniture stores, a telegraph office, a dance hall,
an ice cream factory, and multiple pool halls. Pine Street and Michigan
Street had a number of wood-framed residential buildings, but brick
buildings, mainly two stories high, dominated the scene along Franklin Street. Some of the older buildings featured tall, arched windows,
while the windows on modern storefronts were rectangular and metal
framed. Nearly all the buildings were ornamented by finials, cornices,
brackets, or friezes. Wrought-iron globe lamps lined the street, which
was shared by automobiles, horse-drawn carriages, bicycles, and street
cars.[20] Hussien Ayad worked in one of these brick buildings, a "coffee

house and restaurant on 216 Franklin Street." Wherever they settled in significant numbers—New York, Detroit, Chicago—young Syrians congregated in coffeehouses. They drank Turkish coffee and took their meals together, played games like backgammon, exchanged gossip, debated politics, listened to Arabic-language newspapers being read aloud, and chased away the loneliness of being in a new land. All of Ayad's customers were Arab, and he cooked them Syrian food, which was "easy to make and required little or no measuring or cookbooks," he recalled.[21] Syrian men also established and enjoyed congregating in pool halls, though the police would sometimes chase away the Syrian teenagers who liked to hang out there.[22]

Though Michigan City had its share of Syrian business owners, most Syrians, as in the United States more generally before World War I, were laborers. Many of them worked for the Haskell and Barker railroad car factory. In 1916, for example, all fourteen men listed in the city directory with the last name of Allie ('Ali) were employed there. Some of these men with the last name of Allie might have been immigrants from other countries such as Albania, Turkey, Iran, or Bosnia, but most of them were Syrian. Many of them lived just outside the walls of the factory, which occupied several city blocks in the western part of town, not far from the lakeshore. Linked by the Michigan Central Railroad, the Monon, and several other rail lines to its many customers, Haskell and Barker's red-brick industrial complex included over a dozen buildings that made parts and assembled passenger and freight cars. It produced its own steam and electric power from coal, manufactured gas, and wood. There were separate foundries to fabricate wheels and brass parts, and separate shops for steel cars and wooden cars. It featured an annealing room where metal was slowly cooled, becoming tougher, and a large steam dry kiln room. The factory made its own fasteners, in addition to metal and wooden parts, and it mixed its own paints and stains. Its multiple smokestacks polluted the Michigan City air, but like other factories built around this time, many of its buildings contained skylights, windows, and high ceilings, which gave them an airy feeling.[23]

In the first decade of the twentieth century, according to Hussien Ayad, there were not yet any formal Syrian Muslim "groups or societies to join" since the Syrian Muslims who now lived and worked in Michigan City had come from different villages and areas of Syria. They had to get to know each other first, but eventually "factories and working places" in addition to kinship and hometown ties "brought people together, and produced friendships." It was important to Syrian Muslims in Michigan City that they plant their Syrian and Muslim identities on American soil, and they began organizing themselves into voluntary associations, much like the Syrian Muslims of Sioux Falls. Hussien Ayad remembered that there were several groups at the time. On April 26, 1914, Hussein AbouDeeb Mohamed established Bader Elmoneer, which was also the name of a Syrian Shi'a Muslim association in South Dakota. In fact, this may have been the same man and the same organization, with branches in both cities. There were large groups of Shi'a Muslims in both towns who were connected to each other by shared origins and social and business interests. Hussein Ali Hamood created Al-Ittihad Al-Tibnein, the Union of Tebnine, referring to the village from which several of the town's residents had emigrated. In 1915, Ayad himself formed Zahwat Al-Shabab Al-Islam, or the Glory of Islam's Youth.[24]

Unlike in Sioux Falls, this civic and religious activity did not yet attract public recognition like that of Syrian Christians, including the Syrian Antiochian Orthodox who worshipped at St. George and the Syrian Catholics who established Sacred Heart. The Muslim community was also much less prominently featured in the newspaper than the Jewish community, which had found a degree of acceptance unknown to Muslims. A Jewish team regularly participated in the church basketball league, making the front page when they beat the town's Baptists. Some of Michigan City's most successful businessmen were Jewish, and the philanthropic causes that they led, including relief for European Jews during World War I, elicited significant support from local Christians.[25]

In contrast, Syrian Muslims received public attention mainly as potential criminals or as excellent wrestlers. As the historian Linda Jacobs has revealed, Arab visitors and immigrants became popular entertainers in the United States after the Civil War, often playing on stereotypes of the Middle East and the Muslim Orient as they appeared in vaudeville shows, circuses, and exhibitions, at Coney Island, and on the lecture circuit.[26] The use of one's ethnic identity as a way to develop one's entertainment brand was not unusual, including in sports. Other ethnic groups did the same. In the early twentieth century, wrestling was a popular sport in which Americans of various ethnic backgrounds participated. One of the most popular professional wrestlers in Michigan City was Yussif Hussane, the "Terrible Turk," who hailed from Battle Creek, Michigan. (Wrestling fans will note that several men in the history of the sport have gone by this moniker.) His January 1914 match with the "Russian Lion," Jack Leon, at the Armory was heavily promoted. When Leon did not appear, fans settled for an exhibition between Hussane and another professional wrestler, John Freberg. "Hussane's experience proved too much for Freberg," reported the *Evening News*. "Freberg outweighed his opponent by thirty pounds, and showed considerable cleverness at times." But "Hussane is a scientific grappler and coupled with his exceptional strength and endurance make him a much feared man on the mat." It took Hussane about twenty-five minutes to pin Freberg the first time but then only four minutes the second. According to the paper, the winning move was "a half-Nelson and crotch hold."[27] He had real fans in the city, whose newspaper reported on matches that he held in other places, including Omaha and New York.

The interest in Hussane was more than a passing fancy. There was a vibrant culture of wrestling in Michigan City, and Syrian Muslims played a large role in it. Hussane's match with Leon was heavily promoted by local wrestler Hussane A. Seloom. It was advertised as the "biggest event in wrestling doings ever pulled off here." Tickets sold for fifty and seventy-five cents, and seats on the stage went for one dollar. Hussane developed a following in Michigan City and had "many friends here," according the newspaper. The next month he appeared again in a match at the Orpheum, built in the early 1900s as a three-story opera house that

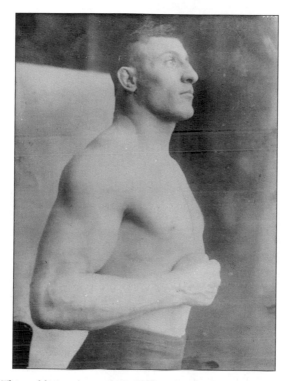

FIGURE 4.1. This publicity photo of Yussif Hussane, the "Terrible Turk," was published by the *Michigan City Evening News* on January 12, 1914. Credit: Wikipedia Commons.

could seat five hundred people. His opponent was Farmer Bill Hokuf of Iowa. It was "one of the best matches if not the best wrestling match ever witnessed in Michigan City." Both wrestlers were admired by the crowd, and "the quick exchange of holds at stages brought the crowd to its feet," according to the newspaper. But "Hussane used his old-time whirlwind style of wrestling," employing the jackknife in his first pin and the half-Nelson in his second. Locals also appeared on the bill that winter night, and a couple of them were Syrian Muslims. "John Levendowski and Alli Hammid wrestled forty minutes to a draw," and the promoter's brother, "Young Seloom" won his match. When headliners like Hussane were absent, local matches drew more modest crowds, like when Hussane A. Seloom defeated Gus Costello of Chicago in April 1914.[28]

Away from the public's gaze, Syrian Muslims in Michigan City also started or expanded their families in this decade. For example, Mary Allie (also known as Mary Teraine and later Mary Unis and Mary Shamey) was born on June 25, 1913, to Alex and his wife, a woman whose name is recorded in US social security records as "Bazar."[29] Mary's father came from the village of 'Aramta and her mother was from Kfar Houne, two villages located in the southern Lebanese mountains about two miles away from one another. Living at an altitude of about three thousand feet, they were used to some snow in the winter, but their hometowns were more temperate than Michigan City. The average low temperature in their villages was only 40 degrees Fahrenheit in the coldest part of the winter, and the average high temperature in August was no more than 77 degrees. Their villages were approximately fifteen miles from the Mediterranean coast, though the journey on mountain roads was not an easy one before World War I. The sometimes rocky and sometimes forested hillsides on and under which they lived were used for grazing goats and sheep, and were particularly well-suited for the growing of herbs like thyme and oregano. The majority of people who lived there may have been Christian, but both of Mary's parents, whose marriage was arranged, were Shi'a Muslims. As Mary recalled, their "livelihood" in Syria "wasn't too good." Her father may have come to the United States first in 1910 and then, around 1911, returned to Syria to bring his wife to America. Like many other Syrians, they sailed to Marseilles and then to New York. Stopping in Providence, Rhode Island, for a brief time, they headed to Michigan City, where several members of Alex Allie's family already lived. They meant to stay just a few years, but they never moved back.[30]

In Michigan City, Mary's family lived around other Arabic-speaking people, both Christians and Muslims. Around the time she was born, Mary's father died. To earn a living, Mrs. Allie took on five or six boarders, charging them to wash and iron their clothes and to cook Arab food for them. It's not clear from the city directory exactly where the boardinghouse was, but there's a good chance it was just across the street from the Haskell and Barker car factory. Many people with the last name of Allie roomed at addresses there. Mary's mother spoke Arabic with them. Like many of the other Syrians in Michigan City, the family often patronized Arab-owned stores, though Mrs. Allie seldom went to the store herself. Groceries were delivered to her home, which became easier when she was able to phone in her order. When she did leave the home, she always covered her head with a scarf, as did many other Syrian Muslim women at the time in Michigan City. If they needed assistance in a legal matter or something else requiring English literacy, Mary's mother said that there was one man in the community they would often call on. Mary's mother also stayed in touch with friends and family back in Ottoman Syria (and then Lebanon), asking someone who was literate in Arabic to write letters for her. There was no mosque at that time in Michigan City, and those who prayed did so in each other's homes and during work breaks in the town's factories. Mary's mother prayed, and she tried to teach Mary how to pray, too, but Mary said that she ran away—"it was too much," she told her mother.[31]

Kamel Osman also remembered people praying in their homes when he was a young child in Michigan City. Born around the same time as Mary Allie, Osman was the child of two Shi'a Muslim parents. His father, Tahan, or Ta'an, was from Tebnine. Like other immigrants, his grandfather and his father had both come to the United States to make money, returning at various times to Syria. Around 1910, he met Zainab Hassan (also known as Zainab Katima or Ghutaymi) in Michigan City, and the couple married on July 20, 1911. His parents told him that there was no formally trained shaykh to oversee the marriage, but that an "educated" community member filled the role instead. Nine months later, on April 13, 1912, Kamel was born.[32]

When Kamel was old enough to go to school, his friend's father told him that the local Catholic school was better than the public school, and Kamel wanted to go to school where his friend went. This interfaith friendship is a reminder that in addition to the conflict that sometimes existed between Syrian Christians and Muslims in Michigan City, there was also cooperation and genuine affection. Kamel's father was working out of town at the time, and Kamel enrolled in the Catholic school. But "three quarters of the teaching," said Kamel, was "religion." When Ta'an eventually learned that his son had been attending a parochial school, he sent him back to public school. "You should learn Muhammad's religion," the father told his son. But Kamel, like Mike Aossey and other Muslims, did not see learning about God from Catholics as any betrayal of his Islamic heritage. He later said that "there is no difference between religions because all religions refer to the same God." Though he may have differed with his father on whether Catholic school was a threat to his faith, he still found something to admire in his father, namely, how his dad helped other people in need. Ta'an, who worked for Haskell and Barker at least some of the time, was always willing to assist any *ibn 'arab*, that is, any Arab person, when they first arrived in Michigan City. He "took them home, fed them, and gave them a couple dollars," remembered Kamel.[33]

Kamel Osman was just a boy when the United States entered World War I, but as in other towns and cities, older Syrian Muslim men were drafted and joined the fight. Michigan City's very first conscript, of any race or religion, was Mohamed Debojah (also spelled Debaja), born in 1890 in Bint Jbeil, a town in the south of contemporary Lebanon. He was likely the same man who was falsely accused of taking kickbacks in exchange for hiring other Syrians at a local factory. On August 8, 1917, Debojah was dressed in a white shirt, a dark jacket, and a tie as he sat down with members of the local draft board. "Holding the flag of his adopted country" in one hand and a pen in the other, he posed with the female clerk of the board as well the insurance agent, coroner, and Haskell and Barker paymaster who composed its membership. "The local Turk," as the newspaper described him, is "28 years old, unmarried, moulder by trade." Examined that very day, Debojah "passed with a standing almost perfect." Debojah was a naturalized citizen of the United States, and "willing to fight for his country" if "the law wants him to," he said. The newspaper spread the rumor that many Syrian Muslims were opposed to his serving in the US military and were even willing to shoot him if he did so. There may have been some opposition to the war. Hassien Moses, still a citizen of the Ottoman Empire, said he was willing to serve in the US armed forces but would not "cross the water and fight against his brothers."[34] Whatever opposition existed, it was not enough to halt the participation of Syrian Muslims in the US military.

Michigan City's quota of conscripts was 130, but, on its first try, the town gave Uncle Sam only 76 men. At least 10 of them were Syrian. In addition to Mohamed Debojah, Hassan Eyade, Shekal Owad, Mike Hedad, George Koure, Hassian Moses, Allie Hassan Derwish, Moses Sead, Mohamed Amon, and Ale Wasine (Wasni) were among those accepted for duty. Relatively few Syrians were given an exemption as a result of their "alien enemy" status.[35] A little over a month later, thousands of Michigan City residents came together to send most of these young men off to war. They mustered at the courthouse on West Michigan, where roll call was taken, and then they marched to the train station where they boarded a "special car on the morning southbound Monon passenger train for Louisville, Kentucky." From there, they would go to Camp Taylor. As they marched together, the Haskell and Barker band accompanied them, as did members of the Rotary Club and the Elks Lodge. People threw coins at the boys, a total of around seventy-five dollars, which was collected for the group's mutual benefit. The local Moose Lodge gave them four thousand cigarettes. "Many men, women, and children wept as they embraced their loved ones, and hundreds of eyes were moistened long before the train departed," the newspaper reported.[36]

But then something happened. The US Army sent Debojah, Koure, and Wasni back home. It was not unusual for Syrians, especially for those whose immigration and citizenship status was unclear, to be discharged after being conscripted. But Debojah said he thought it had something to do with the fact that he could neither read nor write. Whatever the reason, in March 1918, the local draft board decided to send all three men back to the Army. They had to say goodbye one more time as they planned to take a train on the Monon back to Louisville.[37]

The next month, Michigan City mourned the death of the first local soldier to die in the war. He was a Syrian Christian. Services for Edward Shikany, who died of pneumonia at Camp Pike in Arkansas, were held at a Sacred Heart, a Syrian Catholic church. The Rotary Club sent flowers and a representative. A military firing squad and a bugler were present at the burial, and Shikany's casket was covered with the US flag. Later, Sacred Heart added a gold star to its parish service flag. It was one of thirteen stars, representing the number of parishioners who went off to war. Father Michael Abraham gave the sermon in Arabic and English, and after vespers were concluded, the congregation sang the US national anthem.[38]

During World War I there was increased public attention to the discrimination that Syrians, especially Syrian Muslims, faced in Michigan City. Their participation in the war advanced their social status as white Americans. On the very same day that Edward Shikany's death was mourned in the local newspaper, it was announced that Joseph Allie had won a verdict against South Shore Amusement for discriminating against him. The company operated the bathhouse at the Michigan City beach. It refused to give Allie a bathing suit. The newspaper reported that "something was said about 'not wanting that Turk around here.'" So, "Mr. Allie sued the company to recover for the humiliation suffered a result of being refused the use of the bathhouse." A jury of white men took a little less than an hour to deliver its verdict in favor of Allie. He had sued for one hundred dollars; the jury awarded him fifty, not a small sum in 1918.[39] This was more than a victory for one Syrian Muslim. It was a victory for all Syrian Muslims who sought access to white-dominated public space. In the past, Syrians had been shut out of or unfairly policed in the park or on the beach, which were the premier public spaces of Michigan City. The fact that a jury found for the plaintiff was evidence that the town's white citizens were willing to grant more rights to Syrian Muslims.

Allie, who worked for Haskell and Barker, was soon drafted into the armed forces. Just a couple weeks after he won in court, this native of Tebnine was one of over fifty men from Michigan City who left for Camp Taylor in Kentucky. In July, he wrote a patriotic, upbeat letter from camp to let people in Michigan City know that "the Kaiser is in for a first class trimming." He was "very sorry he did not get into the game long ago." The young men with whom he served could "clean up on anything the Kaiser ever dreamed of." Allie said the food at Camp Taylor was delicious. All the Michigan city boys were "feeling fine," he said, and he "urges every citizen do his best to help Uncle Sam win this war." He also praised the support of the Red Cross and the YMCA. Over the next year, the newspaper reported on several of Allie's letters, and he became a regular source of information from inside the ranks. He was happy to tell people back home that he passed the examinations that qualified him for overseas duty. His departure was delayed when he was sent to another unit, but he later reported to Camp Merritt, New Jersey, for his posting in France. At the end of the war he was the last man from Michigan City at his particular post to be sent home; his job was to guard "Uncle Sam's property and keep the camp in running order until the French government gets ready to take it over." It was a painfully slow process, he said. With everyone gone, he wrote, "I certainly feel blue when I read in *The News* and see so many of the Michigan City boys coming home, and me way over here on the other side of the water." He knew that when he was finally given permission to return, he would be so happy that "I would not know what to do with myself."[40]

Joe Allie, a Syrian Muslim who faced down anti-Muslim discrimination in court, had served in Uncle Sam's army alongside Muslims, Christians, Jews, and others from his adopted town. During the war, his letters carved out space in Michigan City for himself and others like him. Even if he should not have had to prove anything, he had done so. He was no longer just a worker at Haskell and Barker or a terrible Turk. Even if there was a bit of exaggeration or inaccuracy in the reporting on his homesickness, it seems he really loved the town for which he had been willing to sacrifice himself. Being so far away, it meant something special to go back home again to Indiana.

Joe Allie's attachment to Michigan City was not unique. The Syrian Muslim veterans of World War I joined with those who only became US citizens in the 1920s to plant Muslim institutions in the city. On April 10, 1924, according to Hussien Ayad, a large number of Syrian Muslims established the Asser El-Jadeed Society, which they also called the New Generation Society. In the 1920s, they purchased an area in Greenwood Cemetery for $825 so that Muslims could have their own section. Then, "we purchased two buildings on 2nd Ave., one as a haven for the incapacitated free of charge; and the second one we made into a club hall for meetings," wrote Hussien Ayad. This second building became their mosque. It was located just a couple blocks from Lake Michigan and the town's busy railroads. "The Temple of Asser El Jadeed Arabian Islamic Society," as it was labeled in a 1936 Sanborn insurance map, was a simple, brick building with a gabled roof. Its short minaret looked more like a chimney than the stereotypically tall towers of Syrian mosques.

In addition to serving as a space for congregational prayers, the building contained a basement banquet hall where families would gather to enjoy Syrian Lebanese food and one another's company. Like many other ethnic-religious communities, this new generation of Muslims met together not only for prayer but also for fellowship. It became a "social and religious center for Middle Eastern descendants throughout the Midwest sponsoring religious events, conventions, and meetings for friends and relatives from Detroit, Michigan, Toledo, Ohio, and Chicago, Illinois."[41] Michigan City was one of the many nodes of the Syrian Muslim Midwest where people gathered to find spouses for their kids, sing songs in Arabic, and do business deals. A photograph of one of those gatherings reveals the diverse generational styles of the congregation. Some women wore dresses and covered their hair with headscarves; some men wore suits and fedoras. But others donned the "Great Gatsby" styles of the Roaring Twenties: women in flapper hats and men in flat hats, also known as golfer's or newsboy's hats.

What happened in Michigan City after World War I occurred in other places in the Syrian Muslim Midwest. In explaining why these

FIGURE 4.2. The New Generation Islamic Society hosted picnics near Lake Michigan. Credit: Julia Haragely Papers, Bentley Historical Library, University of Michigan.

communities bloomed at this time, it is clear that circumstances beyond their control were partly responsible: it was hard to return to Syria in World War I, and then the National Origins Act of 1924 made it harder still to get back in the United States if you decided to leave. Some Syrian Muslims felt it was better to make the best of it in the United States. But there was more to it than that. Syrian Muslims established their ethnic-religious congregations partly as a response to their surroundings. They were influenced by their neighbors—Scandinavian and German Lutherans; Bohemian, Polish, and Italian Catholics; Ahmadi Muslim missions; African American Muslim congregations; Syrian Melkite and Orthodox churches; and Ashkenazi and Sephardic Jews. Syrian Muslims themselves also inspired and imitated one another across the Midwest. Not only were they aware of each other's efforts, but they also visited one another; traveling sometimes hundreds of miles, they celebrated a holiday, a festival, or the opening of a mosque. In the 1920s and the 1930s, as the second half of the book shows, Syrian Muslim communities had the financial resources, the know-how, and the will to form that most American thing, the ethnic-religious congregation.

PART II

1920s to World War II

5

Muslim Life and the Agricultural Depression in North Dakota

The life of Boaley Farhat, the Syrian Muslim pacifist from Rafid, Syria, whose first home in North Dakota was a ten-by-twelve "shack," changed dramatically after World War I. For one thing, he purchased an automobile—and not just for his farm. He bought a car because, he said, it was a form of recreation. As in other parts of United States, the 1920s in Ross and other parts of western North Dakota were the age of the automobile. Fewer Americans traveled by rail. In North Dakota alone, "the number of registered passenger cars and trucks rose from 92,000 in 1920 to 183,000 in 1930." The Federal Highway Act of 1921 funded the construction of a couple thousand miles of new roads in the state. But most of these roads were still unpaved. Major highways like US 2 were graded, gravel roads that, during bad weather, could become impassable. By 1927, there were still "only ten miles of paved federal and state highways" in the entire state. But the more populated cities were different. Minot, the closest major town to Boaley Farhat, had five and a half miles of paved streets in the early 1920s and "at least twenty-four miles of concrete paving by the early 1930's." You didn't need a license to operate a car until 1935, and there were no real traffic signals until 1939. The chance of accidents was high, but driving around town was also an adventure for those seeking a thrill. The fact that the automobile was the primary mode of transportation for "rum-running," that is, for the illegal transportation of alcohol in the era of Prohibition (1920–1933) only added to its sense of youthful danger. Ford was the most popular automobile in Minot, but you could also purchase Cadillac, Chrysler, Studebaker, Packard, Chevrolet, Nash, Flint, Buick, and other makes and models. Sunday drives around the countryside and to the city became a popular form of recreation not only for the elite and middle-class, but for working-class people, too. Over half of North Dakota's farmers owned a car by 1920 and "by 1930," it was "eighty-seven percent." This new form of transportation meant that they didn't have to use a mail order catalogue or be satisfied with the small stores or barber in Ross. Instead, they could go shopping in Minot.[1]

What isn't clear from the historical record is whether Boaley Farhat could fit his ten kids in the car. On June 19, 1922, Farhat, then thirty-five years old, married Miss Rosenna (also spelled Rosanna) Lynch, then eighteen. Just a month before, he had officially become a citizen of the United States. Farhat was ready to put down more permanent roots, as his marriage indicated. It was a civil marriage performed by a judge at Mountrail County Courthouse in Stanley. Lynch was from Bowbells, North Dakota, located near the Canadian border. Both of her parents were Canadians, but all four of her grandparents were from Ireland. From 1923 to 1937, Mrs. Farhat gave birth on the Farhat homestead to five girls and five boys—Alley, Joe, Neddy, Mohamed, Nora, Hassen, Anna, Reteby, Ayesha, and Deneal. They were all raised Muslim and Rosenna learned to cook Syrian food. In the family they spoke English to one another, but when other Syrians would drop by, conversations sometimes took place in Arabic.[2]

Like Charles Juma, the Farhat kids attended the Ross Consolidated School, which was, according to their father, the center of their social and recreational activities. Boaley Farhat said that did not have time for serious hobbies. As a farmer, he worked every day of the year. But his kids joined other children and adult members of the Syrian Muslim community in seeking recreation and pleasure outside of work. "We Syrians used to gather at each other's homesteads and feasted, danced, and played games," Side Abdallah observed. "Baseball was a favorite pastime of many," noted Sam Omar. Hassyn Alla Juma played the guitar.[3]

The Farhat kids grew up in a house that bore multiple cultural influences. The father was a cosmopolitan man. In addition to speaking Arabic, Spanish, and English, he was deeply interested in international affairs. He kept up with goings-on in Syria and the Arab American community by subscribing to *Al-Bayan*, the Arabic-language newspaper published in New York. Before World War I, the editor supported Ottoman rule in Syria. But immediately after the war, the newspaper voiced the hopes of Arab nationalists that Syria would become independent. In 1919, the editor advocated the idea that the United States should recognize and seek to become allies with Hashemite Prince Feisal, who sought to lead a unified Greater Syria from his capital in Damascus.[4] The French military removed Feisal in 1920, and Arab nationalists saw French control in the newly created mandates of Lebanon and Syria as yet more foreign occupation. Boaley Farhat was not alone in remaining concerned about and connected to the political fate of the old country. Sam Omar, for example, read Arabic-language newspapers that would make their way to him, through somewhat complicated means, from Cairo, Egypt, and Damascus, Syria. Even as the 1924 National Origins Act limited the number of people from Syria who were allowed to immigrate to the United States, Syrians throughout the state of North Dakota consumed news from their homelands and continued to donate some of their charitable dollars to various philanthropies there. In 1925, for example, Syrian Christians donated their own money and sought to raise money from their neighbors for victims of the French-Druze war.[5]

As interested as Boaley Farhat and Sam Omar were in the politics of the old country, such commitments did not mean that they were any less engaged in the politics of their new country. Omar eventually became a Democrat, but Farhat, who like Omar got the right to vote in the early 1920s, became a Republican. Since Farhat was a pacifist and a member of the Farmers Union, it seems likely that he was committed to the ideas of North Dakota's progressive Republicans. Today, rural America is often stereotyped as a home to conservative politics. But before and after World War I, some people in North Dakota and other states in the Midwest were among the most radical in the country. Their "rural radicalism" is a legacy understood by historians, but little remembered by the general public in the United States. In Boaley Farhat's county, for instance, one town's postmaster, storeowner and later Pontiac car salesman John Husa, was a declared socialist; he was one of sixty-three Socialist Party members in the town of Belden.[6] There were a few members of the Communist Party, as well. Most North Dakotans were Republicans or Democrats, but, by the 1920s, even the conservatives among them were keen to support reforms that were often first promoted by socialists. Many socialist ideas were popularized in the era of World War I through the platforms of the Nonpartisan League (NPL), which was established by former Socialist Party member A. C. Townley in 1915. Rather than aligning themselves with one or another party, the NPL swung its support toward whichever candidate would support pro-farmer policies while opposing US involvement in the Great War, which was seen as benefiting "the armament trust, munitions grafters and the military clique."[7] Mountrail County went for the Democratic incumbent, Woodrow Wilson, in the presidential election in 1916, hoping that he would keep the country out of the war.[8]

In 1916, the NPL found its candidate for governor in farmer Lynn Frazier, who oversaw the passage and implementation of a whole slate of progressive measures to protect the interests of farmers along with those of laborers, homeowners, women, rural schoolchildren, and children born out of wedlock. Under Frazier's leadership, North Dakota established workmen's compensation insurance and crop insurance, imposed a progressive income tax and estate tax, created a minimum wage for women, offered state-subsidized loans to farmers, and founded a state-owned bank as well as a mill and grain elevator. Frazier was defeated in a 1921 reelection campaign by the so-called regular (or reactionary) Republicans, but supporters of his progressive politics went on to help him and others get elected to the US Senate and House of Representatives. Sometimes accused of supporting Soviet Communism or socialism, the Progressives responded that they were the voices of Thomas Jefferson and Abraham Lincoln, trying to protect the American people from "corporation rule, rule by financial interests with legislation for the financial interests, and against the common people."[9]

Though the progressive Republicans held on to some power in the 1920s, they were not able to protect North Dakota's and other states' wheat farmers from a major agricultural depression. The 1920s are often associated in historical memory with roaring economic growth, especially in the stock market, but in North Dakota the economy depended mostly on the price of wheat and it was in decline. During World War I, the federal government's Food Administration, led by Herbert Hoover, had set the price of wheat at $2.20 a bushel, a dollar below the market price. This was bad enough, but by 1923 the price had declined to ninety cents, which was less than it cost for many small farmers to produce it, especially if they owed money on their land and their equipment. By 1930, a bushel of wheat was worth only sixty cents. Yields also declined. From 1919 to 1930, farmers contended with drought, and rainfall was below average one out of every two years. As a result, by 1929 the Bank of North Dakota had foreclosed on 8.3 percent of its loans to farmers—and the problem would only get worse during the Great Depression.[10]

One reason for the low price of wheat was federal monetary policy. In 1920, the US Federal Reserve increased interest rates and decreased the money supply, which made the price of the US dollar rise against other currencies. US wheat became more expensive compared to wheat from other countries in international markets. Foreign demand for US wheat disappeared and "the collapse of this market brought on a farm depression that continued through 1933, with a brief reprieve between 1925 and 1927." US agricultural revenue decreased by $13 billion. As the price for wheat dropped out, the farmers' land also became less valuable. By 1925, it was worth only two-thirds what it had been worth in 1920—a loss in value of over half a billion dollars.

Then, the banks who lent money to the farmers for equipment, supplies, and land started to fold.[11] Bank failures were a regular part of life for farmers like Boaley Farhat. Farhat said that he "lost . . . thirty-five dollars in the Citizens State Bank." He also lost money held in the Ross State Bank and the Stanley Bank. Sam Omar had lost a lot more: $359 in the Citizens State Bank, "a few hundred in the State Bank of Ross, . . . and $25.60 in the Stanley Bank."

Over the next decade or so, some members of the community, including Hamed Abdalla, Ernest Alley, Abdalla Farhart, Hassen Farhart, and Alex Ganney, decided to return to Syria and Lebanon. Like many others North Dakotans of various ethnic backgrounds, some headed to cities to work in factories. Albert Adary, Saide Alley, Alex Ash, Ahmid Assem, Mahamad Hassan, Raymond Hassen, Salim Hassen, Albert Mostafa, and Morris Osman went to Detroit, a favorite destination.[12] They generally became members of existing Syrian Muslim communities in their new towns and cities. They may have had personal reasons for leaving, but there were immoveable historical forces at work, too. The false promises of the dry-land farming movement—the idea that the short-grass prairie was suited for intensive agriculture—had failed them and other settlers. The international economics of farming compounded the environmental challenge.

Still, many endured. Though events were simply beyond their control, some of the Syrian Muslim farmers joined thousands of other farmers across North Dakota to support one another and to seek better policies from the government. Boaley Farhat as well as Kassam Rameden and Sam Omar joined the Farmers Union. Drawing inspiration and sometimes personnel from the Grange movement, the NPL, the Equity Cooperative Exchange, and other organizations that sought collective solutions to the problems faced by farmers, the Farmers Union became the most effective organizing vehicle for North Dakota farmers. By 1927, its thirteen thousand members were able to sell their grain to the Farmers Union Terminal Association, which weighed their crop fairly and gave them a fair price. Members like Boaley Farhat could also sell their cattle, sheep, and other animals to the Farmers Union Livestock Commission. Farmers Union life and home insurance was available, and with the cooperation of North Dakota's state insurance agency a farmer could purchase insurance on wheat that was being stored before the farmer was ready and able to sell it. The policy protected against "fire, theft, tornadoes, and other hazards."[13] A Farmers Union member could buy lumber, twine, and other supplies through the Farmers Union Exchange, too. It was a popular organization in the northwestern corner of North Dakota, and in 1930 it held its national three-day convention in Minot.[14] That year, the Farmers Union claimed that it had become the largest single grain-marketing cooperative in the country.[15]

Farmers needed to purchase more equipment than ever before as agriculture became more mechanized. "The number of horses on North Dakota farms fell by a fourth" in the 1920s. Farmers in Ross could buy nearly any implement or machine that they would like in nearby Minot, which in 1922 boasted the country's most successful International Harvester dealership.[16] Tractors were so much more efficient, and the gas required to operate them was relatively inexpensive compared to the feed that horses required. The same was true of mechanized harvesting threshers.[17] New plows, still sometimes pulled by horses, also offered improved performance. With new equipment, farmers could cultivate more land, and could do so without hiring additional labor. Mike Abdallah, the man who had tried to make a living farming 40 acres in the Bekaa Valley before coming to America, went from farming 100 acres to farming 240. His best year was 1925, when the price of wheat recovered a little. His family's home got bigger. There were "three large rooms" on the first floor and two rooms upstairs. The basement was a coal shed. In addition, there was a frame barn, a straw barn, and some frame sheds.[18]

It was after this period of modest economic recovery that Mike Abdallah and others were able to erect one of the first buildings in the United States actually built by Muslims for the purpose of communal prayers.[19] "On January 2, 1930," members of the community purchased "four acres" from Abel and Freida Hadey "about 1½ miles east and ½ mile south of the Village of Ross," on land that was once owned by Ahmet Farhat.[20] What they built there did not look anything like the mosques in which they had prayed in Syria. And it did not look much like the churches in town either. It looked like a granary or storage shed. This was a very simple building whose aesthetics reflected the architecture of the barns and houses that they had been putting up on their own farms for a couple decades. The low-hanging, rectangular structure sunk deeply into the ground had walls of concrete with tall window wells on the long sides. It featured a stone chimney and gabled roof, and a wooden shed with two doors served as the building's entrance. It had a total of twelve windows. "At the time of construction," according to a local history, "it was said" to cost "$400." That money mostly paid for the materials, which the community members then used to build the mosque themselves. "The furnishings consisted of chairs, benches, a large rug and heating units," and "when attending worship services, the members would bring their own small rug on which they knelt."[21]

This mosque was not some stubborn attempt to preserve religious tradition against the onslaught of the modern world. In fact, some of the Muslims who helped to build the mosque had not been religiously observant in Syria. Side Abdallah, for example, attended Friday congregation prayers in Rafid "infrequently," but many years later he made sure to tell a WPA interviewer that he "helped to build the first Moslem church here."[22] By using the word "church" to describe the mosque, something that many community members did, Side Abdallah was translating for a non-Muslim audience. The word "church" meant religious congregation, and building one was, in that place and in that time, the most American thing that Syrian Muslim Americans could do. "Every community has their little temple, or church, or mosque. And that was ours," remembered Emmet Omar, who grew up in Ross. Religious congregations were Americans' most popular nonprofit organization in the 1920s—more popular than social clubs or even sports teams in that more Americans were likely to join, attend, and give money to a religious congregation than any of these other civic groups. The fact that the WPA worker asked about religion is itself evidence of how central the institution was to American life. Religious institutions shaped American society as a whole, but especially in North Dakota. By 1936, wrote Elwyn Robinson, "the state had 212 women's clubs, 1,078 Farmers' Union locals, 1,390 secret fraternal societies, and 2,097 churches."[23] Sometimes, attending services at a religious congregation was North Dakotans' only social activity. When asked what forms of recreation she enjoyed, Mary Juma said that "we didn't have any recreation; we only work." But Juma added, "We attend services every Friday."[24]

The religious congregation offered individuals not only a way to develop and perform their morality and respectability, but also the chance to pool their cultural, political, and economic power. The largest immigrant population in the northwestern part of the state was Scandinavian, and many of them were Lutheran. From 1916 to 1926, the Lutheran church grew fast—approximately three-fourths of all new church members in the state became Lutherans, a total of fifty-nine thousand people.[25] Mountrail County was a hotbed of Lutheranism, with over a dozen congregations. These churches increasingly used English in their service during this era of growth. Before World War I, more than half the churches in North Dakota offered a service in one of thirteen languages other than English. After the war, an increasing number transitioned to English as their primary language. But even after this transition, their immigrant members, and their sons and daughters, continued to cultivate ethnic solidarity in their congregations. Assimilation did not mean getting rid of one's ethnic identity. Instead, many Americans sought to plant and weave those traditions into the tapestry of American culture. So when Syrian Muslims built their mosque on the Dakotan prairie, it was a decision that mirrored the pattern of Lutherans and their other neighbors. In order to be American, as American was defined in their part of North Dakota, one needed to practice one religion with one's ethnic group in a religious congregation. According to Sam Omar, many Syrian customs had disappeared in the United States except for religion.[26] Even as Islam was preserved, some of its meanings and functions changed and, for some, became more important.

As "American" as it was to build a religious congregation for one's ethnic and religious community, it also took some courage to build a mosque. Throughout the 1920s, stereotypes of Muslims remained potent in North Dakotan society. Hundreds of articles appeared in the state's newspapers alluding to Muslim "hordes." Other bad words were used, too. Islam was still associated with irrationality, violence, and danger. Even if the claiming of physical space on the prairie for Islam was an attempt by Syrian immigrants to cultivate social acceptance as one of North Dakota's many white ethnic and religious groups, it was still different than building a Christian church. It helped that the mosque was located outside of town, so remote and so inconspicuous that it may not have been noticed by people other than trustworthy neighbors, including the Scandinavians whom Muslims often credited with kindness and understanding. The *Mountrail County Promoter* did not mention it in its weekly listings of religious services. Some non-Muslims lived near the mosque, but it was located in a part of Mountrail County where there was a critical mass of Muslim farms. Families who lived less than a mile away included the Abdallas, Farhats, and Omars, and there were many more families in sections of Ross Township within a few miles.[27]

Behind the mosque, the community established the "Assyrian Moslem Cemetery," where loved ones could be buried in a ritual that combined American hygienic practices with Islamic tradition. According to a local history, "after the body was embalmed," which was not a traditional Islamic practice, "it was washed" and "wrapped in a white burial shroud," which were traditions that the Syrian Muslim community brought with them to the prairie. A "prayer ritual" was also "performed." This was the *janaza*, or funerary prayer. Reciting the first chapter of the Qur'an, a group or congregation of people would say, "In the name of the Most Compassionate, the Most Caring / Praise be to the Lord of All the Worlds / King of the Day of Judgment / the Most Compassionate, the Most Caring." Generally speaking, a supplication is made, repeating some words of the Prophet Muhammad, perhaps asking God to forgive the deceased, to have mercy on them, to cleanse them of sin like the funeral shroud is cleansed of dirt, and to make easy their entrance into paradise. The body is placed in the grave with the head pointing toward Mecca, the direction in which Muslims pray, and is buried. A grave marker is added, as was the case in the Ross "Moslem Cemetery" where dozens of markers can be found today. Among the first people to be buried there was Mike and Lillie Abdallah's nine-year-old boy, Albert Charles Amid Abdallah (1921–1930). Joseph Jaha, less than a year old, was also buried there.[28]

The establishment of a Muslim cemetery served a practical purpose, but it also had a special meaning. There is little more permanent in the United States than cemeteries—as permanent as anything can be in a country that seems to prefer tearing down old structures and starting over rather than preserving its architectural legacy. Though Native burial grounds and Black graves are more likely to be destroyed, built over, or sometimes moved than the cemeteries of white people, some of the oldest existing structures from colonial American and US history are the stones or aboveground crypts that mark people's graves. Where we bury our dead becomes sacred ground, and the act of visiting and maintaining graves is not only an expression of filial piety, sometimes for people we never met, but also a positive affirmation that we belong, in some way, to these places in which our ancestors were buried. For a religious minority, the founding of the cemetery as much as the building of a mosque was another sign that they belonged to the prairie and to America. It demanded recognition and respect for the Muslim dead and also for the Muslims who were living.

Syrian Muslim families continued to grow. Some of their marriages were endogamous, meaning that they married another Syrian person. For instance, in 1931 Mary Juma's son, Charles, married Sada Gader (also spelled Cader, since the Arabic letter *qaf* can be transliterated as a "c," "g," or "k" as well as a "q"). Sada Gader was born on January 12, 1913, likely in Canada although she also lived in Whitewater, Montana. Her parents, Elly Gader and Isha Yesda, came from the same village as the Juma family—Bire in the Bekaa Valley. To marry someone who was connected to a family's village of origin was not unusual among Syrian immigrants. By 1930, the Gader family was living near Ross, North Dakota. Sada, or "Sadie" as she was known, was the eldest of six children, and she had her hands full as an unpaid worker and housekeeper for her parents. The next year, when she turned eighteen, she got married and moved out of the house. Charlie and Sadie had their first child the year after that. During the 1930s, they also welcomed another son and two daughters.[29] There were many other examples of Syrians marrying one another in and around Ross. Sam Omar married Nazira Kurdi; both of them were originally from Rafid. By 1940, they had five children: Fatima, Abraham, Rosie, Sharfee, and Joseph.[30] Mike Amid Abdallah also married another Syrian, who was from his village, Rafid. It was a second marriage for Lillie or Lila Abdallah, who had five children with her former spouse. After marrying Mike, she had six more kids.[31] But other Syrian Muslims married outside their ethnic group, just like Boaley Farhat did. Hassyn Alla Juma wed Nettie Mitchell from Logan County, West Virginia. Nettie was of Irish descent. By 1940, the couple had eight children: Lila, Ellen, Allay, Joseph, Mohamad, David, Mary, and Ahmad.[32]

For all these families, life in the 1920s, during the era of the agricultural depression, was not easy. But the 1930s were worse. Much worse. The Great Depression in combination with below average rainfall "nine of the eleven years from 1929 to 1939" was catastrophic for the North Dakota agricultural economy. Drought from 1929 to 1931 cut down on yields, but the rain came back, temporarily, in 1932. That was a blessing and a curse as yields increased and a higher supply pushed down prices. A bushel of wheat was going for thirty-six cents—during the war, it had been $2.20. As the debt of farmers continued to rise and foreclosures increased, the Farmers Union supported more radical solutions. The group endorsed government-guaranteed prices for crops, refinancing farmers' debt at low interest rates, and a new bankruptcy law that would forgive farmers' debt in proportion to how much their land was actually worth. In 1932, most members of the Farmers Union voted for Franklin Roosevelt for president and William Langer for governor. Even before Roosevelt was sworn in, Langer began to tackle the state's fiscal crisis. He announced that he would raise the price of wheat by forbidding anyone to ship wheat outside the state. His action did not hold up in court, but it managed to raise the price a bit as the market bid it up on fears of a reduced supply. Most importantly, he placed a moratorium on foreclosures on state- and privately financed debt so only the federal government could foreclose on properties in North Dakota. The Farmers Union praised the move, and its newspaper proclaimed that "human rights are more sacred than property rights." Some local sheriffs continued to foreclose on people's properties, but in one of the more dramatic acts of resistance against this law enforcement action, "angry crowds of farmers abused officials, making them slop the hogs, scrub the barn floor, and walk home." Near Williston, a group of farmers purchased all the equipment at farm auction for pennies on the dollar and gave it back to the farmer. Foreclosures became a public safety risk, and Gov. Langer called out the National Guard to put an end to sheriffs' sales and restore order. Charles Juma, son of Mary and Hassen, said that Langer "saved this state."[33]

But the farmers couldn't catch a break. In 1933, drought resumed. That year, the average personal income in North Dakota was less than half that of the country as a whole—$375 per person on average in the United States versus $145 per person on average in North Dakota. The price of land declined. Farmers were still struggling to pay back loans and pay taxes on their land. The next year, 1934, was the driest year ever recorded in the state. It was not as bad as the Dust Bowl of Texas, Oklahoma, and the rest of the Southern Plains, but "dust storms occasionally made travel by plane and auto hazardous," wrote Elwyn Robinson. "Here and there drifting soil covered fences, ditches, and farm machinery." There was little water and sometimes no feed for livestock, and the all the dust was bad for everyone's lungs, including the animals'. The federal government stepped in, offering twenty dollars a head for cattle.[34] Mike Abdallah "was forced to sell thirty-nine head of cattle to the government because I didn't have feed for them." He admitted that "it was hard to have to sell my cattle to the government for so little money but they would have starved if [I] had tried to keep them." In the middle 1920s, he had farmed 240 acres, but by 1939, he farmed only 160. The droughts of the 1930s convinced Abdallah to concentrate his efforts on raising sheep, whose water consumption was perhaps one-tenth of that needed by a dairy cow. By 1939, he had "106 head of sheep, 9 cows, and 7 horses." He did not own a tractor. The Depression also took a toll on his grown sons, and one of them moved to Minnesota to find work. His grown daughters got married and moved out. Teenagers Fatima, Hamid, and Hassan and eleven-year-old Mary were at home because they didn't have any money to pay school expenses.[35]

Their youngest brother, Toby, born in 1930, lived at the Grafton State School, which had been established as the "North Dakota Institution for Feeble-Minded Children" in 1903. Like many such institutions, the school emphasized practical training for its residents, who helped to grow their own food if they were able to do so. It is not clear what Toby Abdallah's life was like at the institution. He died in 1953 and was buried in the Moslem Cemetery in Ross with other members of his family. But during Toby's time at the Grafton State School, as it was renamed in 1933, it became North Dakota's most horrific center of eugenics medicine. Out of the 1,049 forced sterilizations completed in the history of the state, 634 of them were performed on disabled children at the school. Over 60 percent of all those sterilized in North Dakota without their consent were people with mental disabilities. And the peak period of such grotesque practices was from 1933 to 1938. During the Great Depression, the number of residents increased so quickly that the institution struggled to find adequate space for everyone. Many families were poor and hungry. The economic strain of the Great Depression made it more difficult to care for children in general, but especially for children with disabilities. Many of them ended up living at the Grafton State School. The Abdallah family had a special burden to bear when, relatively late in their lives, Toby arrived and they did not have the time, money, and know-how to take care of him. It is possible that the state encouraged them to send Toby to Grafton.[36]

That part of their lives made them different from other Syrian Muslims in Ross, but they were not alone in their poverty. Boaley Farhart faced the same challenges as Mike Abdallah: "My greatest loss came in

FIGURE 5.1. Sam Juma, Alley Omar, Frank Osman, H. A. Juma, Charlie Juma, Alley Gader, Floyd Sheppard, Hamid George, Albert Hadey, Mike Abdella. Undated. Credit: Photo MN/24–10, State Historical Archives of North Dakota.

1934 when I had to dispose of so many cattle at such low prices, thirty-two head in all." He said that the Depression had lowered his standard of living. "I can't provide for my wife and ten children as I would like to."[37] Sam Omar, the man from Bire who came to North Dakota in 1902, said something similar. After the crash of 1929, he could no longer make a good living at farming. He had to sell twelve head of cattle in 1934. By 1937 and 1938, he said, "we lived on what cream we could sell."[38] Side Abdallah had to sell "five cows to the government in 1934." Hassyn Alla Juma could no longer afford to pay his taxes on his forty acres. "I don't know whether or not they will take it from us," he worried. That year, tax foreclosures resulted in the transfer of two million acres of land to county ownership in North Dakota.[39]

The Depression was harder on some Syrian Muslims than others. At Mary Juma and son Charles's house, the drought had made it impossible to make any money farming, and "we didn't have enough cattle to make money on," remembered Charles. They were left with a couple dairy cows. They could not make payments on their loans and became tax delinquent. In 1938, they lost title to their land through foreclosure and went on federal relief. It was humiliating when Charles asked the federal relief worker if they could get a pair of shoes for Hassen and Charlie Jr. When Everal McKinnon visited their house in 1939, he described the furniture as "old and worn" and the inside of the house as "clean but shabby-looking." The exterior of the house had never been painted. In the 1930s, Mary Juma became ill, and one of her legs was amputated. Mountrail County paid her hospital bill. This strong woman, who not only had farmed for decades but also peddled alongside her husband in cold Canadian and US winters, lamented that she could no longer help out very much. "I miss my work, both indoor and outdoor," she said. Sitting in a wheelchair, Mary Juma visited with her grandchildren, who spoke Arabic with her but English with their parents. "I like to hold the baby," she remarked. She also visited the mosque on Fridays, and "sometimes friends stop in to talk for a while." The Depression "has made living hard, but I don't worry." She testified that she still enjoyed life.[40]

Those who lived through the Great Depression are well known for their stoicism and for taking small pleasures out of life when possible, and Syrian Muslims were no exception. "I have always enjoyed life," Mike Abdallah said, echoing the sentiments of Mary Juma. Mike Abdallah's family, for example, liked to listen to the radio and take joyrides in their car. Some of his kids learned to play the mouth organ and the guitar, and his boys would go on treks to hunt and trap in the nearby hills. "They like the sport of it," Mike Abdallah said, "and the cash they get out of it." The women in the family did all their own sewing, and they kept the house "exceptionally clean," according to the WPA's Everal McKinnon. When a guest came for dinner, they could still afford to offer him a nice meal. McKinnon wrote that they served him well-seasoned chicken stew with potatoes, onions, tomatoes, and other vegetables cooked in a broth. The menu included fried potatoes; "a plate of homemade cheese (made from sweet milk); . . . homemade cookies and cake and plum sauce and tea."[41] And, as with most meals, it was served with Syrian bread. Making various kinds of flatbread was something that Syrians did wherever they went in the Americas. "A Syrian enjoys his flat bread as a Norwegian enjoys his lefse," proclaimed a local history. It was often baked on the large, flat metal top of a coal-fired stove. It may have changed by the time she wrote it down, but Sada Gader Juma's recipe for the bread included yeast, sugar, warm water, salt, oil, milk, and flour, which was kneaded until it was "soft and pliable." She let it rise until it "doubled in size." Then, forming the dough into balls, it was made into small rounds, and those rounds were "flapped, slapped, and tossed" until it was "almost paper thin." It didn't take long for the flat, round loaf to "bubble and brown."[42]

This tradition of bread-making and the community that nurtured it in North Dakota survived in part with the help of state and federal aid, as several community members testified. In 1933, farmers began to receive relief, which sometimes came in the form of groceries or feed for livestock, by way of a state emergency relief agency funded by the Federal Emergency Relief Administration. Thousands of North Dakotans also found work as WPA employees; they transformed the state as they built roads and bridges, dug wells, served school lunches, created outdoor recreation facilities and state parks, and recorded the history of various ethnic groups. In 1934, what would become the federal Farm Security Administration began to coordinate relief for farm families. By 1938, "more than 25,000 farm families were receiving grants from the Farm Security Administration." The next year, when several of the Syrian Muslim farmers were interviewed by the WPA, the number of farm families on relief had increased to 31,000.[43] In addition to the Juma family, the families of Mike Abdallah, Sam Omar, and Hassyn Alla Juma all received federal relief.

"The relief situation is all right," claimed Boaley Farhat, "as that is the only way some people can exist." Side Abdallah agreed: "The relief given to the poor people is a fine program." It was "as good as it can be," remarked Hassyn Alla Juma. Mary Juma said that both the FSA and the WPA were "good because they help us poor people." But there was also criticism. Sam Omar thought there was too much "graft and chiseling." Mike Abdallah's opinion was that the FSA was "O.K." but the office in Stanley was "no good." He also asserted that the WPA was not run properly: "I don't believe that enough deserving and needy people get jobs because they [don't] know the right people or because of politics." He had worked for the WPA "for about a month in 1936." Based on his own experiences, he concluded that the government was not "helping enough" in North Dakota compared to other states. But he also said that he was not "smart enough" to diagnose all the problems with federal programs: "If I was," he added, "I wouldn't be a poor farmer with sheep to take care of and cows to milk."

One factor that may have influenced the views of Mountrail County farmers toward federal policy was the Land Utilization Program (LUP), created as part of Franklin Roosevelt's New Deal legislation in 1934. The LUP identified vast areas of the Great Plains as better suited for grazing animals than raising wheat and other crops. The federal government appropriated tens of millions of dollars to purchase more than ten million acres of what it deemed "submarginal" land. It was supposed to take wheat-producing land out of production, reseed it with drought-resistant prairie grass, and create large, scientifically managed grazing areas that could be used by ranchers. The idea was supported by Syrian Muslim farmers in western North Dakota. They were the sodbusters who had tilled up the shortgrass prairies and had tried to grow wheat there for two or three decades. Their experience taught them that without steady rains their prairies were not capable of supporting intensive agriculture. That's why Mike Abdallah became what he called "a poor farmer with sheep to take care of." Based on his experience, he believed that "this part of the state should be used for grazing." Side Abdallah agreed: "Going back to grazing would be the best bet for this state." As did Sam Omar and Boaley Farhat. But when the LUP began to buy land in North Dakota, the government purchased "very little cropland at all." Instead, the LUP bought tracts in the "badlands along the Little Missouri River. Here the soft, silty and clayey bedrock erodes from hills and cliffs into piles of stony rubble devoid of vegetation." This part of the state never grew wheat, not much anyway. So the LUP ended up taking land that was not yet used for agricultural purposes and turned it into grazing land.[44]

Not all of the federal programs designed to help farmers in North Dakota and other states were unsuccessful, however. North Dakota was abuzz with talk about agricultural policy, and everyone from the local farmer to the US president tried to find a solution to a crisis that would not abate. Roosevelt's specially appointed Great Plains Committee issued *The Future of the Great Plains* in 1936, and the report outlined dozens of ideas. Among them was a belief in the value of soil and water conservation; the next year, the North Dakota legislature passed an Agricultural Conservation and Adjustment Act designed to assist with the implementation of federal policy at the local level. By 1938, each locality in North Dakota had its own county agricultural conservation association. Working under the provisions of the Agricultural Adjustment Act of 1938, local conservation associations performed a variety of tasks that benefited Syrian and non-Syrian farmers alike. For one, as the name of the organization implied, the organization promoted soil conservation by paying farmers to plant grass seed and build small dams on their properties to manage water flows and reduce soil erosion. It offered loans to farmers against the value of their wheat and other crops that were in storage either on the farmer's premises or in community granaries or public warehouses. The leaders of the associations were elected, thus putting the implementation of federal farm policy into the hands of locals.[45] All of the Syrian Muslim farmers interviewed by the WPA workers were members of their county agricultural conservation association, and several held the organization in high esteem. "I belong to the Agricultural Conservation Association," said Mike Abdallah, and "if it weren't for this there wouldn't be any money in trying to raise a crop."

Even if most North Dakota farmers took advantage of the federally funded programs of Franklin Roosevelt's New Deal in the 1930s, many of them did not support Roosevelt's foreign policy. Their leader was US senator Gerald Nye, who was elected in 1925 as a progressive, pro-farmer Republican who blamed many of America's woes on big business. Nye developed a national reputation as an anticorruption reformer and antiwar advocate; he was what his opponents called an isolationist. In the US Senate, Nye uncovered President Warren G. Harding's Teapot Dome scandal, one of the most infamous cases of corruption in US history. In the 1930s, Nye led a special investigation of the munitions industry. He saw World War I as a conspiracy of interests among politicians, bankers, and, most of all, the defense contractors and others who sought to profit from the war. In 1935 and 1937, Nye led the effort to pass the Neutrality Acts, which prohibited the US president from taking sides between any two countries at war and also banned selling, giving, or transporting arms to any of the belligerents. Most people in North Dakota and in the United States more generally agreed with Nye in 1937—in one public opinion poll, 70 percent of them said that the US decision to enter World War I was an "error." After Japan invaded China in 1937 and then Germany invaded Poland in 1939, many in the United States began to see war as inevitable. But in North Dakota, even after Germany invaded Norway in 1940, most farmers were still opposed to war. The Farmers Union opposed implementing a draft. Some national antiwar activists like Charles Lindbergh were anti-Semites who saw World War II as a Jewish conspiracy. Nye may have implied or fostered similar views, but his public statements focused on the idea that US national interests were best served by avoiding war—any war. He said that President Roosevelt's foreign policy was leading inevitably to US involvement, and he called for his fellow citizens to resist prowar propaganda.[46]

When asked in 1939 whether the United States should join the war effort against Germany, many Syrian Muslims, like Sen. Nye and other North Dakotans, opposed US participation. Farmers Union member and Republican Kassam Rameden, a veteran of World War I who saw action at the front, said that America "should stay at home" in what would become World War II. Boaley Farhat was a pacifist who opposed all war. Sam Omar favored the US fighting in World War I, but not in World War II. Mike Abdallah thought of fighting in World War I as a "good cause," though he was opposed to fighting in World War II as well. "I don't see that we can do any good, not enough to pay for what it would cost in lives and money both," he suggested. "The European countries, it seems, have to have war every so often anyway," he continued. "I'm tired of reading and hearing about the troubles over there." Abdallah observed that since Syria and Lebanon were now under the control of France, they too would be swept into the conflict. He added, however, that he did not "know anything about the Old Country" anymore since "it had changed a lot since I left there." Mary Juma laughed "heartily" when she was asked about US participation in the war, saying that "Hitler must be stopped some way, shooting him if necessary." She also lamented the human suffering: "It must be terrible in Europe now with the war raging." Like many others citizens of her state, she seemed to blame war profiteers, at least in part. "Greed and jealousy make the innocent suffer," she proclaimed.

But after the Empire of Japan attacked the US naval base at Pearl Harbor, Hawaii, in 1941, opposition to the war fell silent. Sen. Nye and the entire congressional delegation from North Dakota voted to declare war. As in World War I, North Dakota's Muslims registered for the draft, as required. Many of the children were simply too young to participate—for example, all of Sam Omar and Hassyn Alla Juma's kids were under eighteen. Some North Dakota–born Syrian Muslims turned eighteen during the war, but were never called up for or were exempted from service. Hassan Abdallah, Mike and Lillie Abdallah's boy, was born in 1925 and registered in 1944. Under his employment category, it said: "staying at home on the farm." Boaley Farhat's eldest son, Alley, was also old enough to serve. He registered when he was nineteen in 1943 and served until 1946. He was a technician fifth grade in the US Army, the equivalent of a corporal.[47]

World War II had a profound effect on Ross's small Syrian Muslim community. The war is often credited as ending the economic hardships of the Great Depression, and this was true in North Dakota. But the rains played an important part, too. "Every year from 1940 to 1944 had above-average precipitation," wrote Elwyn Robinson, "and 1941 was the wettest on record." Wheat yields increased, and the additional supply was needed during wartime. So farmers received a higher price. A bushel went for $1.53 in 1945. The price of cattle also increased. The resulting windfall meant the end of federal relief for most farmers, who no longer needed grants-in-kind or cash payments. About sixty thousand men and women, more than 10 percent of the state's population, were serving in the US armed forces, and schoolchildren pitched in to help meet the demands for farm labor. Farmers were also able to purchase more tractors and equipment. Bank deposits tripled. Many farmers paid off debts. Charles Juma bought back the land he had lost due to tax delinquency.[48]

At the same time, the demographic and economic trends that had threatened the life of the Syrian Muslim community in the 1930s continued during the war. Unlike Cedar Rapids or Detroit, the little hamlet of Ross never had an industrial base or a diversified economy. The war did not transform North Dakota in the way that it did other states. It remained almost wholly agricultural. Out of $225 billion in defense contracts, North Dakota received $9.6 million. Able to pay off its debts, the state government chose to save for a rainy day rather than invest in industrial infrastructure. Even as farmers as a whole benefited during the war years, farm foreclosures actually increased as the state moratorium on foreclosures expired. Farms got bigger, and the number of farmers decreased. Several farmers started over in Montana. Some of those who left the farm to serve in the armed forces never came home, and other laborers went to work in the expanding factories of other states. Side Abdallah, like many others, headed for Detroit. During the war, about 165,000 people left the state. The population of North Dakota was shrinking.[49]

This is the main reason why, over the long term, the Syrian Muslim community in Ross—but not in the Midwest overall—was unable to sustain itself. Some Muslims converted to Christianity. Others stopped practicing religion altogether. These same trends occurred among other Muslims in other places, too, but there was a difference between Ross and Cedar Rapids, where there was a critical mass of Muslims and a way of life that sustained that community. Ross was always a community of small farmers. It remained so for decades. And small-scale, intensive agriculture in western North Dakota became increasingly untenable after World War II. Some Syrian Muslims would live in Mountrail County their whole lives; some of their descendants live there still. Mary Juma's boy, Charles, eventually left the farm and moved to the nearby town of Stanley. He became a Lutheran. He spoke fluent Arabic until he died in 1985. He could claim Islam as part of his heritage, but he was no longer part of a living Muslim community.

Over time the Syrian Muslim community ceased to exist. The mosque fell into disrepair and was taken down in the 1970s. The children and grandchildren who remained in the area often proudly claimed their Muslim forebears but did not practice Islam. Richard Omar maintained the cemetery out of filial piety; in 2018, it was listed on the National Register of Historic Places. Several Muslim journalists and filmmakers visited the site, and it became part of Muslim American lore. Occasionally, a relative of one of the original Muslim families is still buried there. Sarah Omar Shupe, the former spouse of Alley Omar, donated money to have a small mosque built on the site of the original.[50] Though some may feel sad about the community's disappearance, many Muslim Americans who discover it today are amazed that it existed at all. Its memory is now preserved as an irreplaceable artifact of the Muslim heartland.

Cedar Rapids' Grocery Business and the Growth of a Muslim Midwestern Town

In the 1920s, Hassan Igram, the man who had worked for the Cedar Rapids Gas Company, decided to try peddling for a while. Although the day of the pack peddler was largely finished, it was not unusual for Syrians to do some peddling here and there between jobs or to supplement incomes. According to his son, Abdullah, Hassan Igram peddled around Iowa and then decided to join a few other Syrians in Macy, Nebraska, located on the Omaha Reservation just over the Iowa-Nebraska state line. He operated a general store and met his first wife, Goldie Gregg, there. The daughter of farmers, Goldie was just sixteen, maybe seventeen when she married Hassan in Sioux City, Iowa, on November 28, 1922. Hassan was in his mid-twenties, perhaps as young as twenty-four or as old as twenty-seven. Goldie was one of several children living in her parents' house, and it was not unusual to be married at a young age in rural America at the time. Shortly after getting married, the couple moved to Cedar Rapids. By 1924, they were living on the top floor of a two-story, wood-frame house and operating a grocery store on the lower level of 511 M Avenue West. Just a few hundred yards from the Cedar River, the house was located in a newly developed section in the northwest part of town. That year Hassan Igram became a naturalized citizen of the United States. The next year, in 1925, Goldie gave birth to their son, Abdullah, who was born on September 14.[1]

Unlike rural North Dakota, the Cedar Rapids economy was roaring in the 1920s, and Hassan Igram exemplified the entrepreneurial success of the white ethnic immigrant during this era. Cedar Rapids rapidly paved its streets in the 1920s to meet the demand of consumers who by 1920 could choose among fifty different makes of automobiles for sale by local car dealers. By 1925, there were sixteen thousand automobiles in the county. Tall, nine- and ten-story buildings were built downtown. Women, who gained the right to vote nationally in 1920, helped to support the expansion of the public school system, voting to issue public bonds for the building of new middle schools. Cedar Rapids more than tripled in land area. In 1926, "the city added thirty-one square miles to its previous fourteen square miles."[2] Its population was over fifty thousand. It also became the seat of Linn County, and May's Island, located in the middle of the Cedar River, became the site of a new City Hall and the Linn County Courthouse. The Linn County Courthouse was erected in 1925 as a Beaux Arts–style building with a colonnade of ten large Ionic columns.[3] Seven stories tall, City Hall was built in 1927 in a neoclassical style to honor the veterans of World War I. Its observation tower was composed of a "Greek colonnaded temple above which rises a symbolic sarcophagus." It also featured a large stained-glass window designed by artist Grant Wood. Hassan Igram knew these buildings well. In fact, the very first court case tried in the town's new superior court room was a small, three-way employment law dispute involving Igram and Company. The judge ruled for the employee and for Igram and Company, which netted $34.16 from another company.[4]

As in Sioux Falls, South Dakota, the corner grocery store became a pillar of economic activity for both Christian and Muslim Syrians in Cedar Rapids. But by the 1920s, more efficient distribution networks and the widespread commercial use of refrigeration meant that dry good stores were converted into grocery stores, which carried a much larger variety of goods. This was the heyday of the neighborhood grocery. Italians, Bohemians, and others opened small stores throughout the city. Between World War I and World War II, the number of those stores owned by Syrians increased dramatically. In 1925, approximately five of Cedar Rapids' more than two hundred grocery stores listed in the city directory were operated by Syrians; just ten years later, the number had jumped to around twenty.[5] Hassan Igram was one of the founding figures of that expansion. Working with Albert Kalell and Abdo Omar, he

purchased additional locations for Igram stores, and later he also cooperated with the Sheronick family and others to coordinate marketing
and purchasing for Syrian-owned stores.[6]

The Igram stores offered fresh meat and produce, kept cold in display
cases made by Frigidaire, then owned by General Motors. C.R. Food
Products supplied the store with fresh poultry, while Butter-Top baked
the bread and other goods and Hutchinson's made the ice cream. Farmers would sometimes supply the store's fresh vegetables, but during the
winters, vegetables were mainly purchased from a wholesaler. Many of
Igram's customers, unlike the Igram family, did not yet have refrigerators
at home. They still used iceboxes, which were not as effective, especially
in keeping things frozen. As a result, customers came more frequently
to the store, sometimes once a day, and the store became an essential
community gathering place for Arabic speakers.[7] But the stores catered
to non-Syrian customers, too.

Igram believed in the power of advertising to build his customer base
beyond his own ethnic and religious community. Hassan Igram and his
partners passed out handbills with weekly specials and, beginning in the
late 1920s, placed a number of newspaper advertisements with those specials. The store carried items that some Muslims may or may not have
consumed—for example, it stocked cans of pork and beans, offered Fi-
delity cooked ham, and sold lard, which was still popular in American
gastronomy at the time. (Igram carried oleomargarine and butter, too.)
Advertised meat specials included picnic hams for sixteen cents a pound,
sugar-cured bacon for twenty-three cents a pound, and fresh wieners for
fifteen cents a pound. In 1928, a near-full-page newspaper ad celebrated
Igram and Company's fifth anniversary and invited all of Cedar Rapids to
come the next day, Saturday, September 22, for a party. Free cigars were
offered to the gentlemen and treats for the "ladies and children." Dozens
of items were put on sale to celebrate the day, from canned fruits, sar-
dines, and tobacco to flour, sugar, White King washing powder, bananas,
bread, macaroni, gingersnaps, and fig bars. That year, Igram and Company opened a new store, its third, at 835 North Thirteenth Street East.

Then, on January 4, 1929, Igram and Company No. 4 was established on Mount Vernon Avenue when the group took over the Biondo Brothers grocery. In addition to visiting one of the four locations, consumers could get home delivery for any order totaling two dollars or more. After the Great Depression hit, the newspaper advertisements promised that Hassan Igram "has a heart when he marks prices."[8]

Another major Syrian name in the grocery business was former peddler and dry goods salesman Abdo Aossey, the man from Insar who had gotten his start with Hassen Sheronick. Aossey had stores in Urbana and Vinton, Iowa, but eventually moved to Cedar Rapids. Unlike Hassan Igram, Aossey did not marry an American. In 1922, he traveled back home to Insar "to wed the sweetheart of his youth." He had become a US citizen in 1920, and so he knew he would be able to reenter the country with his US passport. Thomas Allbones, his business partner, spent $1,000 to accompany him on what the *Cedar Rapids Evening Gazette* described as a tour of the "Holy Land" and Europe.[9]

Abdo's sweetheart was Hasibe. Her father was a Shi'a Muslim shaykh, or leader, who performed key functions in Insar. As one of two village religious scholars, he issued rulings or opinions regarding the application of the Shari'a, or Islamic law and ethics, in cases of marriage, divorce, inheritance, and other personal matters. Hasibe's father was also an educator. He held regular classes, instructing students in the Qur'an, the Arabic language, history, and modern science. Traditionally trained shaykhs like her father were often educated not only in matters concerning the Qur'an and the traditions of the Prophet Muhammad, but also in subjects such as logic, science, and philosophy. He apparently believed in the power of knowledge for women as well as men because he made sure that Hasibe and a sister attended classes and learned to read and write. Hasibe was also kept from working in the fields. In 1923, when she was about sixteen years old, Hasibe was married to Abdo. The idea that she was his "sweetheart," a romantic notion fictionalized in novels and depicted in silent films, was obviously an embellishment. The marriage was arranged for Hasibe and Abdo, who had returned home for the purpose of marrying a woman from his village. The only problem with their match was that Hasibe refused to go to the United States. She had never left the "borders of her village." In fact, Hasibe had never even left her house by herself. She feared that she would be "lonesome" in America. Abdo stayed in the village long enough for her to become pregnant, but still she would not leave with him. Abdo had been gone long enough from his store, so he left Hasibe in her parents' house and returned to Iowa without her, at least temporarily. He steamed over the Atlantic in the *Olympic*, a ship operated by the White Star Line, and arrived in New York on November 28, 1922.[10] He kept trying to convince her to join him. In the summer of 1926, he again went back home to see his family—the newspaper reported that the purpose was to visit his mother but surely it was also to convince his wife come to Iowa.[11] In 1927, he finally succeeded, and Hasibe moved to the United States.[12]

It was not always easy for a Syrian or Lebanese person to enter the country in 1927, as the Aossey family knew from personal experience. In 1924, the US Congress passed the Johnson-Reed Act, also known as the National Origins Act, which implemented a racist immigration quota system that largely excluded people from Asia, Africa, and Southern and Eastern Europe while favoring immigrants from "Nordic" countries in northwestern Europe.[13] Legal Syrian immigration was virtually cut off, with the exception of wives and children of male US citizens. Though Syrians had been classified as white by the US courts, their whiteness was insecure. They had participated in and built US society for decades, but their culture was still vulnerable to being characterized aa "unassimilable," perpetually foreign.[14] The National Origins Act discriminated against non-white foreigners and also threatened the legal citizenship of Americans who were seen by the government as potential "illegals." Abdo Aossey's brother, William, experienced this consequence firsthand. In 1927, a big headline of the *Cedar Rapids Gazette* article proclaimed, "Vinton Business Man Held at Texas Border as an Alien." The article noted that William and Abdo were "well-known locally" as grocers and merchandisers, and had lived in the United States for eighteen years. "William Aossey, 32, did not find it hard to get into the United States when he came here as a penniless boy from Syria some eighteen years ago," declared the *Gazette*, "but now that he had prospered and is proprietor of a $30,000 business, he is having trouble getting back into this country from Mexico, where he went on a visit recently." Held in Brownsville, Texas, because, according to the US Bureau of Immigration, there was no record of him ever entering the United States in New York, he waited for help from the attorney that Abdo hired for him. He told them he was a US citizen, but they didn't believe him.[15] About a week later, he was allowed to reenter the United States after the secretary of labor's office intervened "on account of Aossey's long residence in this country."[16] But the matter remain unsettled. In 1940, William Aossey appeared before a US Immigration and Naturalization Service inspector at a local police station to determine his residency and make him eligible to apply for citizenship.[17]

Though discrimination against Syrians and other Americans perceived as "foreign" threatened to and sometimes did deprive Syrians of their social status as white people, Syrian Muslim grocers in Cedar Rapids continued to prosper. Several of them had earned enough money to send remittances to their relatives in Lebanon and Syria, and they also traveled there. Abdo Aossey went back to Insar twice in the 1920s. And Hassan Igram took his whole family to the old country in 1929. In April, Hassan, Goldie, and six-year-old Abdullah Igram drove their car to Pennsylvania and then boarded a ship in New York for a journey back to Hassan Igram's hometown of Joub Jennine. They first stopped in Portugal, where they visited the National Museum. The gold coaches of Portuguese monarchs were impressive, Hassan Igram said. They also visited Algiers, Naples, Istanbul, and Athens, where they saw the Acropolis. Finally, after almost a month of touring, they arrived in Beirut around May 15, and went from there to Damascus and then to the village. They stayed in Hassan Igram's hometown until October. Hassan Igram brought gifts for his friends and family, and one of the most surprising to many in the village was American-made fruitcake. They loved it, according to Hassan Igram: "Those who shared in eating it looked as if another piece would not have been refused." Igram said that while Damascus and Beirut were modern cities, they were still using cattle to pull plows in Joub Jennine. The modern education system impressed him, though, and people in both the village and the city were anxious to learn new trades and make themselves successful, he said. The main problem was Syria's French occupiers, who imposed harsh taxes on the people, according to Igram. During the family's many months there, they toured the country and spent time with friends and family. They returned in the autumn on the beautiful and impressive RMS *Majestic*, known as the "world's largest ship," from Cherbourg, France. Finally coming home to Cedar Rapids on October 29, the family settled back into their upper-floor apartment above the 511 M Avenue store. The local paper featured an extensive write-up of their adventure and included a photograph of the beautiful young couple and their handsome son, Abdullah.[18]

Abdullah Igram returned to school and, by the fall of 1930, received public recognition for his perfect, punctual attendance. He was a student at Harrison Elementary, located half a mile directly west of his house on M Street. Abdullah was one of the first students to use the new school building there. The slate-roofed, brick English-style building, whose capacity was 560 students, featured large windows and a "doorway of Tudor Gothic design." Implementing the latest developments in education, its science labs had experiment tables with running water and the younger students sat in chairs rather than at fixed desks. Linoleum was installed everywhere but the gymnasium to reduce the noise of footsteps. Over a dozen large oak trees provided shade to the five-acre plot on which the building was erected. Harrison School offered not only reading, writing, and mathematics, but also drama, art, and music. It was a place that encouraged its students' imaginations. When the kids took an interest in a spider's web on the grounds, for example, the sixth-grade science teacher launched a lesson plan on spiders. Science class also incorporated "kite contests, pocket gardens, nature calendars, air pressure experiments, and moon movies."[19]

Not everything about young Abdullah's life was easy. One of the scarier aspects of living above a grocery store during this era was the constant threat of robbery. In December 1930, the *Gazette* reported a stickup at one of the Igram stores and a foiled plot to rob the M Street store above which the family lived. At the store on Thirteenth Street, the perpetrator, later discovered to be a man named Robert Tillman, told employee Sam Madlon to stick up his hands and warned that he would shoot him with his "blue steel, 32-caliber revolver." Igram's partner, Omar Abdo, was also there, and happened to be on the telephone. His call ended, and he was told to stay put in his chair. The perpetrator reached across the store counter and took the bills and half dollar coins. He got away with thirty-seven dollars as he leisurely exited the store and walked north on Thirteenth Street.[20] Not two months later, it happened again: "a lone bandit entered the store, lined up three occupants of the place against the wall, and took the money that was in the cash register." Sam Madlon and Omar Abdo were there once more. But instead of walking slowly north on Thirteenth Street, the robber sped away in a getaway car, a method of egress used much more frequently starting in the 1920s.[21]

Things were also going awry at home. There was trouble in the marriage. On July 17, 1931, Judge Atherton B. Clark granted Hassan Igram a divorce from Goldie. The *Gazette* listed the reason as cruel treatment, but Linn County court records say the real reason was adultery.[22] By this time in Cedar Rapids, divorce was a regular part of life. In fact, in 1930 the county divorce rate ranked twenty-third in the United States. But this case was unusual in at least two ways. First, by a ratio of four to one most divorces were granted to women rather than men. Second, almost no one sued for divorce on the grounds of adultery—only 1 percent or so.[23] As historian Glenda Riley points out, court decisions seldom tell the full story about what really happened between husband

and wife, but whatever occurred between Hassan and Goldie, it must have been difficult for their son. Though the full record of the case no longer exists, it seems clear that Hassan was granted custody of Abdullah because his mother was the one accused of adultery. By 1932, Goldie had moved out and was renting a small room elsewhere. That same year, Hassan married a different woman, Fatima Hamed, and she moved into the second-floor apartment on M Avenue. Goldie Igram remarried in 1933, becoming Goldie Lee.[24] She sued Hassan for half of the property that her ex-husband had acquired during the marriage, but Judge Clark dismissed the suit.[25]

Hassan and Goldie Igram's marriage was not the only union under stress during the years of the Great Depression. Abdo Aossey's brother, Mike, had a rocky one, too. In the early 1920s, Mike returned to Cedar Rapids from Detroit, where he had been working as an electrician for Ford Motor Company. He tended to Abdo's business when Abdo went to Insar to marry Hasibe. Mike became a US citizen and later moved to J Street in Cedar Rapids. Around 1928, he rented a gas station that had a small grocery attached. That same year, he was injured in a serious car accident. He was trying to pass someone on the Lincoln Highway one and a half miles outside Cedar Rapids when he struck Elmer Magnusson. "Both machines were demolished," reported the *Gazette*. To make matters worse, the ambulance speeding to the scene of the accident overturned. Eventually, Mike was taken to the hospital where he was treated for a broken leg and other injuries.[26] While he was still in the hospital, his grocery store was robbed twice. In one of the thefts, "cigars and candy made up the loot."[27]

Despite that, he said that things were going fine until, in 1929, he married a woman from Vinton, Iowa, whose family did not approve of Mike. Her name was Iola McElroy. He was twenty-five to twenty-seven years old; she was twenty. They were married in secret by a justice of the peace in nearby Waterloo. The Great Depression was hard on him, not because of the economy, he said, but because of his in-laws. Mike and Iola started moving around a lot. Around 1931, he moved from Vinton to Cedar Rapids and then to Detroit. During these years, he picked up whatever work was available. At one point he sold eggs and cheese door-to-door. His first child, a girl, was born in Dearborn, Michigan. His wife and daughter returned to live with her parents, and he soon followed. His in-laws, he said, turned his spouse against him. They didn't "believe in progress." Still, the marriage continued, even if the situation was difficult. The family moved back to Cedar Rapids, where after one more try running a gas station, Mike Aossey got into the grocery business in the mid-1930s. In 1934 he opened his own grocery on 2324 J Street SW, across from Wilson School. In 1935 he had a daughter. Iola would file for divorce in 1944.[28]

What is perhaps remarkable is how much Syrian Muslim grocers like Mike Aossey endured and even prospered at the same time that so many of their fellow citizens were out of work. "People have to eat" was a common way of explaining why these grocery stores succeeded even in hard times. Other Syrian Muslims besides Mike Aossey opened neighborhood groceries in the middle of the Great Depression and succeeded. Negebe Sheronick, the daughter of Hassen Sheronick, was one of them. She moved to Cedar Rapids in 1930 and ultimately established a store with her husband on 1436 L Street SW. Hassan Igram helped to get them started. "We worked, done real good," Negebe later remembered.

Along with raising children and helping to run the family store, Negebe became an important figure in the Syrian Muslim community. She had always been a hard worker. Negebe brought formal education, leadership experience, and resilience from having grown up in the Bekaa Valley. One of the few girls in the village to attend school, she studied written Arabic and other subjects for eight years. Later, in 1922, her father supported the hiring of a female teacher to make sure girls in the village had better educational opportunities. In addition to her studies, Negebe worked for her father. She was what she called a "boss," overseeing sharecroppers in her father's fields. Hassen Sheronick had no sons, and she was the eldest daughter. It was "unusual for a girl to do that," she said, "but it was necessary." The workers respected her, as she "hired and fired, [and] carried out her father's commands." Like many people in her village, she had experienced hardship at the hands of the country's French occupiers, including the Senegalese troops in the French military forces. "No woman dared show her face," she said, recalling the abusive actions of the soldiers. Joub Jennine was located on the Damascus Road, and French troops demanded quarter. In 1925, during a popular revolt by Druze forces against the French, her father, who was a leader in the village, was forced to leave, at least temporarily. She got married and left for America. She first moved to Toledo, another town with a significant Syrian Muslim population, and worked as a storekeeper with her husband. There, she gave birth to H. A. also known as Sam, and to Amy. In 1930, the family moved to Cedar Rapids. In Iowa, she became part of an active group of Muslim women committed to the well-being of the Muslim community as a whole.[29]

Fatima Igram, Hassan Igram's second wife, also became an active community member. Born Fatima Hamed on June 27, 1916, in Fayette County, Iowa, about sixty-five miles north of Cedar Rapids, she was the daughter of Hussein Sam Hamed and Sherifa Jabara. They were dairy farmers who immigrated to the United States before World War I from Joub Jennine, Hassan Igram's and Nagebe Sheronick's hometown. Fatima attended rural Iowa schools. Like many children of immigrants, she couldn't speak English when she entered first grade. But she quickly learned. Fatima was the oldest of eight children who grew up around a few other Syrian Muslims in Fayette County and spent time with non-Syrian friends, too. Her family owned a pump organ, and they liked to listen to the Victrola record player. There was an incredible market among Arabic-speaking Americans for Arab American music, which was recorded on 78s in the United States. As a farming family, they did not take time off for Islamic holidays. They "were just like any other day," she said. "We really didn't observe that many," Fatima remembered, but during Eid al-Adha and Eid al-Fitr, the two most popular Islamic holidays, they would pray and eat Syrian food. Like other religious minorities in Iowa, including Jews, the family marked Thanksgiving with an American meal, embracing the holiday as part of a shared American civil religion. And even if it was not an Islamic holiday, Christmas was a special time when "Mom would get gifts for the kids."[30]

Though they did not strictly observe all Islamic religious practices, Fatima was raised in a proud Syrian family that did not hesitate to tell other farmers about their culture and religion. In 1930, a long story about the family appeared in the *Cedar Rapids Gazette* entitled "Mohammedan Farmer of Fayette Lives Up to Christian Principles by Pinning His Faith on 260-Year-Old Koran." Written by his friend and neighbor Ray Anderson, a seemingly liberal-minded Presbyterian, the article made that case that a Muslim was as capable of being a loyal American citizen and an ethical human being as any Christian was, perhaps more so. It acknowledged that Sam Hamed rejected a belief in the divinity of Jesus Christ and was "just as staunch a Mohammedan today as the day in 1901 he was smuggled out of his native city [of Joub Jennine]." But Anderson dismissed the idea that such theological differences were all that important, and he challenged the stereotype that all Muslims were oppressors of Christians. Sam Hamed was a good man who paid his debts, didn't drink, and was bringing up his children the right way, according to his neighbor. He was an excellent tenant farmer, and one of the article's four illustrations showed Sam and others threshing a bountiful harvest of oats. The kids, who helped out on the farm, were all involved in 4-H, the organization founded in 1902 to help rural youth become better farmers and homemakers. Abe, his eldest son, was pictured with his Holstein that won awards at the West Union Fair and the Waterloo Dairy Cattle Congress. A picture of Mrs. Hamed, who belonged "to the neighborhood women's club," and her children standing by their car was also included. The fourth illustration was of a remarkable, hand-copied family Qur'an that had been passed from father to son for more than two centuries. Noting how much the family valued it as an heirloom, Anderson thought that this Qur'an was "probably the oldest in Iowa."[31]

In 1931, the same year that Hassan Igram got divorced, the Hamed family moved to a farm at Robins, Iowa, just a few miles north of Cedar Rapids. Hassan Igram began to visit his old friends from Joub Jennine,

FIGURE 6.1. Abe Hamed, Fatima Hamed Igram's brother, won awards for the Holstein he raised as a member of 4-H. Credit: Photo Hallick 010a, Arab American National Museum.

and six months later, he married their eldest daughter.[32] She was around sixteen years old; he was about thirty-four. Over the next decade, Fatima gave birth to two boys and a girl at home, with Dr. C. T. Houser attending. She also raised Abdullah. In the mornings, Hassan would come up to the apartment and eat breakfast with the kids before they went to school. Because Harrison Elementary was so close to the house, the kids would come home for lunch and the family often ate dinner together, too. The apartment felt big to Fatima. It included three bedrooms, a living room, dining room, kitchen, and sun room. It had indoor plumbing and was heated by a coal furnace—Hassan would "get up in the night and go down to the basement" to add fuel. Hassan Igram handled the family finances and the store management. He kept the grocery store's books in Arabic. Fatima waited on customers, cooked for the family, and cleaned. She bought the family's clothes at local department stores such as Craemer's and also Newman's and Killian's. As soon as they were old enough, the kids helped their father, Hassan, in the store, which was open seven days a week, generally from early in the morning until evening with a break on Sunday afternoons. Fatima didn't drive but she used the Inter-Urban train to get around town and beyond. She also had a telephone in her home, and she visited her parents on their farm "two, three times a week, sometimes more." The family liked to listen to the radio together, and they would sometimes go to one of Cedar Rapids' many public parks. Abdullah loved five-cent movies on Sunday.[33]

Around the same time that Fatima married Hassan Igram, there were important changes in the family's business. Igram's fourth store closed by 1932, as various partners took control of their own stores. But the Kalell, Sheronick, and Igram extended families still cooperated with one another as they bought supplies in bulk and advertised together in order to lower or share costs. Hassan Igram and Albert Kalell would also invest in the real estate, buying and selling property and houses in Cedar Rapids. By 1934, Igram changed the name of the M Avenue store in northwest Cedar Rapids to include his partner, Joseph Kalell. That year, Igram and Kalell celebrated the store's eleventh anniversary with another huge sale. Delivery was now free. The store offered an even greater variety of goods, including Wheaties, Bisquick, fresh milk, Russell's Velvet ice cream, veal steak, Armour bacon, and, now that Prohibition had ended, different kinds of beer: Miller, Pabst, Manhattan, and Hunter's. For the anniversary, Igram and Kalell ordered a huge cake. Before distributing pieces of it to customers, they held a competition and gave a prize to the person who came closest to guessing the cake's weight.[34]

During the Great Depression, the grocery store became a trusted financial institution. Customers would cash their paychecks, remembered

Fatima Igram, and "they'd buy groceries." Igram and Kalell also offered credit to purchase groceries, and then when the customer would get paid every week or two, they would settle their accounts. If they had fallen on hard times, their credit would be extended. Many of the customers were like family, and Fatima Igram remembered that her husband "carried quite a few. He helped them out." According to his son, Abdullah, some of them were never able to pay him back.[35] Igram, like other grocers, also received payment from the county for some of those bad debts, as dozens of entries in the newspaper show.

The Igram children may have helped at the store, but they were also devoted to their hobbies, especially music. If you grew up in Cedar Rapids between World War I and World War II, it was hard to avoid music, which was ubiquitous in the public schools. Each day children sang songs like "My Country 'Tis of Thee" and "The Thrift Song." School music instruction included everything from the "Rooster Song," which ended with a "rousing 'Cock-a-doodle-doo!'" to the "Turkish March or Haydn's *Surprise* symphony." Winners of various musical competitions were offered free tickets to see the Minneapolis Symphony or the St. Louis Symphony when they came to town. Cedar Rapids' civic organizations, including churches and fraternal groups, almost always included music in their public meetings.[36] Music was in the Cedar Rapids air, and it was not surprising that several Syrian Muslim kids became able musicians. Abdullah Igram, for example, played the cornet. His passion for music led him to perform not only in school but also in classmates' churches. Abdullah played a song titled "The Sweetest Story Ever Told" at a Calvary Baptist Church concert on March 3, 1938. He also competed in the American Legion's drum and bugle corps amateur contest. Each of Abdullah's brothers and sisters played a different instrument—Emily played the piano while the other two boys played trumpet and saxophone. Hassan and Fatima Igram paid for private music lessons.[37] They were not the only Syrian children who were devoted musicians. Wanda Aossey was also recognized publicly for her musicianship.[38] Sam Sheronick, Nagebe Sheronick's boy, played the accordion at a meeting of the Divine Science church, one of the country's many metaphysical groups devoted to spiritual healing and other esoteric practices. Sine Killel sang as part of a trio at the same service.[39] Amy Sheronick, Sam's little sister, sang in an Americana concert that was part of the Parent-Teachers Association Dad's Night at Van Buren Elementary.[40]

Religion was also an important part of many people's lives in the Syrian Muslim community. Part of that importance was manifested in how Arabic-speaking Muslims moved around the Midwest to marry one another, celebrate one another's accomplishments, or start a business together. Traveling by car or sometimes by train, they went to and from the major Muslim Midwestern towns—Toledo, Detroit, Chicago, Sioux Falls, Cedar Rapids, Michigan City—creating a regional network of Arab Muslim life. There was a lot of movement to and from Detroit and Toledo, for example. H. K. Igram, who was Hussan Igram's brother, moved to Cedar Rapids from Toledo, Ohio, in 1932 and opened a confectionary shop. He remembered that Islam was well-suited to the life of the American merchant. It was "not difficult to keep Islamic practice like daily prayer or fasting during Ramadan" in the United States, he said. "Nothing to it!" If you had to work on Fridays, "when it's time to pray, you just stop and pray where you are." When he peddled, he prayed in the nearest field. Once he owned a store, he would "pray right on the floor, any place in the store, in the back room," and "if a customer comes in, it don't make any difference; they like it. They knew you were praying. They all know how the Muslim prays." H. K. Igram emphasized that the salat, or prescribed prayer, had to be performed properly, even if someone thought it was strange: "when you pray, you have to bow—damn right—it's no good without it."[41]

In addition to praying in one's store, Muslims sometimes met in each other's homes to pray together. By the early 1930s, they obtained space for communal prayers in one of Cedar Rapids' many fraternal organizations such as the Západní Česko Bratrská Jednota (ZCBJ), or Western Bohemian Fraternal Association Hall, and the Czech-Slovak Protective Society, both located on the southside of downtown Cedar Rapids.[42] During this era, Hussien Karoub, one of Detroit's most prominent imams, visited and sometimes led the community in prayers, also teaching some Arabic classes.[43]

Muslim mothers applied Islamic ethical norms in their childrearing. Hasibe Aossey raised her daughters strictly, as she had been raised. She refused to let them wear a bathing suit when they went swimming, for example. But it wasn't quite a strict as it had been for Hasibe. In Insar, when she was a child, women did not shake hands with men who were not family members. As the daughter of a village shaykh, she was expected to wear a headscarf when in public. It was a custom—one that she would later criticize—that she continued to practice in the United States for more than a decade after arriving. Rather than wearing a headscarf, she would sometimes wear a dusting cap. Once, when an imam from Detroit came by the store in Cedar Rapids, she was uncovered. She "escaped through a back window before he could see her and covered her head."[44]

But Islam was more than a set of behavioral rules for Syrian Muslims in Cedar Rapids. It was also a source of knowledge, which was valued for its own sake. Having been educated in the Bekaa Valley, Negebe Sheronick valued the study of religion not in isolation from other forms of knowledge but in concert with them. Having arrived fairly recently from the old country, Sheronick became a bridge between American-born Muslims and the learned traditions of their old-country ancestors. She studied Czech at a Bohemian night school. She also subscribed to and read Arabic-language newspapers published in the Syrian diaspora, including New York's *Al-Bayan* and *Mirat al-Gharb* and Detroit's *Al Hayat*.

Sheronick became one of the major players in the campaign to erect a mosque in Cedar Rapids. When it came to raising the money to build the mosque, "women did most of the work," she said, "but men were very helpful," too. Woman leaders like Fatima Igram, Negebe Sheronick, and Hasibe Aossey were extraordinarily productive people. Hasibe Aossey was typical in that she took care of the kids and the house while also working in the family grocery store and volunteering for the Muslim community. She said that she liked it that way. As they sought to build a public home for their ethnic-religious community, these women first established a fraternal lodge called Zahrat al-Ihsan, known in English as the Rose of Fraternity. One of the organization's primary purposes was to raise money to build a mosque. It did so by charging dues and holding public fundraisers.[45] In 1934, for example, the club put on a February dinner and a dance at the Moose Hall attended by 600 people. Since the total population of Muslims in Cedar Rapids may not have been more than 150, it is clear that many non-Muslims came out in support. Even more people—1,100—came to the next benefit, which was held in November in the same location. Supper was served and then the dancing commenced.[46] A 1936 "Oriental Benefit Supper" was held at the ZCBJ Hall. The dancing was from 9 p.m. to 12 a.m., and tickets were fifty cents each. The 1939 the "Oriental Benefit Supper" was held at the Czech-Slovak Protective Society Hall; tickets went for seventy-five cents.[47]

Negebe Sheronick later remembered that one of these dinners netted $600 for the club. She said that both men and women sold tickets. Wearing a label that featured the names of both the club and the mosque on the shoulder of their clothing, they "went from store to store," telling storekeepers that it was a "mosque benefit." Some of the store owners bought as many as fifty to one hundred tickets. The club continued to hold fundraisers throughout the 1930s. The women would bake pita bread and Arab sweets. Sometimes, they helped Syrian Christians from St. George cook Syrian food for church fundraisers, and the women at St. George returned the favor, helping to cook for Rose of Fraternity dinners.[48]

On February 2, 1934, the Rose of Fraternity formally established its bylaws, which contained seventeen articles and a preface. On this document, the name of the organization is translated not as the Rose of Fraternity but as the "League of Bountiful Flower." Like many historical Muslim documents, it begins by invoking the name of the "Most Merciful God," and the "Lord of all creatures, the king of the day of judgment." It offers prayers upon the Prophet Muhammad and his family. The preface then set out the intentions of the unnamed community members who wrote the document: "The Arabian Mohammedan community, who took the city of Cedar Rapids as their home, have met and decided to organize a league to be of Religious-Educational-Fraternal nature." The reason to do so, the charter explained, was to promote "the Arabic-Islamic name," to "perpetuate their beautiful . . . customs," to "keep the Arabic Language alive, and to permeate the spirit of Islamic teachings." To achieve that mission, the League implicitly acknowledged the reality that there were both Sunni and Shi'a Muslims in the community, pledging to "promote . . . love among the several Mohammedan sects." It also hoped to encourage cooperation with non-Muslims. Like many other religious bodies in the United States, the bylaws set out a democratic leadership structure in which a board would be elected by all members through "a secret ballot at the end of each calendar year."[49]

In March 1935, the city of Cedar Rapids granted a $4,000 building permit to Rose of Fraternity Moslem Order for a "church" and a school to be erected at 1335 Ninth Street NW.[50] Construction began immediately, although the land on which the mosque was built may not have been transferred to the community until April, when A. Hamad evidently gave it to the Rose of Fraternity lodge for one dollar.[51] Located just two blocks east of the new Harrison Elementary School—it was on Abdullah Igram's way home—the mosque was built in the middle of a modest residential neighborhood composed mainly of small one-story, wood-framed houses.[52] Besides the fact that it was a mosque, the Rose of Fraternity temple blended easily into the built environment. It, too, was a small wood-framed building—twenty-four feet wide and forty feet long, just 960 square feet (or 90 square meters). Despite its diminutive footprint, it was designed, like so many American religious structures, to be more than just a place of worship. It was a community center, or what Syrians called a *nadi* (club, lodge), that contained a formal place for Islamic prayer as well as common areas for socializing, eating, public programs, and teaching youth. A March 1935 article in the *Gazette* said that it would be "used for meetings of the Rose of Fraternity lodge, for religious services and for a school in which the Arabic language would be taught." The city of Cedar Rapids required buildings on this street to face west, which meant that the rectangular building could not be pointed (southeast) toward Mecca, the direction in which all Muslims perform ritual prayers. As a result, community members had to form their prayer lines diagonally, facing a corner of the building when they prayed together.[53]

Construction finished in about four months, and on June 16, 1935, a dedication ceremony was held. One newspaper article said the final cost was $5,850, and Negebe Sheronick similarly remembered that it ended up costing around $5,000. Hundreds of Muslims came from "Sioux City, St. Paul, Chicago, Fort Dodge, Detroit and other Midwestern cities" to celebrate its opening. Some of them were contributors, having been solicited by Cedar Rapids Muslim community members who traveled to various cities asking for donations.[54] "Notable guests" included the "Rev. H. Karoub of Detroit," that is Imam Hussien Karoub of Detroit, and "Dr. Sufi M. R. Bengalee of Chicago." Bengalee's presence signified the ecumenism of the event and of the mosque more generally. He was neither Sunni nor Shi'a but instead a member of the Ahmadiyya community, a modern Muslim reform group that would be rejected later by many other Muslim Americans as heretical or unorthodox. But the 1930s were different. During this decade, Muslims in the United States were as likely to cooperate with one another across sectarian lines as they were to disagree with one another. Nearly all those interviewed later by Alixa Naff stressed that there was little real difference between Sunni and Shi'a Muslims, and they sometimes seemed annoyed that Naff, who was Christian, assumed that it would be otherwise. Mike Aossey's idea that God could be found in many places and by many people, that God could be called by many names, was one repeated by other Naff interviewees. That universal view seemed to be a fundamental theological orientation among many of these founding figures in Cedar Rapids, and it was reflected in their public relations as well. They emphasized, over and over, that people of any "denomination," meaning, those from any religious community, were welcome to visit their mosque or enroll in their Arabic classes.[55]

On Thursday nights, the community held its social meeting and then Fridays they had prayers. The large, first floor was used as a lecture hall and a masjid, that is, the place where Muslims make their prayers of prostration. When it was prayer time, chairs would be removed and rugs would be put down on the floor. Children attended prayers with their parents. "Most of the time" a man would read the Qur'an, said Fatima Igram, but sometimes a woman would do it. Congregants would gather downstairs for social events. The basement had a "kitchen, restrooms, and a dining area." The basement would also be used for Arabic and other classes. Sundays were popular days for families to gather in this Christian-majority town. During summers Muslims would come for communal prayers "carrying picnic baskets" and held "day-long picnics."[56]

The rhythm of weekly activities at the mosque was similar to that of local churches. In this way, the Rose of Fraternity quickly became just another Cedar Rapids religious congregation. Generous coverage in the *Gazette* spread news about the community, but the personal contacts between Muslim grocers and non-Muslim customers as well as relationships between Muslim and non-Muslim schoolchildren also resulted in meaningful local knowledge of Muslims. By the 1930s, many in Cedar Rapids were used to living in a religiously diverse city. In addition to Catholic, Orthodox, and Protestant Christians, there were followers of metaphysical, esoteric groups such as theosophists. The state of Iowa was awash with religious groups and denominations, and no one group was dominant. The idea that religious diversity could be a social asset rather than the cause of conflict was enshrined in the creation of the University of Iowa's School of Religion, funded by John D. Rockefeller in the middle 1920s. Muslims were not included in the original community advisers for the project, but the School of Religion faculty did eventually reach out to the community in Cedar Rapids. In 1945, University of Iowa music professor Addison Alspach and religion professor Marcus Bach recorded the call to prayer and Qur'an recitation at the Rose of Fraternity lodge.[57] It is also clear that religious discrimination and prejudice toward Muslims remained, as it did during this era toward Jews and Catholics. But some in Iowa publicly embraced religious tolerance and actively cultivated interfaith cooperation among Protestants, Catholics, and Jews. Perhaps most well known in the 1930s was the Brotherhood Trio of Rabbi Eugene Mannheimer, Rev. Stoddard Lane, and Father Robert Walsh, whose road show employed "self-deprecating humor and mutual teasing" to convince "small-town audiences" that religious diversity was a positive development.[58]

Even if the beliefs of different religious communities differed, many if not most of them were united in their commitment to public service. Religious congregations did much more than conduct religious rituals, and the Rose of Fraternity was no different. Like other religious communities in town, it also offered public programs that welcomed the general public to its building. The community even invited non-Muslims to lead events there. In 1935, for example, the lodge held a Sunday evening program featuring speeches and musical performances by youth. Speakers included "B. L. Wick, who spoke of the Hawaiian Islands and foreign countries which he has recently visited; Royal Holbrook who spoke on 'Beauty and Opportunity in Iowa'; Kamel Hind, teacher of Arabian [Arabic], on 'Wisdom and Character'; Sam Allicks on membership; and Dick Richards of Oelwein [another town in Iowa] on 'Good of the Community.'" Children from the Hamed, Sheronick, and Igram families performed "patriotic and religious songs."[59] Later anniversary celebrations would include Arab dancing, which would be performed in the lodge, not the actual prayer space.[60]

In 1936, a headline in the *Gazette* proclaimed that local "Boys Master Reading of Koran in Arabic Language." Abdullah Igram, then twelve years old, and Hussen (Sam) Sheronick, just seven years old, gave a public recitation of the Qur'an at the mosque to prove their bona fides as what is called *muhafiz al-qur'an*, or a preserver of the Qur'an. Though a few Americans had memorized the Qur'an before this date—some enslaved African Americans knew the Qur'an by heart before the United States gained its independence—this was the first time, according to the Cedar Rapids community, that a formal Muslim school located in the United States had succeeded in training Muslim youth in the traditional science of recitation. Abdullah and Hussen were taught by Kamel Hind, who conducted classes for eighteen young Muslims every night from 6 to 8 p.m. and on Saturday mornings from 9 a.m. to noon. The community provided Hind with room, board, and spending money. The newspaper also explained to its readers that the "Koran is held to be a transcript of divine revelations made to the prophet Mohammed and contains 114 chapters." The boys, it said, had started their intensive effort to memorize the text in July 1935.[61]

That same year, the temple celebrated its anniversary with a program that featured Muslims and non-Muslims. Visitors came from across Iowa and beyond. Elaine Graham, Lucille Mann, and Margaret Hamad sang "To a Wild Rose." Participants belted out Arabic songs and some performed "native" dances. Several speeches were given in Arabic. "Intense patriotism as well as a cry for universal brotherhood was brought out in every speech. Several speakers mentioned their pride in the 'Stars and Stripes' and each such reference was greeted by hearty applause." It seemed that members of the Rose of Fraternity were anxious to perform their loyalty to the United States. But such loyalty did not keep them from supporting the hopes of Arabs abroad for freedom. The anniversary was dedicated to Arabs in Palestine, who were at the time revolting against their British occupiers and Zionist settlers. Attendees donated $294 toward Palestinian relief efforts.[62]

Birth and death and other life cycle events were commemorated by the ethnic-religious community around the mosque. As in North Dakota, non-Muslim recognition of these events, at the local level, would translate Islamic practices into meanings that local Christians could understand. For at least some non-Muslims in Cedar Rapids, Islam was not the strange ways of "them" but just another American religious practice. The mosque and the ethnic-religious sense of community that it fostered became a pathway to participate in the public culture of Cedar Rapids. Even in the most intimate rituals, non-Muslims were often involved. For example, the community utilized local non-Muslim funeral homes, like Turner's, and following the sanitary, legal practices of their locale, Muslim bodies would sometimes be embalmed (contrary to Islamic legal tradition, which forbids this practice.) Even then, however, the body would be ritually washed and covered with a shroud, and the *janaza*, or funeral prayers, would be offered.[63] In 1934, Hassen Sheronick, who was manager of the Kilell grocery store, died. Turner's funeral home was assigned to care for the body, and Imam Karoub came from Detroit to lead the *janaza*. He was buried in Cedar Memorial cemetery.[64] Another of those who was mourned was Abdo and Hasibe Aossey's infant son. The local newspaper's death announcement used the same words it would use in the case of Christians: "Funeral services for the infant son of Mr. and Mrs. A. A. Aossey . . . who died at 6AM Tuesday will be held in the Moslem Temple at 1PM Wednesday. The Rev. Mr. Hende," that is, Kamel Hind, "will officiate and burial will be made in Cedar Memorial Park."[65]

The congregation was a center point of their lives; so many different activities took place there. In 1937, the Rose of Fraternity again celebrated its anniversary. This time, Iowa secretary of state Robert E. O'Brian, former president of Morningside College in Sioux City, was slated as the headliner for the event. Prayers would be offered. The junior members of the temple were to sing songs in both Arabic and English, but the paper noted that "all parts of the program have been arranged so they may be understood by those visitors who do not speak Arabic." The lodge expected Muslim visitors from across Iowa and from Detroit and Toledo.[66] The temple anniversary also prompted the newspaper to include information for the general public about the religion of Islam. It explained that Muslims considered Christ to be a prophet and that "they refer to [the] deity as Allah, the Arabic interpretation of God." Before they prayed at the mosque, the *Gazette* explained, they would purify themselves by washing. The prayer ritual would then be conducted in Arabic, and they would turn their heads both left and right as they prayed. The

Gazette featured similar coverage in 1937 of the Muslim "Pilgrims' Day." Muslims in Cedar Rapids, it explained, would "join 475 million through-out the world" for the holiday. The writer of the article got confused, and seemed to think that Eid al-Fitr, which marks the end of Ramadan, and Eid al-Adha, which occurs at the end of the annual hajj, were one and the same thing, but the tenor of the coverage was positive. It noted that "all Moslems" were invited "to attend services" which would be held at 8 a.m. at the temple.[67] An article the following year in 1938 announced the celebration of Eid al-Fitr, the "Ramadan Holiday," and correctly de-scribed the meaning and nature of the holy month of fasting.[68] Another article published a year later explained that pious Muslims prayed five times per day: "At dawn, noon, mid-afternoon, sunset and evening, they face toward Mecca with the age old vow of devotion to God and Allah."[69]

This fair-minded, sympathetic press coverage of Muslim people and Islamic religion in Cedar Rapids came about partly because the Muslim community had organized itself as a religious congregation, and the *Gazette* supported the idea that American religious freedom naturally led to the existence of difference religious communities. But the acceptance of this local Muslim congregation, like the acceptance of the local Jewish synagogue, was never complete. Christianity was not only the religion of the majority; it was also in some instances what literally *counted* as reli-gion. In the city's 1937 directory, for example, the Rose of Fraternity was neither acknowledged as part of the city's fifty-seven churches nor was it listed under other associations or clubs. The imam was also excluded from the list of the city's clergymen.[70]

But the Moslem Temple continued to assert itself as part of Cedar Rapids' multidenominational religious scene. In 1939 it held a unity rally with Syrian Christians from St. John. As usual, Arabic songs and Arab dance were on offer. In addition, Gayle Woolson, a member of the Baha'i faith, spoke on "unity, brotherhood, and peace."[71] Like other religious congregations, the temple sometimes received complaints from the neighbors that there was too much noise.[72] But this did not rise to any sort of crisis for the community. So long as the community was patriotic and did not attempt to overturn established social conventions, like patriarchy or white supremacy, it could be celebrated as part of the American community. Muslims were to be incorporated rather than shunned.

The mosque actively cultivated a Muslim identity not to isolate from the rest of the community but to become part of it. These Muslims saw no contradiction in being fully Muslim and fully American. Today, some observers might scoff at the idea that the same grocers who sold pork and beer in their stores could also be devoted Muslims since the consumption of pork and liquor are prohibited in most interpretations of Islam. But this was not a rare phenomenon at the time in Muslim America. Muslims in Detroit and Toledo also owned bars and stores that sold liquor, and many of them contributed to their local mosques. There is no contemporaneous evidence that these Muslim grocers felt deeply wracked by guilt or saw any major problem with their situation. Perhaps some did. But at the very least, the historical record invites us to reserve judgment when looking back at these pioneering families who sacrificed their time, talent, and resources to establish Muslim religious congregations.

It is also important to remember that not all Syrian Muslim social and religious life revolved around the mosque. As he looked back on his life much later, Mike Aossey felt that he had not "mixed with Syrians in Cedar Rapids much." He continued to do business and socialize with his family, but his friends were as likely to be non-Syrians as they were to be Syrians. For example, when his daughter, Wanda, celebrated her eighth birthday in 1938, the party was thrown by Wanda's mom and by Mrs. Gerald Clark; other guests included the Link, Garrison, and Hamilton families.[73] This feeling of being separate from the Syrian community was a product partly of Mike's adolescence. Mike grew up in the American villages of Urbana and Quasqueton, where his non-Syrian friends—"the boys"—were like a family to him. His own biological brothers were too busy working. They did not celebrate Islamic holidays together, Mike remembers, and he went to church instead of making Islamic prayers with his brothers. He left the protective umbrella of his brother, Abdo, as a teenager to work in Detroit. Later, he found more "brothers" in the Odd Fellows, a fraternal organization in Cedar Rapids. Even though he was taught to read and write Arabic in Syria, he did not subscribe to Arabic language newspapers like some others in the community did and he did not continue to use written Arabic.[74] The community was not without its internal disagreements, either. In 1935, Negebe Sheronick's husband, Aleck (or Ali), was sued by a relative, Sam Sheronick, for $400.[75] Negebe Sheronick later described how she and her husband were cheated by a relative, although it is not clear if it was Sam.

The Muslims of Cedar Rapids developed a critical mass of families, successful businesses, and social networks that not only sustained the mosque, but were also a vibrant part of a Syrian diaspora and a growing US Muslim community. Links to the old country through the arrivals of community leaders such as Negebe Sheronick and travel back and forth helped to preserve a sense of Arab identity and belonging. In 1939, just as World War II broke out in Europe, Hassan Igram's parents, seventy-four and seventy-two years old, came to visit the Igram family in Cedar Rapids. Though it was more typical for American children to visit their parents in Syria, the transoceanic journey of the parents to America ex-emplified the ongoing connections of Syrians in Cedar Rapids to family and village in French-occupied Lebanon and Syria. That year, the elder Igrams finished their farming season in Joub Jeninne, where the oats and wheat were not completely harvested until August. Once seasonal rains began in September, it was a good time to leave. Worried about submarines and the dozens of warships that they saw in Gibraltar, the Igrams kept their life belt floatation devices at the ready while aboard the *Nea Hellas*, the Greek ocean liner that brought them to New York in September. Hassan and Fatima Igram along with Fatima's mother went to greet them.[76] It must have been one of the last such visits, which be-came increasingly rare. Travel to and from Syria and Lebanon would become more difficult.

Some parts of Syrian Muslim life continued largely unaffected by the war. The Islamic Youths of America, the youth club of the mosque, kept meeting. Among those initiated in 1940 were "Sine Kalell, Sammy Sheronick, Doris Hamed, Emogene Sheronick, Sammy DeHook, Eddy Kaliell and Alex Sheronick."[77] For a time, their adviser was the itinerant imam Shaykh Khalil bin Ibrahime Al-Rawaf.[78] Some of these Muslim youths reached out to other Muslims across the United States and Canada. Mohammed Omar and Abdullah Igram published a journal called the *Americo-Moslem*, which they distributed to Muslim communities in North America.[79] Sam and Amy Sheronick starred in Wilson School's three-act play based on Booth Tarkington's *The Fighting Littles*.[80] Muslim-owned groceries kept opening—H. K. Igram built a new store in 1941 out of concrete block on 820 Sixth Street SW.[81] His request to transfer his license to sell cigarettes and beer from the old store was approved by the city council that year, but his permit to erect a neon sign in what was a largely residential neighborhood was denied.[82]

As in World War I, there was a significant movement of people in Iowa that opposed military intervention in the European war. *Cedar Rapids Gazette* editor Verne Marshall was the leader of the national No Foreign War Committee, and used the pages of the newspaper to rally others to his anti-Semitic positions on US involvement in the war.[83] But there is little evidence of any public opposition by the town's Muslim citizens, perhaps because there was little possibility for this ethnic-religious minority to dissent. The lessons of political repression among Iowa's German, Bohemian, and other white ethnic communities during World War I had been well learned. And by December 7, 1941, when Japan attacked the Pearl Harbor naval base in US-occupied Hawaii, whatever opposition there may have been became moot. Muslims in Cedar Rapids fought and supported the American war effort in a variety of ways. Among the many Muslims from the Cedar Rapids community who served in the military were Sam Aossey's boys: Emmett, who was a technical sergeant at Camp Gruber, Oklahoma; William, who was in combat more than one hundred days straight at the South Pacific front; and Mike, who was an air corps member in Amarillo, Texas.[84]

Abdullah Igram sought to aid the war effort first by collecting defense stamps "with the aim of procuring a $100 defense bond," which he wanted to give to his school, Roosevelt High.[85] Once he graduated, he prepared to enter the military. On February 16, 1942, Igram, then eighteen years old, registered for the draft. He began active duty in the US Army on March 27, 1943. This cornet player and student of the Qur'an qualified for the Army Specialized Training Program (ASTP), "the largest military training program during World War II." Designed to help soldiers meet the technological challenges of warfare while also aiding US higher education in wartime, the ASTP took place in over 220 colleges and universities. After passing a rigorous examination and completing basic training, Abdullah Igram attended the University of California, Berkeley. Going to accelerated classes in his uniform, he studied engineering and other subjects as he also completed military drills with fellow soldiers. On October 15, 1944, he was posted abroad, spending a total of fifteen months out of the country. Igram was part of the Army Signal Corps, which oversaw communications during the Army's various military campaigns, often by connecting one unit to another via long-distance radio. This was no small task in the South Pacific, where victory over Japanese military forces required careful planning and effective implementation of amphibious assaults. Under the command of Gen. Douglas MacArthur, Igram served for a time at a base in New Guinea. As part of the 4025th Signal Service Group, he was also credited with participation in the 1944 Battle of Leyte, which was the beginning of the campaign to dislodge Japanese forces from the Philippines, and the 1945 Battle of Luzon, which eventually expelled the Japanese Imperial Army from the Philippines' largest island and its capital, Manila. Igram remained in the Pacific theater afterward, and came home on January 13, 1946. He was honorably discharged on January 20.[86]

It was still hard for Abdullah Igram to be recognized as a Muslim in the US armed services. It upset him that, unlike the Christians and Jews with whom he lived and fought, he was not allowed to indicate his religious preference on his dog tag, the identification tag generally worn as a necklace by those in the armed services. When he first received his dog tag, it had "P" for Protestant on it. Igram was not a Protestant. The sergeant told him he could leave it blank. Not only was this an insult to him, but it also meant that if he died while in service, his body might have suffered a fate similar to that of South Dakota's Joe Chamie, who was buried under a cross. Who would say the *janaza* for him? Igram had no problem supporting the war. He just thought he had a right to be recognized as a Muslim when he put on the uniform.

Like most Syrian Muslim men, Syrian Muslim women also supported the war. Cedar Rapids even had its own Muslim "Rosie the Riveter." Machine operator Aishy (or Ichey) Sheronick, born in Syria around 1899, moved to Cedar Rapids after marrying Mehmud Sheronick in 1920. When she first arrived in the United States, she told *Gazette* reporter Louise Lux, "I cried for months and begged my husband to take me back to Syria." But she adjusted and became one of the many women who helped to establish the Rose of Fraternity mosque (and later helped to build the mosque in Toledo, too). When US manufacturers mobilized to produce armaments and supplies for the war effort, Aishy Sheronick was one of the many women who took factory jobs. Around October 1942, she was one of the first female workers employed by the Loftus Company. It was the first time she had ever worked outside the home. She learned to operate various machines in the plant and in 1943 was making "export shipping boxes." Some of them were packed with meats for the troops at Wilson and Company, where her husband was, as it turns out, a box packer. Their son, Private Aleck Sheronick, joined the military in May 1942, and one of their other children worked in a Detroit factory building airplanes. According to the newspaper feature, Aishy Sheronick liked working at the plant and believed that every woman who could work should do so. "Whenever I see a friend who isn't busy enough," she said, "I tell her to get a job and start helping to win this war." When the reporter asked whether anyone helped her with housework, she said that her daughter sometimes did, but that everyone was working outside the home. "Sometimes I think they want me to have too much work to do so I'll think I can't keep working," she said. They worried that she was "overdoing it." But Aishy Sheronick was determined to keep working until "the war is won."[87]

The Syrian and Lebanese Muslim women and men of Cedar Rapids were, perhaps first and foremost, hard workers. They created things. From the grocery stores to the mosque and their contributions to the war effort, they embodied a Muslim American identity that rooted Islam and Muslims in the cultures of the American Midwest. There were moments from 1920 to World War II when some non-Muslims in Iowa recognized them not as foreigners but as a white ethnic community that built civic organizations, practiced a faith other than Christianity, and devoted their lives to US victory in World War II. Syrian Muslims still faced discrimination regarding their religion, their not-quite-white skin color, their foreign accents, and their immigration status. But like Bohemians, Greeks, and Jews who also lived in Cedar Rapids, many of them chose to protect and support one another by creating a strong sense of community and building the organizations and networks that would sustain them. They tried to "blend in" and succeed not only through their entrepreneurial activity, political loyalty, and engagement with non-Muslim friends and neighbors, but also by establishing that, like most other Americans, they, too, had a religion. Like some Muslims across the Midwest and around the country, some of them married Christians or stopped practicing any organized religion whatsoever. But the remarkable story of Cedar Rapids' Syrian Muslim community is not a story like that in North Dakota; it is instead that they remained Muslim as a way to assimilate into US society. They did not see any contradiction between preserving their faith and becoming American—they insisted that Islam *was* an American religion.

7

From Sioux Falls and Michigan City to Detroit, Capital of the Muslim Midwest

Aliya Ogdie Hassen became a teenager during the 1920s in Sioux Falls, South Dakota, and the fashions, silent movies, and speakeasies of that decade indelibly shaped her identity as a woman. Six decades later, she still remembered her first movie. She was about ten years old when she saw *The Sage Hen*. It played for several days at the Olympia Theater during the week of February 27, 1921. The Olympia, built in 1909 on South Phillips Street, was one of seven theaters in town. It was an elegant two-story building ornamented with a large marquee and corbels between its second story and the roof. The theater was about a half hour walk southwest of Aliya's house. On her way, she would have crossed the Big Sioux River. The theater held as many as 387 people, and the family of owner Otis Adams sometimes accompanied the playing of its moving pictures with music. The showings of *The Sage Hen* were advertised in the *Sioux Falls Argus-Leader*. Starring Gladys Brockwell and Lillian Rich, the movie was a "gripping tale of the old west" about a woman who was driven out of her hometown by gossip. The title of the film referred to a "strange woman of doubtful character" who chose to leave her son at a young age rather than ruin his life. "With tragic heroism," the movie's newspaper advertisement explained, "she sacrificed herself for her boy." Years later, after the protagonist had managed to cobble together some sort of life, she was threatened by still more gossip. But then her grown son came to her rescue. Aliya Ogdie Hassen may have sympathized with the protagonist, but she would not wait on a man to save her from a sad life. She would save herself.[1]

After World War I, there were important changes in Aliya Ogdie Hassen's life. Around 1920, the family moved from North Weber to 1422

East Sixth Street. On North Weber, they had lived on the same street as some other Arabic-speaking families, but on East Sixth, their immediate neighbors were the Butlers, Lowreys, O'Hearns, and Vandivers, and it appears that no other Syrians were living on the same street. Their arrival in the neighborhood was a hard one. Alex Ogdie had purchased the property and obtained a building permit so that he could erect a concrete-block grocery store. Twenty-three neighbors joined together to oppose him, objecting to a "Syrian store" in their neighborhood. Syrians seemed to lack the necessary power to challenge such discrimination. There were perhaps only 150 of them in a town that had grown to a size of 25,202. Sioux Falls was overwhelmingly white; there only 83 Black residents counted in the 1920 census.[2] The petition of Ogdie's white neighbors indicated that their opposition stemmed specifically from the fact that it was a *Syrian* grocery. The fact that Syrians had been part of the community for over two decades and had become well-known for operating first dry goods and then grocery stores did not give the neighbors pause. It seems that no important public figure stuck up for Alex Ogdie, as some had done for other Syrians before World War I. Opinion was unanimous. Perhaps the neighbors were worried that the store would function as other Syrian groceries did—as a meeting place for Syrian people. For whatever reason, the city commissioners agreed with the petitioners and instructed the city building inspector to revoke Alex Ogdie's building permit.[3] Ogdie hired a lawyer and appealed the decision, explaining that after receiving his permit he had contracted with Fanebust Construction for over $1,000 in sewer improvements and would lose a considerable sum if he backed out of his contracts. But the city commission "stood firm."[4]

There is other evidence that the patterns of anti-Syrian and anti-Muslim prejudice and discrimination that existed in the early twentieth century took place in 1920s Sioux Falls. The newspaper remained full of anti-Muslim articles, explicitly framing "Mohammedans" and "Moslems" as tyrants, misogynists, anti-Christian bigots, and purveyors of violence.[5] Various speeches given about Muslims in the town's churches and other civic associations portrayed Muslims as either pathetic victims or cruel victimizers. When Syrian Christians or Muslims were invited on the rare occasion to attend events that discussed Syria or the newly formed French mandate of Lebanon, they were not featured as speakers. In 1920, for example, when the women of the Congregational Missionary Society met to discuss Syrian culture, the speakers were non-Syrians—but a Syrian guest, Mrs. Haggar, was invited to prepare a "delicious Syrian dish" for the event.[6]

Nativism, the movement spreading across country that opposed the presence of foreigners in the United States, took hold in Sioux Falls. One newspaper article warned about Syrians, Black people, and Hungarians "engulfing" the "Anglo-Saxon minority" in various New York neighborhoods, making it impossible for white people to live there.[7] This atmosphere of xenophobia negatively affected Syrians across the country, including in Sioux Falls. The Klan was active in some parts of South Dakota. Foreigners were associated with danger, and many ethnic groups were unable or unwilling to claim their linguistic and cultural heritage in public.[8]

Syrians were sometimes the victims of violent attacks. In 1920, for example, Bert Kinnison was found guilty of assault and battery for attacking grocer Alex Hammod with a knife, cutting him "severely" in the head and arms.[9] In 1924, a tussle broke out between Aliya's mother, Fatima Ogdie, and two men named James Lane and John Barnhardt. Fatima said that the two men struck her during the argument—which was about the ownership of a lumber wagon—but the charges against the men—not for assault, but for disturbing the peace—were dismissed in municipal court.[10] Syrians also sometimes fought each other, and some seemed to have more than their fair share of trouble with the law, perhaps because they were more likely to be targeted by law enforcement. A number of Syrian boys were put "under surveillance" because they were suspected of participating in an organized gang that stole coal from the Illinois Central Railroad; grocer Mahmoud Swiden pled guilty to contributing to the delinquency of minors for buying their stolen goods.[11] It is not unreasonable to assume that Syrian boys learned early that they would have trouble finding social acceptance and equal opportunity in 1920s Sioux Falls.

Whatever their conflicts with one another and with non-Syrian Muslims in Sioux Falls, the community still came together to celebrate its Arab cultural heritage, mourn the deaths of each other's family members, and socialize with one another. Muslims in Sioux Falls never built a mosque like Muslims in North Dakota, Iowa, and Indiana did, but they were connected to other Syrian Muslims in the Midwest. When Alex Side died in 1920, for example, about fifty people were reported to have attended the funeral prayers. Side had lived in Sioux Falls for two decades, and worked with Sam Hallick at a basket store on South Main. Held at Burtch Chapel, the funeral prayers were led by A. Abas from Crookston, Minnesota, and mourners came from as far away as New York. Side was buried, like Aliya Ogdie Hassen's parents, in Mt. Pleasant Cemetery.[12]

Believers also sometimes prayed in each other's homes and in what Aliya described as a storefront. As in other places in the Muslim Midwest, both Sunni and Shi'a Syrian Muslims performed the salah, the prayers of prostration, together.[13] The community also welcomed Ahmadi missionary Muhammad Sadiq to Sioux Falls in 1921. Hosted by the Swiden family, Sadiq came to lecture about Islam and Muslim reformer Ghulam Ahmad, who preached against religious wars and encouraged cooperation among Muslims and non-Muslims.[14] Well-known among Muslim leaders of all sects and racial backgrounds in Detroit and Chicago, Sadiq had established one of the first Muslim American newspapers, the *Moslem Sunrise*. In addition to seeking connections to other Muslims for religious purposes, some community members cultivated ties to the greater Syrian diaspora by joining Syrian diasporic political groups and by reading Arabic-language newspapers. Even though Alex Ogdie never learned to read, someone would read to him. He was upset when the French and the British partitioned Ottoman Syria into separate mandates after World War I—Lebanon and Syria going to the

French, and Palestine and Transjordan going to the British. The demise of Hashemite Prince Feisal's Arab government headquartered in Damascus, Syria, was particularly troubling. In August 1920, French general Henri Gouraud demonstrated French control over the country by touring the historic Umayyad Mosque and the tomb of Salah ad-Din, or Saladin, the founder of the Ayyubid dynasty who repelled the Crusaders from Jerusalem. Alex Ogdie cried when he heard the news.[15]

At home, Aliya Ogdie learned about Arab culture and history as well as contemporary politics, and at school, she found meaning in her classes on art, music, and literature. Known by her classmates as Ella, she attended Bancroft School, just two blocks south of her house. As she wrote later, one teacher there, Miss Barlow, "had great faith" in her.[16] Aliya was likely thirteen then, since Grace Barlow was assigned to teach at Bancroft School in 1923.[17] The following year, Barlow was assigned to teach at Whittier School, where Aliya Ogdie had just matriculated as a high school student.[18] Barlow was active around town in the public recitation of literature, and it is clear that her teaching and example deeply influenced Aliya's writing, especially the hundreds of poems that Aliya later dedicated to her teacher. By fourteen, Aliya was writing romantic poetry about flowers, birds, and the changing of the seasons, and then by fifteen, about love, despair, and trauma. In addition to studying English, Aliya took a real interest in art. At Whittier, she was one of five enrolled in a special poster art class, which met daily for eighty minutes.[19] Located less than half a mile east of her house on Sixth Street, Whittier was normally a primary school, but in 1924 it became home to a class of ninth graders that included Aliya. Sioux Falls voters authorized expenditures of $1.2 million in new or renovated school buildings, and Roosevelt High was still under construction in 1924. The new two-story, fireproof Whittier had already been completed, and it featured all the modern amenities—a gym, auditorium, laboratory equipment, and the best in "heating and ventilation."[20]

That year, Aliya Ogdie also won a musical memorization competition. Her prize was a phonograph record, compliments of the Williams Piano

Company. Whittier racked up more records than any other school.[21] The memorization competition took place in the Sioux Falls Coliseum, a red-brick auditorium built in 1917 that could seat twelve hundred people in its balcony and eighteen hundred "in removable chairs on its floor." There were five doors to the front entrance of the thirteen-thousand-square-foot rectangular building, whose brick exterior was topped by a façade of soaring paned windows beneath a box-gabled roof. It was the town's main convention center, and its aura of importance emanated not only from its architecture but from the fact that in 1919 President Woodrow Wilson had visited there to promote the League of Nations to an overflow crowd.[22] It must have felt good to win a competition held in her hometown's premier public venue.

Aliya had dreams for her life that were very different from the expectations of her mother. The 1920s are often associated in US historical memory with women who firmly rejected buttoned-up fashions, stiff language, and hairstyles that belonged more to a bygone Victorian era than to the first decades of the twentieth century. Though images of "flapper girls" have been exaggerated in remembering this decade, there was an element of truth in the stereotype, and it clearly applied to some of Aliya Ogdie Hassen's adolescence. Sioux Falls was a small, conservative white town, but people there listened to jazz music and drank bootleg liquor, too. In 1921, the same year in which Aliya saw her first movie, parents in Sioux Falls were starting to worry about flapper dresses and hats, which were sold by the BeeHive and other stores in town. According to one syndicated column in the newspaper, "mothers were to blame for [the] daring stunts of flappers." A mother "knows the danger to the girl of going about with perhaps a single garment under her dress, her stockings rolled, and her skirt so short as to expose her knees." Even worse, the column cried, young ladies were having intimate conversations with young men. All of this unconventional behavior was a "maelstrom of daredeviltry" putting the modesty and safety of young women at risk. Men could not be trusted to control themselves, the column warned.[23]

Aliya liked the new short haircuts and the knee-length skirts, but her mother had a different view. She made Aliya wear dresses that came down to her calf. When Aliya decided on her own to cut her hair short, her mother beat her. In addition, Fatima Ogdie did not allow Aliya to go out of the house by herself. She had to be accompanied by a brother or her father. Her father was the easy one, she said, but he left the decisions about his daughter's honor up to Fatima. On occasion Alex Ogdie would "take a drink" of "corn whiskey," and he invited Aliya to smoke with him. He was an insomniac, and when he "couldn't sleep," he would wake her up and they would smoke tobacco in the water pipe together.[24]

Perhaps because Aliya was becoming what her mother saw as something of a wild child, she was married off at the age of fifteen. She was not the only girl to marry young: "because there were never enough boys their age to marry, girls were married to men many years older," Aliya later remembered. Some of these arranged marriages worked and some did not. Syrians were not the only Americans who were stricter with their girls than their boys, nor the only ones who married off their girls at a young age. Of course, Syrian brides were not the only women to resist such practices. This was a moment of generational rebellion for many. But in the 1920s, Aliya Hassen said, only a few American-born Syrian Muslim women rebelled. Her cousin "ran off to go on the stage," and she knew someone who was "put in a reform school" when she refused to go through with an arranged marriage. Aliya did not rebel, at least not at first.

On September 9, 1925, in Monroe, Michigan, she married Nijabe (sometimes spelled Nigabe) Kadoura, who was born in Syria around 1887. Aliya later said she was "tricked into agreeing to marry a much older man by her cousins." That year, she penned a poem entitled "Betrayed," perhaps inspired by the "loss of faith" that occurs when those closest to us betray us. "How fervently we wish we had / been tortured first," wrote this fifteen-year-old, "rather than learn that we / have been betrayed."[25] Her mother, whom she said had pressured her to get married, was a witness at a ceremony over which Probate Judge Carl Franke presided. Ten months later, on June 18, 1926, sixteen-year-old Aliya gave birth to her first child, daughter Amelia.[26]

Even if it was not unheard of for a fifteen-year-old to be married, Aliya's poetry written that year makes clear that she thought, even then, it was wrong that she had been married to an older man. And the particular man to whom she was married made it much worse—he was not a problem because he was an Arab; he was a problem because he was mean and sexist. From the beginning, according to the poem "Who Cares," her husband falsely accused her of infidelity for even looking at younger men and answering "a smile or a word from some lad." He was obviously insecure about her "beauty" and "youth." He was "old" and had no true "longings" or cravings, which made real intimacy with him impossible. Her wedding night was not about love and romance, she wrote, but about his own insecurity and his domination of her: "While I into the bridal chamber / went, compared with you a babe / In my innocence you reveled / As with a new toy / And in my stark terror / Never once pitied my plight." She would smile and laugh when he cursed her. But no matter what she did to make the marriage work, it did not matter. Aliya began to feel helpless. She wondered whether God was "cruel and unfair," whether the difference between "good" and "bad" had any meaning anymore.[27]

Aliya did not reject God, but she did ruminate on the meaning of Islam and on religion more generally. She developed an interest in comparative religion as a way to think about the meaning of life. Sioux Falls had its share of religious diversity, but in Detroit, Aliya would have been exposed to an even greater variety of religious philosophies and practices. Detroit's lively religious scene included large numbers of religious seekers and thinkers who practiced esoteric and metaphysical traditions such as theosophy, Rosicrucianism, and spiritualism.[28] In the 1927 poem "Content," Aliya mused on these different life paths to happiness. She acknowledged that some people found contentment in raising children, the acquisition of material wealth, the writing of poetry, or the seeking of pleasure. But all those paths were fundamentally different than the paths of those who found their meaning in religious creeds. The Christian priest sought to be like Christ in the embrace of "brotherly love." The "Moslem imam" was exalted by the belief that "Allahu Akbar, La Ilahi [God is great; there is no god] / Illa Hum [except Him]."[29] But by far the figure who received the deepest, longest treatment in the poem is the Hindu yogi. The yogi may be regarded as superstitious by the "civilized world," she wrote, but they are noble beings. They sit and sit by the Tigris river, "with no thought of self," relying on "passing pilgrims to feed them bread / While Mother Earth is their contented bed." When they finally experience what Aliya calls a vision, "they are led / By unknown forces, among men / for whom their hearts bled. / They go thither and yon trying / to abolish sin. / Forever striving to better the / race of men."[30] Aliya's interest in yogis was not a passing one. She became a longtime practitioner of yoga.

Even as she became interested in and influenced by religious traditions other than Islam, Aliya Ogdie Hassen remained attached to the religion of her youth. At some point, she even jotted down references from the Hebrew Bible and New Testament that foretold "Mohamed's coming" and other aspects of Islamic doctrine. The poem "Mohamed's Creed (1927)" repeats a central theme of Islamic religion in explaining how the mission of the Prophet Muhammad was not to create a new religion but rather to affirm the universal religion that God revealed through the prophets from the beginning of human history. The poem begins with the pronouncement that "Allah hu Ahad! [God is One], the Moslems teach" and declares that God is "summad," or self-sufficient. It goes on to explain Islamic beliefs about the virgin birth of Christ and Jesus's miracles—beliefs shared by Christians and Muslims. "To Mohamed," the poem continues, God "sent / through the Quran / A message of oneness with / out stain or flaw." Aliya lamented that religion was sometimes a source of strife when, in truth, "The Lord answers all prayers / of men / No matter the race or creed."[31]

While her thoughts turned to God in these years, most of the poetry that she wrote as a married teenager portrayed the emotional canvas of her life, her sadness and anger, but also her determination. The year after she was married, in 1926, she composed "Jealousy," whose narrator would walk the streets at night to forget the thought of a person whose "jealous hate . . . turned you into the devil incarnate." The narrator protests that there is no basis for such "distrust," proclaiming, "how unstained is the virgin / soul of me." The poem prophesies that the devil will one day repent and plead for forgiveness, but that it will be "too late," concluding that "jealousy is not of love but / of inferior hate." Being a young mother was hard, too. "I am alone in this dark, cold room," began "Agony of Spirit" (1928), "And haunted by the face of / my child. / Her calling voice resounds / from the gloom. / Heartbreaking calls, that are / driving me wild." Aliya may have been feeling despair during these years, but she also wrote about the importance of a "never say die" approach to life. In "Spunk," she forthrightly acknowledged her unhappiness but vowed to go on: "that seems the way with me / but if I cry and pray to die / What good will it do me?" she asked. It was better to "laugh" in the face of life's troubles. Aliya's poetry also spoke of longing. One poem hinted at forbidden love that would "bring about your fall." Another poem, titled "Throughout the Night," depicts the narrator in the arms of a lover, "with my head pillowed on / your breast / I felt safe and content 'til / break of day / And all my fears were laid to rest." And then the narrator wakes up, and realizes it is all a dream.[32]

Not all of her desires went unfulfilled. In an interview with Grant Farr many years later, Aliya said that during this time she would sneak out of the house sometimes to go dancing. And Detroit was a great place for that. The tonier nightclubs had strict dress codes, and bouncers made sure that people behaved themselves. There were many smaller, more working-class joints as well. Hundreds of people attended dances in hotel ballrooms. Wearing the kind of short skirts and haircuts that Aliya admired, they danced the Charleston and the Black Bottom. A dance marathon could last more than a day.[33] Aliya's husband was less than pleased with his young wife. In her poem "Tongues," written in 1927, Aliya depicts a woman who, like the sage hen, was a victim of "evil tongues." Yes, she was "wild about dancing and driving too / Just try to remember she is / younger than you. / Her nature demands thrills / and adventure 'tis true." The poem pleaded that no good could come by "stifling these longings." There was no "dishonor" in being true to "thine own self."[34]

During these years, her husband, Nijabe Kadoura, was an autoworker, like so many Arab Americans in Detroit. Henry Ford's relatively high wages at his assembly line in Highland Park, called the "Crystal Palace" because of "its façade of windows," attracted hundreds of Syrians to what became known as the Motor City. As in Cedar Rapids and Sioux Falls, there was already a burgeoning community of Syrians there by the end of the nineteenth century. But Detroit's incredible growth outpaced those towns'. By 1920, the city had almost one million residents. Before World War I, many Syrian workers lived around and worked in Ford's Highland Park plant, just outside the city limits of Detroit, and then after the war, they took jobs at Ford's gargantuan, mile-long River Rouge Assembly plant in Dearborn. In the 1920s, the town of Dearborn annexed more land and grew "from 2,470 to more than 50,000 residents." Arabic-speaking workers largely settled east of the plant, in the "single-family frame bungalows, frame duplexes, and multi-unit apartment houses" of Dearborn's Southend. Among those who worked for Ford Motor were two Syrian men who would become the city's most prominent imams in this period: Shi'a leader Kalil Bazzy and Sunni leader Hussien Karoub. Historian Sally Howell documents how these men and other Syrian Muslims helped to build over a dozen different Muslim institutions or associations in the first half of the 1900s. Unlike Muslims in most smaller towns, they sometimes joined American-born Black Muslims, Turkish Muslims, Balkan Muslims, Afghans, Iranians, Bengalis, and Indian Muslims in founding these groups, and at other times, they focused mainly on Arabic-speaking populations.[35]

In 1927, Nijabe Kadoura's address was listed as 2430 Faber Avenue, about five blocks northwest of the Dodge Main auto factory in Hamtramck, just outside Detroit. The neighbors included the Kowalczyk,

Trzeciak, Filion, and Vhalick families. The next year, the family's address was 1099 West Lantz; the neighbors were the Bower, Lindholm, Sullivan, and Sturm families. By 1930, Nijabe Kadoura was renting a place for thirty-five dollars a month at 1251 Ferney Avenue across the street from Ford's River Rouge plant.[36]

The River Rouge Assembly contained a total of 15.7 million square feet of floor space. Covering two thousand acres, one and half miles wide, the Ford plant was initially designed to build warships for the US Navy in World War I. It was converted in the 1920s to a massive assembly plant in which everything from the engine block to cylinders, manifolds, and eventually safety glass was produced. Huge freighters brought all the raw materials, including the ore and coal needed for the fabrication first of iron and, by 1926, steel. At the time of its construction, the foundry was the largest on the planet. The plant also produced all of its own electricity, supplying excess power to the Ford factory in Highland Park and sometimes to the Detroit Edison utility company. In addition to manufacturing nearly all the parts that were used in the Model T, which was actually assembled in Highland Park until the model was retired in 1927, the River Rouge Assembly built Ford tractors and then, in 1927, the Model A car. Though a manufacturing facility, it was designed to be an attractive complex. Henry Ford's architect added "light and air" to the buildings though the use of glass in the high ceilings and walls. In 1930, more than one hundred thousand people worked there.[37] Little training was required as workers became part of the factory's machinery, performing simple tasks over and over.[38] When Nijabe Kadoura moved across the street from the plant, he joined a white working class with immigrants from across Europe and the Levant. Some of their neighbors were born in the United States, but others were from Yugoslavia, Romania, Czechoslovakia, Syria, Hungary, and Turkey.[39]

Her husband may have been making a decent wage, but Aliya was miserable—"very unhappy" is how she put it once. She decided to "walk out" of her marriage. It was a bold decision. She felt like "divorce was unheard of" in the Syrian community, even though the number of divorces was increasing among Syrians in the 1920s. But she refused to live like the "sage hen" whose story she saw on the silver screen when she was still a girl. By 1930, she had taken three-year-old Amelia with her and moved back in with her parents in Sioux Falls—long enough to be counted in the US census and in the 1930 Sioux Falls city directory.[40]

Aliya returned to Michigan by August 11, 1931, to file for divorce on the grounds of extreme cruelty. In Michigan, there was no such thing as a no-fault divorce. A person could seek an absolute divorce only on the grounds of adultery, physical incompetency, desertion, drunkenness, or imprisonment; one could also bring divorce papers from another state. However, if a person filed for a divorce "from bed and board," a provisional form of divorce like a legal separation, then one could claim other reasons. "Extreme cruelty" became the most popular category for petitioners because it was so subjective. It often had nothing to do with anything physical, but was defined legally as including, for example, a husband who falsely circulated injurious rumors about his wife's character.[41] Though Aliya did not seek absolute divorce, in the end the court ruled for one. The divorce decree was made official more than a year later on October 22, 1932. Her husband did not contest it. Aliya received no alimony.[42]

She was on her own in the middle of the Great Depression, and it was the worst possible time to look for work. Joblessness, homelessness, and hunger were now a normal part of life in Detroit and across the country. During the Great Depression, demand for automobiles plummeted, and Detroit was hard hit. The city did not have enough money to provide welfare for those who needed it. When Nijabe Kadoura lived across the street from the River Rouge Assembly before the fall, approximately 128,000 people worked for Ford Motor. By August 1931, Ford employed a total of 37,000 workers, representing a "drop of 91,000 employees." The remaining employees were told to work harder and faster. Ford refused to contribute to local charities, even though "40 percent of the city's total welfare allocations were being distributed to unemployed workers of Ford." The year that Aliya was divorced, laid-off Ford workers marched to the employment office of the River Rouge Assembly to demand jobs and relief. Ford security forces and Dearborn police fired tear gas and live ammunition, killing four protesters.[43]

Aliya took a job as a clerk in a dime store and lived on Howard Street. She was poor, but she felt free to live the life that she had dreamed about. She started going to speakeasies, drinking and dancing until the wee hours. Aliya became what she described as "movie mad," going to the cinema with some roomers. She "had to hold down three jobs" just to get by. For her meals she would go to a cafeteria that sold "two-cent vegetable courses and five-cent meat courses, [and] one cent . . . bread." She lived in "house-keeping rooms." One of her few luxuries at the time was that "she and friends would pool money one or two times a week to buy ingredients for beef stew or chicken."[44] The soup kitchen was nearby, but she refused to go there just as she refused to accept any public assistance.

Then, in 1932, Aliya, twenty-two years of age, remarried. A Christian clergyman performed the service as she wed Ernst Weldon, a thirty-five-year-old white, blue-eyed Christian man from Buffalo, Alabama, who also lived on Howard Street.[45] Weldon was a disabled World War I veteran who may have run a modest gambling business out of his barbershop.[46] If he did so, it might not have been very successful or perhaps he gave it up, because sometime in the 1930s, Aliya remembered, the couple had trouble making their rent. Fortunately, their landlady was patient when they missed rent and even loaned them money. Weldon had helped her open the boardinghouse, and the landlady was glad to return the favor. A few years after they were married, Weldon's health deteriorated. He entered the hospital for a long stay in 1936, and he was transferred to a veterans' hospital in Outwood, Kentucky, in 1938. Weldon seems to have been hospitalized for the rest of his life; he died in that same Kentucky hospital, and his body was sent home to Alabama for burial in 1948.[47]

Aliya was diagnosed with tuberculosis in 1938, the same year that her husband was transferred to a hospital in Kentucky. She spent six months in the hospital herself. Looking at the Aliya of 1938, it is hard to imagine

FIGURE 7.1. Aliya Ogdie Hassen, who loved to dance, was a pioneer of the Syrian Muslim Midwest; born in western South Dakota, she became one of the most remarkable Arab American Muslim community leaders of the twentieth century. Credit: Arab American History Museum.

how important her work would become to Muslim and Arab communities in the Midwest and on the East Coast after World War II. In the 1930s, as she remembered later, she was not very engaged with Syrian or Muslim communities. She felt betrayed by some of her own family members and she had been pressured into an early and terrible marriage to another Syrian Muslim. Aliya was not involved in the town's Syrian or Lebanese clubs in the way that many other Syrian women were. She still remembered God, but found communal solidarity more on the dance floor and in juke joints than in Muslim religious circles.[48]

Aliya Hassen's life in this period is a helpful reminder that Syrian Muslims were diverse. Some members of the community, like Aliya and

Mike Aossey of Cedar Rapids, did not always find their most intimate social connections among other Syrian Muslims, while others did. Some stayed put in towns such as Cedar Rapids and Michigan City, and some moved to Detroit. Some lost touch with relatives in the old country, and others nurtured those ties. Some people returned from long stays in the old country to resettle in the United States.

Osman Chamie, another Sioux Falls native who lived in the same neighborhoods as Aliya Ogdie, also ended up in Detroit, but his journey involved a decades-long detour through Syria and Lebanon. His story gives us a sense of all the different paths that Syrian and Lebanese Muslims took to get to the big city. Related in some way—it's not clear how—to Joe Chamie, the Sioux Falls immigrant who was killed during World War I and buried in France, Osman Chamie began his life in Sioux Falls. Born in 1907 to Mahomet, or Mohammed, and Sadie, or Side, Osman's family operated a dry goods store first on 219 West Sixth Street, near the Ogdies' first residence in Sioux Falls. Family members Joe, Hassan, and Samuel Chamie also roomed there.[49] By 1910, Mohammed had partnered with Mamod Beraney to sell dry goods, clothing, shoes, and notions at Chamie & Beraney on 431 North Weber. Their narrow one-story wood-framed house was part of a larger complex that at different times served as a Syrian restaurant, grocery, confectionary, and billiards hall.[50] Many Syrian Muslims lived on North Weber during this era. Within a couple years, Fatima, Alex, and Aliya Ogdie would move there, too.

It is more than a coincidence that both Osman and Aliya eventually went to Detroit, but Osman's path to the Motor City was different than Aliya's. In 1912, Chamie and Beraney's Sioux Falls store went bankrupt. On February 6, the *Argus-Leader* published one of several notices that the store's general merchandise and fixtures, worth approximately $3,500, would be sold at auction by the bankruptcy trustee. Just one day later, Osman's mother, Side, aged thirty-one, died of a heart attack at Dunham Hospital.[51] Osman was five years old. The next year, Osman's father decided to return to Syria, where he hoped to remarry. His vil-

lage was Qaraoun, located in the Bekaa Valley not far from Joub Jennine and Rafid. He took Osman with him. Mohammed remarried, but
he returned to the United States in 1914 to work. Osman was raised in
Qaraoun by his stepmother. He attended a government-run school, and
the curriculum, until the French took over, included Turkish language
and the Qur'an. Dissatisfied with the results, his father paid for him to
enroll in a Protestant missionary school, and Osman became fluent in
the reading and writing of formal Arabic. He went to school until 1921,
and received the equivalent of what he called an eighth-grade education.
After that, his father asked him to start working in the fields, and eventually Osman became a grain trader. But life for the teenager wasn't all
work. He loved to dance the *dabka*, or Arabic line dance, at village parties. He learned to play the finger cymbals; the *rababa*, a long stringed
instrument played with a bow; and the *mijwiz*, a double-piped reed
instrument.[52]

In the late 1930s, Osman Chamie decided to move to the United
States. "We took a chance," he later admitted. The Great Depression was
ongoing, and in 1937, the recovery was delayed by what historians often
call the Roosevelt Recession. The national unemployment rate was 15
percent, and "in Detroit 135,000 people were still unemployed."[53] Rather
than moving back to Sioux Falls, the place of his birth, Osman headed
to Detroit. He had read about the "hunger and foreclosures on homes,
and the bank failures . . . the soup lines and dry bread," but the same
newspaper, which was published in Zahle, Lebanon, and mailed to his
village, also told him about Detroit and its automobile industry. Letters
sent back to the village from immigrants described ample work opportunities there, and his father advised him to go to Detroit, too. Leaving
his spouse and children, he sailed across the Atlantic with his brother
Abdullah on the *Alaunia*, arriving in the country of his birth on November 18, 1938. (Mrs. Chamie and his children would not come until 1947).
He moved in with Uncle Sam Chamie at 3328 Marie in Dearborn. For six
months, he looked for work but couldn't find any. A friend helped him
get a job with the Works Progress Administration, whose local office was

located in Highland Park. He worked on building roads, often loading dirt on trucks. As he recalled, he earned forty dollars a month and the job was easy. Rather than receiving that money in welfare, he said, he preferred to work for it. He believed that President Roosevelt deserved credit for getting the country "fired up again." After six or seven months of that, he finally found work in 1940 at Ford Motor Company, where he earned seventy-five cents an hour.[54]

During these years, workers at Ford organized for better wages and working conditions. Beginning in 1936, the United Auto Workers (UAW) union held "sit-down strikes" at various auto plants; "workers occupied the factories and locked themselves in." Ford did everything possible to prevent the union's success, staffing its own secret police force with "gang members, bouncers, boxers, and convicts." The Michigan Prison Commission paroled about five prisoners a week; Ford employed them as enforcers. Approximately 10 percent of the ninety thousand employees at the Rouge factory worked for the so-called Service Department, and thousands of them were used "to brutalize any and all workers suspected of union activities."[55] At first, Osman Chamie, who lost two fingers on his right hand from his work at Ford, did not join the union, at least not officially. He paid dues secretly and much of the union's work, he said, was "hidden and underground." But open conflict between management and labor eventually erupted; "there were battles." The union's coalition of white and Black workers held strong. One reason was the UAW's secretary-treasurer, a Syrian Lebanese man named George Addes who worked to keep the UAW unified.[56] The strikers occupied the plant until Ford permitted the union to operate openly. In 1941, Ford agreed to increase wages by five to fifteen cents per hour for its fifty-three thousand employees.[57] Osman Chamie ended up working for Ford for three decades, though he regretted doing so. Osman did not enjoy the work. He wanted to open his own store, he admitted, but he "didn't have the courage."[58]

Kamel Osman of Michigan City also worked for Ford in the 1930s, and his life path uncannily paralleled that of Osman Chamie in another way. Like Chamie, Kamel Osman arrived in Detroit not from his Midwestern hometown but from Lebanon. In 1921, Kamel traveled with his mother and father to Tebnine, their town of origin. Kamel's father used his earnings from America to build a home and to purchase two pieces of land. Young Kamel, nine years old, was enrolled in a school where he learned both French and Arabic. He already spoke colloquial Arabic, but within three months he learned how to read and write standard Arabic, too. He also studied the Qur'an.[59]

In 1928, when Kamel was still a teenager, he returned to the United States. But rather than going to Michigan City, he moved to Dearborn, Michigan. He was enrolled in the fifth grade because, after many years of education in the south of Lebanon, his Arabic and his French were better than his English. He "pronounced English words with a French accent." When "kids in school made fun of him, he beat them up." As a result, Kamel "was thrown out of school." His uncle, who disciplined him for the incident, then reenrolled him in school and his English improved. But the troubles with his uncle continued. That same year, the uncle threw him out of his house. Kamel said his aunt made him do it. Whoever was responsible, these relatives abandoned a teenager to the city streets of a country he barely knew.[60]

And then came the crash of 1929. Like 150,000 other people in Detroit, he did not have regular work. A quarter of all workers in the United States were unemployed. Kamel became homeless. And he remained homeless for eight years. He slept in public parks sometimes and, joining 186,000 other train hoppers, found shelter in railroad cars. "A quarter of US children were malnourished," and Kamel Osman experienced food insecurity, too.[61] "I was so hungry," he remembered. His father was in the United States, but according to Kamel, he was unemployed sometimes and had "his own problems." Kamel's mother and sisters were still in Lebanon, and so his dad had to support them. Kamel said he was too proud to ask his dad for help. One time, his father sent him fifteen dollars and he bought some new clothes. Kamel picked up odd jobs. He washed dishes, sometimes seventeen hours in a row, earning maybe a dollar per day. In the early 1930s, he got a job as a milkman for five dollars a week. He picked up some work in a Highland Park factory for thirty-five cents an hour, but after two or three months, he was fired.[62]

In the middle 1930s, however, things started to improve for Kamel Osman. A friend of his got him a job selling newspapers. He then worked for the WPA, mainly as a custodian, for five or six weeks. He also applied for a job at Ford Motor Company, but "was turned down because he had a bad left eye." His uncle asked Ford employee Ali Turfe to help him get the job. Kamel Osman was finally hired in 1935, laid off for six months, and then rehired. For nine years, he worked for Ford, receiving thirty-six dollars a week—more money than he had ever seen as an adult worker. The working conditions there were not ideal, however. "Coercion and surveillance" of employees were used to "control the shop floor."[63] When someone would report in sick, the company would send an investigator to the worker's home to verify the worker's claims. Similarly, when a worker wanted to use the bathroom, a supervisor would check to see whether they had actually done so. "If there was no evidence of using the bathroom," said Kamel, "the worker would be fired." To make matters worse, there was no privacy in the restrooms. "The toilets had no doors," he remembered. Plus, "no smoking was allowed" while at work, and if you drove any car to the employee parking lot that was not a Ford, you would be fired. You had to wear a blue shirt to work or you would be sent home. You could also get fired for union organizing. Eventually he had enough, and in 1941, he became what he described as a professional gambler. In 1944, he was arrested by Dearborn police on the suspicion that he was running various gambling schemes at the River Rouge Assembly. The police stopped him and his wife for speeding after observing the exchange of brown paper bags with people in another vehicle. There were mutuel tickets and "adding machine tape" plus $650 in the bags, allegedly showing that Osman was running some type of betting pool in which he paid the winners and kept a cut for himself. When the police searched their home, they found more gambling paraphernalia.[64] Osman left the gaming business and went back to work as an autoworker.

Ford Motor loomed large in the lives of Syrian Muslims in Detroit. So many of them worked there. For example, another Syrian Shi'a Muslim from Michigan City whose family found employment with Ford was Mary Ali Unis Shamey. Mary was only one year younger than Kamel Osman, but unlike Kamel, she moved directly from Michigan City to the Detroit area. In 1919, the Ali family resettled in Highland Park, Michigan, where her maternal uncle worked for Ford. They lived in the heart of the Arab community on Victor Avenue, where "there were grocery shops, coffee houses, and Arabic restaurants." According to the 1920 city directory, Riza Allie and Abbas Hassin had fruit stands. Addah Arif ran the barbershop. Mashike Mohammed was in charge of the pool hall. Restaurants included Nassar's, and Hassan and Hassan. Hassan Michl and the Gazey Brothers has grocery stores. Muslim real estate developer Mohammed Karoub also owned an apartment complex on the street.[65]

Then, in 1926, the Ali family moved to Dearborn's Robertson neighborhood. Mary may not have grown up in Lebanon, but she grew up in an Arabic-speaking community. She communicated with her mother, who did not know English, in Arabic. Her mother maintained "her ties with [the] homeland," asking "somebody who could read the write" to pen letters to people in Lebanon. Mary learned about the traditions of "the old country" from her mom, who gave her pride in her identity. She also had a lot of Arab Christian friends in Dearborn, and like Kamel Osman and many others, she would visit their churches. Later, these Christian Arab friends would visit the mosque. Her friends would spend the entire weekend with her family sometimes. She was not allowed to spend the night at other people's houses, but her mother was happy to host the kids at her house. She also went to their families' weddings, shared the same food, and knew each other's cultural traditions. Mary's identification with her Arab identity did not mean that she avoided non-Arab people or non-Arab culture. When she lived in Highland Park, for example, Mary celebrated Thanksgiving, Easter, and Christmas with her friends, and the family put up a Christmas tree on more than one occasion. Her mother, she said, was not very strict with her, allowing Mary to move around outside her own Arabic-speaking world: she would "take her to Western movies and pick her up when the show [was] over." Mary learned about her own womanhood from people other than her mother. She had her first period, she said, at school; her mother had not talked to her about menstruation. Mary completed the eighth grade in Dearborn, where she attended a Catholic school at least part of the time. She had friends of "many nationalities" and from the many ethnic groups that attended school with her.[66]

But when it came to marriage, Mary wanted to marry an Arab man. His name was Sam Hussein Unis, a veteran of World War I who worked at Ford until his death in 1943. He was a union member. The marriage was not arranged. She met him at a grocery store in Dearborn and they got to know each other for six months before getting hitched in 1937. It was her decision, Mary Ali said, but out of respect, her husband "asked her mother and father-in-law" for permission, a tradition honored by many American grooms. When she married Sam, Mary didn't have to move far. She went from one house to another in the same neighborhood. The groom rented their first home, which is also where they were married. A shaykh "performed a religious ceremony with the presence of the family members and relatives; they had a dinner there" and "then the married couple left the same day for a small trip to Bowling Green, Ohio."[67]

As a married woman, Mary continued to enjoy the Arab community in the Detroit area. She was proud to welcome friends and neighbors to her new home; "my door was opened anytime," she said. The heart of Arab culture was *karam*, or generosity, she believed. Cultivating community through shared cultural experiences, including leisure activities, was essential to this culture of reciprocity. "People started to go out for picnics," she recalled. "When they had mahrajans [festivals], they would rent parks for two or three days." Those already well-versed in the *dabka*, or line dance, would lead others who wanted to participate. The *'ataba*, a genre of rural Arabic music popular in Ottoman Syria, was also sung. It is not clear from Mary Shamey's description exactly how the songs that she heard were performed, but generally speaking the *'ataba* was a

FIGURE 7.2. Mary Unis Shamey smiles at her daughter and son on Robertson Street in Dearborn, 1942. Credit: Arab American National Museum.

"non-metric strophic folksong" originally "improvised by a solo poet-singer accompanying himself on the rababa."[68] There was real sisterhood in the community, as well. During these outings, women would sit by themselves so that they could talk without the men overhearing them.[69]

Both Kamel Osman and Mary Shamey were members of the Progressive Arabian Hashmie Society.[70] Incorporated in 1936, the Society "was opened" in 1937, according to historian Sally Howell, "as a mosque and social hall on Dix Avenue in the heart of the business district of Dearborn's Southend." One thousand people came to the dedication of the building, located inside the former Union State Bank, a two-story, neoclassical structure. According to the newspaper, it did not look much like a mosque from the Middle East, but "the inside of the building has been painted and decorated to make it look as much like the real thing as the structural difficulties permitted." Circuit Court Commissioner William J. Cody was on hand to dedicate the building, as were Sunni leader Hussien Karoub and other Sunni Muslims.[71] On the one hand, Hashmie Hall was explicitly a Syrian (and Lebanese) Shi'a Muslim group. The name "Hashmie" refers to the Banu Hashim, the clan of the Prophet Muhammad, his daughter Fatima, his cousin Ali, and his grandsons, Hassan and Husayn—the family lineage in which religious authority is vested and from which spiritual power flows for Shi'a and other Muslims loyal to the family of the Prophet. On the other hand, the Hashmie Society's politics were not sectarian as much as they were pan-Arab, expressing a desire for unity among the Arabic-speaking people of what had become Syria, Lebanon, Palestine, Transjordan, and other polities of the Middle East. In 1939, for example, the group hosted a speech by Dalal Safadi, the daughter of a Damascus teacher who was educated at an English-speaking school in Bethlehem and was teaching in Baghdad, Iraq. Her appearance embodied the progressive, pan-Arab unity to which members of the mosque aspired. Many also opposed the British and French occupations of what used to be Ottoman Syria; speaking on behalf of the group, Joseph Fayz and Abdallah Berry protested publicly against the French repression of Lebanese politicians in 1943.[72] Like other members of the Hashmie Society, Mary Shamey maintained this commitment to pan-Arab politics her entire life.[73]

In Detroit, it was possible to support a local Shi'a Muslim congregation while also dreaming of a nonsectarian Arab political future.[74] Unlike some other towns in the Syrian Muslim American heartland, Detroit had Arabic-speaking and Muslim populations that were large enough to establish multiple religious congregations. In 1935, some other Syrians helped to create El-Bokka League, a name referring to the Bekaa Valley in Lebanon, and in 1938, they "broke ground on Dearborn's first Sunni mosque." Whatever rivalries existed among these Muslims, the leaders of Detroit's various Arab Muslim congregations still came together to mark important events with one another.[75] In 1939, the (Shi'a) Hashmie Society hosted Sunni leader Abraham Alwan and others for the end of Ramadan, and also to "burn the mortgage" on their building on Dix Avenue.[76]

So, in the first half of the twentieth century, Detroit became not only the capital of the automobile industry but also the capital city of the Syrian Muslim Midwest. Historians have pointed to the difficulty in determining exactly how many Muslims were in Detroit, but there were so many that there was no way all the Muslims could know one another—this was not a town like Sioux Falls or Cedar Rapids. It was surely an exaggeration, but according to the *Free Press*, there were forty-five thousand Muslims, many of whom were ethnically Arab.[77] Whether or not someone lived in or visited Detroit, nearly everyone in the Syrian Muslim community across the Midwest had a connection to it; the city linked together the networks of marriage, religious community, economic opportunity, and cultural activities around which Syrian Muslim life in the Midwest revolved. So many Midwest Muslims, such as Mike Aossey of Cedar Rapids, worked for at least a little while in Detroit. Other Muslims coming from Cedar Rapids, Sioux Falls, or Michigan City made more permanent moves after World War I.

These social, religious, political, and familiar networks were strong but not exclusive. Syrian and Lebanese Muslims maintained ties to people on the East Coast and often to family and friends in the old country, too. Some also had ties to African American, Iranian, Turkish, South Asian, and European Muslims. Detroit's diasporic community of Syrian Muslims reflected not only the influences of the Arab Middle East, but also the regional and local histories of the Midwestern towns and cities in which so many Syrian Muslims had settled and raised their families. Several families from Ross resettled in Detroit after living in western North Dakota for a decade or more. When Aliya Ogdie married Nijabe Kadoura in Michigan, she brought her memories of the Dakotan prairie, of Sioux Falls, and her poetic sensibility to a union with a man who was born in Syria but had lived in Toledo, too. Osman Chamie of Sioux Falls and Kamel Osman of Michigan City resettled in Arab Detroit after having spent years in French-occupied Lebanon, and they brought native fluency in Arabic as well as habits and cultural practices from Lebanese towns undergoing change after World War I.

As much as the Syrian and Lebanese Muslim community of Greater Detroit reflected all these influences, there were also major events that in many cases forged the identities of community members as social and political citizens of the United States. World War II was one of those powerful national events that shaped the lives not only of those who went off to war but also the lives of their family members back at home. Nearly everyone in the country was affected by the war. Massive government spending lifted Detroit and the rest of the country out of economic depression. The number of unemployed people in Detroit declined from 135,000 to 4,000 by 1943. President Roosevelt vowed that America would be the world's "arsenal of democracy," producing whatever the Allies needed in the war effort against the Germany and Japan. No cars were produced for three years. "General Motors and Ford Motor Company were, respectively, the first and third highest-producing companies of military equipment in the country." The federal government brokered a deal between union and corporate leaders to ban strikes at the time, but as billions filled the coffers of the corporations, workers still had little control over working conditions and salaries. When they staged wildcat

FIGURE 7.3. Allie Joseph Said was born in Michigan City, Indiana, moved to Dearborn, and served in World War II. Credit: Julia Haragely Papers, Bentley Historical Library, University of Michigan.

strikes, they were accused of supporting the enemy. There was tremendous pressure on all working people, including Arab American workers, to make sacrifices for the good of the country.[78]

On the home front, members of the Arabian Hashmie Society joined other groups to organize the community in support of the war effort. Hashmie Society president Joseph Fayz partnered with leaders of the Polish Legion and the Federated Italian-American Societies to serve on the planning committee for the Americans All Win-the-War Congress to be held in 1944 at Cass High School.[79] As in World War I, the military service of Syrian and Lebanese Muslim Americans had long-lasting and important consequences and implications for the community's political and religious orientations. Sometimes, the stories of their service were the stuff of high drama. For example, Allie Joseph Said, who was born and raised in Michigan City, was living at 1638 Mulky Street in Dearborn and employed as a metal worker for Ford Motor Company when he signed up to do his duty.[80] Said was assigned to the 331st Engineers of the Army Air Forces and was stationed in Alaska. In February 1943, Sgt. Said came to the attention of Major General H. L. George for his leading role in rescuing Lt. Joseph P. Donahue, who had been lost in the wild. The general's letter of commendation said that Said undertook a "heroic hike over the trails for some twelve hours under trying sub-zero temperatures" in the rescue effort.[81] Said's hometown newspaper filled in some of the details of the dramatic rescue. According to reporter James Gleason, "two-fisted, husky Allie Said carried a wounded companion on his shoulders for 12 hours over Alaska's rugged terrain, delivering him at a base hospital and saving his life."

But at the time that the general's letter of commendation was making its way to Alaska, Said "climbed aboard a transport plane at White Horse, Alaska, with ten others on Feb. 6 to fly to an officers' training school in the U.S." According to Gleason, "over the perpetual snow of the Canadian Rockies in British Columbia, the big plane disappeared." Fellow service members said that "search in the gigantic snow drifts among the limitless expanse of frozen crags is impossible." Allie Said's mother, Sarah Said, was devastated. She began buying "newspapers by the armful, scanning each picture of soldier groups hoping someday, somewhere, to see a picture of her son."[82]

Several years later, in September 1948, some hunters from the United States stumbled upon the remains of Sgt. Said and the other men aboard the plane. It had apparently crashed into one of the three mountains around Tuchodi Lakes in the Rockies of northern British Columbia. Some of the headlines about the discovery focused on the fact that the plane was carrying tens of thousands in cash and large amounts of gold bullion, dubbing it the "Gold Plane." It was normal for military planes to carry cash and gold back and forth between the lower forty-eight states and Alaska during this time. But for Said's family, there was a meaning more sublime than the sensational and salacious suggestion that the crew of eleven had almost got away with the gold. Sarah Said sent at least two telegrams via Western Union in September and October 1948 to ask that her son's remains be sent home to her. On November 8, 1948, Major James Smith of the Army's Office of the Quartermaster sent his deepest sympathies to her, writing that the Army had identified his remains and would transport them to the next of kin from San Francisco for final interment. The letter also explained the events that led to his death: "Aircraft Type C-47 Number 43–20084 on which he was aboard crashed on 5 February 1943 while on an administrative flight from Ft. Nelson, British Columbia, to Ft. St. John, Canada." There was no radio contact "with the plane after the take-off" and the Army search for plane, conducted over a span of five months, was unsuccessful.[83]

Funeral prayers were finally held for First Sgt. Allie Joseph Said on January 12, 1949, at Arabian Hashmie Hall in Dearborn. The Rev. Mohamed Allie Asker officiated and members of the 331st Engineers of the Air Transport Command participated as well. The service, held in the heart of the Arabic-speaking Shi'a Muslim community of Dearborn, brought together Islamic rites with the symbols of US public culture. A Muslim sacred space incorporated the symbols of US nationalism. A program for the service, provided by the Army, included a picture of Sgt. Said and a patriotic poem that eulogized Said as someone who had fought "for country and his flag" and had been called "home" by "the great Commander." Those in attendance likely had many different emotions when attending the event, but one of those feelings must have been communal pride. Syrian Muslim Americans had been seeking public recognition of their identities as both US patriots and members of the global Muslim community since the days of World War I. At that time there were no religious congregations where someone like Joe Chamie of Sioux Falls could be mourned. Of course, the Muslim community could still perform funeral prayers together, and they did so when they laid people to rest. But that was different from the public recognition of a burial that took place in a sacred space of one's own, a religious congregation that was created by and for the community. In the United States, where religious congregations were the single most popular form of voluntary institution in the country, the performance of a funeral in a mosque fused Islam into the American religious fabric in ways that no other ritual could. There was no sacrifice more meaningful in US public culture than dying for your country as a member of its armed forces, and the places where fallen service members were mourned gave sacred meaning not only to the dead themselves but also to the nation for which they had died.

There would be many more battles inside the US military for the recognition of Islam as the religion of some service members. Abdullah Igram of Cedar Rapids led that cause in the 1950s, and it goes on, even today. But the presence of anti-Muslim prejudice and discrimination—a lack of acceptance of Muslims in the military and the society at large—did not mean that Syrian and Lebanese Muslim Americans felt any less proud of their service during and after World War II.

Syrian Muslim life during World War II was in some ways the culmination of their efforts since World War I to establish identities, institutions, and ways of life that were both wholly Muslim and wholly American. The Syrian Muslims of the Midwest were not alone in these efforts—Syrian Muslims from the East Coast also played an important role in this shared endeavor. But the Syrian Muslim Midwest was different. There were more mosques, more associations, more schools, more networks. The Midwest was truly the beating heart of this community.

The summer breeze of Lake Michigan, the bitter cold of the western Dakotas, the jazz music of 1920s Detroit, the sound of trains on the Rock Island Line, and the casual greetings and love affairs and fights with non-Arab neighbors—all those things unique to the times and places in which they lived—became as much a part of their lives as their connections to the old country and their commitment to their ethnic and religious community. Many of them did not see any contradiction in that. They sought acceptance as white people who happened to practice Islam, at least some of the time. Of course, they had diverse political views, social habits, and cultural practices. But their ties to this place were unmistakably meaningful. They had become people of the heartland.

Conclusion

A Big Party in the 1950s

On August 2, 3, and 4, 1957, twenty-five hundred Muslims, perhaps more, from various racial, ethnic, and national backgrounds came together at the luxurious Hotel Statler in Detroit to celebrate the sixth annual convention of the Federation of Islamic Associations in the United States and Canada (FIA). The program was impressive. The director of the new Islamic Center in Washington, DC, was slated to lead the Friday congregational prayers, and America's best-known Islamic religious teachers, many of whom lived in the Midwest, offered various seminars and discussions. Included in their number were Mohamed Jawad Chirri, a postwar immigrant who had been a leader in Michigan City before being recruited to Detroit, and Vehbi Ismail, the leader of the Sunni Albanian community in Detroit. There was also talk of politics with Fayez Sayegh, director of the Arab Information Center in New York.

If the convention was educational, it was also social. Every night, conventioneers like Kamel Osman of Sioux Falls and Dearborn chose among various entertainment options. You could listen to Arab classical music, do some Arabic line dancing, and on Saturday, you could cut a rug with the Carlos Rivera Orchestra. The events were scheduled to last until 2:30 a.m. Looking back on the event many years later, its coordinator, Detroit Islamic Council chair Charles Alawan, remembered that "it was a lot of fun." The final evening of the convention featured a gala banquet. Diplomats from Egypt, Syria, and Jordan were invited along with Michigan governor G. Mennen Williams. A huge, exquisitely dressed crowd—men in suits with bowties or neckties and women with dresses and strands of pearls—filled the large hall. Many were Syrian and Lebanese, but there were Muslims from all backgrounds, and there was a very large contingent of US-born Black Muslims, who had been establishing their own mosques since the 1920s.[1]

The event would have been impossible without Syrian Muslim Midwesterners' decades of work to build Muslim communities and institutions. It was a culminating celebration of the Midwest as the Muslim American heartland. Muslim immigrants who arrived after World War II were essential to the growth of the community, but they were building on a foundation laid by Syrian Midwesterners who labored to organize Muslim public life even before World War I. In the 1920s, African Americans, Arab Americans, and South Asians established Islam as a religion that was, in many ways, typically American. Postwar immigrants, much less those who arrived after 1965, would have been less likely to create successful Muslim American institutions if the groundwork had not already been completed.

The FIA was created by World War II veteran Abdullah Igram. Already well-known in his hometown of Cedar Rapids, Igram rose to the nation's attention in 1953, when *Time* published an account of his effort to convince President Eisenhower's administration to allow Muslims to indicate their religion on their dog tags. Echoing the approach of Cedar Rapids' Rose of Fraternity lodge, the FIA insisted that Islam was an American religion, and that Muslims not only owed their full allegiance to the United States but that in turn the United States owed them respect and recognition.[2] Though the FIA included organizations from across the United States and Canada, a significant amount of its support came from the Syrian and Lebanese communities of the American Muslim heartland. It was no accident that a military veteran trained in the science of qur'anic recitation and reared in the town of Cedar Rapids was its first leader. Abdullah Igram embodied the skills, orientations, values, and ambitions of the Muslim Midwest.

He was one of many Midwestern leaders of the group. Aliya Hassen also emerged as a leading intellectual figure in the FIA. Moving to New York after World War II, she became a private detective and wrote pioneering popular scholarship on Muslim women's history for the *FIA Journal*. She also befriended Malcolm X and worked to further interracial, international, and interethnic solidarity among Muslims in the United States and abroad. Eventually she returned to Detroit and cofounded the Arab Community Center for Economic and Social Services (ACCESS), which became the country's largest community-based Arab American nonprofit organization.[3]

How did a woman born to peddlers and homesteaders in Sioux Falls, South Dakota, become such a prominent national leader in the Arab American community? Some may be tempted to see Aliya Hassen's journey from the rural Great Plains to Detroit and New York as the familiar story of a girl from the Midwest who ditches her small hometown and its supposed narrow-mindedness to find success in a big, generally coastal city. But that tired tale ignores the truth that Aliya's upbringing in Sioux Falls made possible her later accomplishments as an Arab American leader. There she developed many of the traits and interests that would guide her for the rest of her life. During Aliya's adolescence, Sioux Falls was no isolated town in the middle of nowhere. It was a river city connected as well by rail and road to a booming Midwest in which Arab and Muslim traditions were taking root. The Muslim heartland ran right through Sioux Falls just as it did through Michigan City, Cedar Rapids, Ross, and Dearborn. Aliya Hassen was part of a regional community that taught her about her Arab Muslim heritage and encouraged her to embrace it. Like other Muslim Midwesterners, Aliya Hassen was raised in a cosmopolitan environment where Syrian Midwesterners were proud of their hometowns and the fact that they had built Muslim communities there.

By the 1950s, many Syrian Muslims celebrated the success of their communities while also using their power to further the cause of religious freedom, equal rights, and Arab self-determination. Even if the mosque in Ross, North Dakota, declined, Syrian and Lebanese Muslims preserved their religious identities and nurtured the life of their mosques in Cedar Rapids, Michigan City, Dearborn, Toledo, Cleveland,

Chicago, and beyond. In so many ways, they had achieved dreams the community had first articulated at the beginning of the twentieth century. Their efforts to build wealth, to pass their religion on to their children, and to embrace both Arab and American cultures had come to fruition, at least to an important degree. Syrian Muslim Midwesterners had the confidence and connections to assert their interests and to expect equal treatment. There *was* government and popular discrimination against Muslims during this era, but most of it was directed toward African American Muslims, not Arab American Muslims.[4] It may be hard for those of us who have grown up in blatantly anti-Arab and anti-Muslim times to believe just how much Syrian Muslims had risen in the social order of the Midwest.

But it was not to last.

In fact, one incident at the 1957 FIA Convention foreshadowed the nature of the problems to come. Detroit city council president and acting mayor Louis Miriani cancelled his scheduled appearance to welcome people to Detroit because he said some of its speakers were "anti-Eisenhower, anti-foreign aid, and anti-American." The story was picked up by the Associated Press (AP) and ran in newspapers as far away as the *Bradenton Herald* in Florida. According to the AP's reporting, one of the speakers was criticized "by some Zionist groups." Charles Alawan issued a statement: "we are stunned that the acting head of an American city would refuse to welcome a religious group, especially in a country that is dedicated to religious freedom." Dr. Garland Hopkins, one of the Christian speakers at the convention, declared that Miriani "will have done a wonderful job of assisting Russia," referring to the idea that Communists would use the snub to recruit Muslims worldwide to their side in the Cold War. Miriani pointed out that he "had appeared before Congressional committees in support of the Eisenhower Doctrine of the Middle East and had always been a political supporter of Mr. Eisenhower."[5]

What the incident showed was that US foreign relations inevitably influenced the way Muslim Americans would be perceived, no matter what they did in the United States. It was as if Syrian Muslims had been returned against their will to the days before World War I, when they were called Turks and it was assumed that such people were America's natural enemies. Miriani's cold shoulder demonstrated that the acceptance that Syrian Muslims achieved in the towns and cities of the Midwest was precarious. In the 1950s, when Syrian Muslims exercised more power than they ever had, they could still bear the brunt of lingering negative attitudes toward non-Christian, non-white people. If the United States engaged in a foreign policy dispute with Arabs and Muslims, it was not hard to predict that Arabs and Muslims in the United States might lose their social status as acceptable ethnic and religious minorities. They might become the Other, the enemy even. Even though they were as American as you could be.

This is, in fact, what happened. Increased anti-Arab feeling and discrimination also occurred in the wake of the 1973 OPEC oil embargo, when many oil-producing countries protested US favoritism toward Israel by refusing to export oil to the United States. After the 1979 Iranian Revolution, anti-Muslim feeling and discrimination also increased. It did not matter that Iranians were, for the most part, speakers of the Persian language. The people who had been part of "us" became "them" again. "Them" is so often an amorphous label. The first war against Iraq in 1991 furthered both anti-Arab and anti-Muslim prejudice, which became much, much worse in the wake of 9/11, when the war on terrorism led to increased hate crimes and discrimination against Muslim Americans and those perceived to be Muslim (whether Arab Christian, Sikh, or Hindu). The government's hypersurveillance and unfair prosecutions of Muslims for immigration violations recalled those times in the early 1900s when federal officials stoked fears of Syrians through similar actions.[6]

In this way, the war on terror was a war on ourselves. The government tried to weed out the people whose ancestors had been planting roots in the heartland for more than a century. It was a cruel irony when in 2015, Mike Pence, then the Republican governor of Indiana, tried to ban Syrian refugees from settling in the same state where the Republican governor who preceded him in office, Mitch Daniels, was the grandson of Syrian immigrants. There were clear differences between Mitch Daniels and Syrian refugees, but perhaps the most obvious was that Daniels was Christian whereas many of the refugees were Muslim.

The Muslim Midwest changed in other ways, too. The 1965 Immigration and Naturalization Act jettisoned the racist quotas that had severely restricted Arab immigration since 1924. Perhaps a million new Muslim immigrants from North Africa and the Middle East as well as South Asia and other regions arrived in the United States by the end of the twentieth century. They altered the landscape of Muslim America as they established almost one thousand mosques in a period of three decades. Most Muslim American mosques in the Midwest, including those founded by Syrians, came to be operated and governed by immigrants who arrived after 1965. The history of these institutions prior to 1965 was sometimes forgotten.[7]

This is why remembering the heartland Muslim past is important for all of us in the region, no matter what our religion or race. Syrian Midwestern Muslims have left a legacy through which we can celebrate our struggles for a better society but also face the fears, resentments, and ugliness that sometimes mar our region. We can conjure these ancestors who help us realize that at times we needlessly make strangers out of neighbors and enemies out of friends. Their stories can help us face a past that too many of us are forgetting. As much as anything, their life examples help us rekindle our dreams of what we might become in the future. Yes, the Midwest was born through the taking of Native lands and the expectation among many that white Christians would be dominant in those spaces. Those of us who have inherited this past, those who benefit from it or are traumatized by it, are left with the question of what to do with that historical reality. Do we accept lazy stereotypes of the Midwest, past and present, as exclusively white Christian territory? Or do we call upon the voices of all our Midwestern forebears to acknowledge our interconnected past? Can we use their stories to imagine a different future for those of us who are, inevitably, attached to this region? Some of us can't help ourselves. Some of us have little control over where we live. No matter what our situation, I hope we don't give up on this place. Our beautiful, haunted, powerful heritage beckons us to repair wrongs and to keep the dream of a more loving heartland alive.

ACKNOWLEDGMENTS

Librarians and archivists across the Midwest made this work possible. My thanks go to IUPUI librarian Teodora Durbin, whose skill in locating and obtaining sources is second to none. I also thank Sara Lowe, who gave me essential assistance. Matthew Jaber Stiffler and Elysa Bisoski of the Arab American National Museum provided generous advice and many of the photographs that made it possible for me to imagine what Syrian Muslim Midwestern life looked like. Andrea Glenn at the Indiana State Library made sure I could access the Michigan City newspapers. Michelle Burkhart and Christine Long at the Michigan City Public Library went digging in their collections for sources. At the University of Michigan, Diana Bachman and Madeleine Bradford of the Bentley Historical Library helped with the papers of Aliya Hassen, Julia Haragely, and other key figures. Doris Peterson of the University of South Dakota University Libraries, Christopher A. Schnell of the Abraham Lincoln Presidential Library in Illinois, and Laura Sandowsky and Becki Plunkett of the State Historical Society of Iowa provided important information.

If historian Alixa Naff had not labored for decades to record the oral histories of Arab Americans, I would not have the data I needed to explore their lives in such detail. I wanted to take a fresh look at those interviews, and so I intentionally avoided rereading her book, *Becoming American*, until I was largely done with my own work. Even if some of my conclusions are different, let there be no doubt that my work would not exist without hers. When I met her at the Smithsonian in 1993 as an intern at the American Arab Anti-Discrimination Committee, I had no idea how much her work would come to mean to me. She was a community-engaged scholar, and I am also grateful to the hundreds of

Arab Americans who supported her work. Those oral histories are now housed at the Smithsonian's National Museum of American History, and I thank Christine S. Windheuser, Joe Hursey, and Kay Peterson, who helped me take full advantage of them.

Local historians across the Midwest deserve so much credit for curating and collecting information I used in this book. Sometimes typed, sometimes privately printed, local histories about Ross, North Dakota, and Michigan City, Indiana, provided information that I could not find anywhere else. Equally important were oral histories recorded by citizen scholars and volunteers in North Dakota, Indiana, and Iowa. These interviews provided information that I could not find in Alixa Naff's interviews or local newspapers. I also took full advantage of the many books of historical photographs that have been published in the last couple of decades. Let me also say a special word of thanks to Bob Drahozal at the Cedar Rapids History Center, who not only shared primary sources on Cedar Rapids but also told me about the human geography of Syrian and Lebanese Muslims in town.

As a graduate student in the 1990s, I was trained as an analogue researcher. The card catalogue had been digitized by this time, but I still used the printed and bound *Reader's Guide to Periodic Literature* and traditional microfilm. It took me a while to catch up with the digital research revolution. Paul Mullins mentored me in the effective use of digitized city directories and Sanborn insurance maps, which made it possible for me to pinpoint where my subjects lived, what their dwellings looked like, and who their neighbors were. In addition, the digitization of newspapers made my research much more efficient. In the cases of Ross, North Dakota, and Michigan City, Indiana, I still had to use actual microfilm, since these newspapers had not yet been digitized. It was fun, to be honest, to visit a library, sit down at a machine, and go page by page looking for random allusions to Syrian Muslims. But with regard to every other town that I covered, I was able to utilize keyword searches—names, events, and so on—to identify relevant newspaper articles through Newspapers.com. The other major trove of digital sources that I used were found on Ancestry.com, which has digitized census data, ship manifests, birth and death certificates, military records, and more.

Several colleagues supported my research and writing. Rana Razek shared copies of homestead records from her own archival research—an incredible act of generosity—and became one of my most important conversation partners on this topic. Her suggestions for revision were essential. Sally Howell advised me from beginning to end, and she offered constructive criticism and questions to ponder. Modupe Labode, my teacher on all things Midwestern, was one of the inspirations behind this project, and she gave me wonderful feedback that I incorporated into the final draft. Drs. Howell and Labode gave me literally hundreds of notes. I am so thankful to them. Jon Butler read grant proposals, wrote letters of reference, and inspired me with his approach to the religious history of the Midwest. Thanks to Kambiz GhaneaBassiri and Mohammad Hassan Khalil for writing on my behalf, too. In my department, Matthew Condon, David Craig, Tom Davis, Andrea Jain, Peter Thuesen, Joseph Tucker-Edmonds, and Rachel Wheeler read parts of the manuscript and offered lots of encouragement.

I was also influenced by the incredible work that has been published in just the last decade or so on Midwest history and Arab American history. Two of the most important books that I read about the Midwest were Kristin L. Hoganson, *The Heartland: An American History*, and Jon Lauck, Gleaves Whitney, and Joseph Hogan, eds., *Finding a New Midwestern History*. A few of the books in Arab American history that influenced me were Hani J. Bawardi, *The Making of Arab Americans: From Syrian Nationalism to US Citizenship*; Stacy D. Fahrenthold, *Between the Ottomans and the Entente: The First World War in the Syrian and Lebanese Diaspora, 1908–1925*; Sarah Gualtieri, *Between Arab and White: Race and Ethnicity in the Early Syrian American Diaspora*; and Sally Howell, *Old Islam in Detroit: Rediscovering the Muslim American Past*.

When it came time to publish the book, my editor, Jennifer Hammer, was patient, supportive, and ever-wise in helping me realize my goals.

Veronica Knutson offered able assistance. I was fortunate to work once again with editing, design, and production director Martin Coleman and with copyeditor Dan Geist. Special thanks go to cartographer and illustrator Scott Schiller, who went above and beyond in designing the two maps included in the book. I am so pleased that one of them was adapted as the book's cover.

Family and friends helped. Regan Zwald, my spouse, gave me advice and delighted in many of my discoveries, and she also made essential edits to the final, copyedited manuscript. Jeremy Rehwaldt assisted with copyediting and offered many important suggestions for improvement. Susan Saffa Curtis, my mother, shared memories and also photos and clippings from family scrapbooks. I talked farming with Jeanne and Jerry Zwald, my in-laws. Hiba Alami translated some Arabic for me, and made my own translations sharper.

I received strong financial support for the project from the Indiana University School of Liberal Arts in Indianapolis, the IUPUI Institute for the Arts and Humanities, and the Indiana University Presidential Arts and Humanities Program. I was especially grateful that the university continued to fund research during the challenging time of the COVID-19 pandemic.

NOTES

INTRODUCTION

1 Interview with Adeby Coury by Rick Coury, May 24, 1980, 13, in Faris and Yamna Naff Arab-American Collection Archives Center, National Museum of American History.

2 Stacy D. Fahrenthold, *Between the Ottomans and the Entente: The First World War in the Syrian and Lebanese Diaspora, 1908–1925* (New York: Oxford University Press, 2019), 6, 14, 16, 25.

3 David F. Good, "American History through a Midwestern Lens," *Wirtschaft und Gesellschaft* 238, no. 2 (2012): 435–47.

4 Michael C. Steiner, "The Birth of the Midwest and the Rise of Regional Theory," in *Finding a New Midwestern History*, ed. Jon K. Lauck, Gleaves Whitney, and Joseph Hogan (Lincoln: University of Nebraska Press, 2018), 18.

5 Ibid., 3–24.

6 Jon Gjerde, *The Minds of the West: Ethnocultural Evolution in the Rural Middle West* (Chapel Hill: University of North Carolina Press, 1999), 19.

7 Sarah M. A. Gualtieri, *Between Arab and White: Race and Ethnicity in the Early Syrian American Diaspora* (Berkeley: University of California Press, 2009).

CHAPTER 1. MUSLIM SOUTH DAKOTA FROM KADOKA TO SIOUX FALLS

1 Interview with Aliya Hassen by Grant Farr, Dearborn, Michigan, June 2, 1980, Naff Collection, National Museum of American History.

2 *Find a Grave*, Alex Ogdie (1862–1937), Mount Pleasant Cemetery, Sioux Falls, South Dakota, https://www.findagrave.com.

3 Interview with Aliya Hassen, 8; *1900 United States Federal Census*, Sioux Falls Ward 2, Minnehaha, South Dakota, 16, www.ancestry.com.

4 *Sanborn Fire Insurance Map from Sioux Falls, Minnehaha County, South Dakota*, Sanborn Map Company, July 1902, www.loc.gov.

5 National Parks, Visitation Statistics, Badlands, www.nationalparked.com.

6 Herbert S. Schell, *History of South Dakota*, 4th ed. (Pierre: South Dakota State Historical Society Press, 2004), 7, 253, 256. Descriptions of the Ogdie land are based on personal observations using Google Earth, which also shows the distance from the homestead to the town of Kadoka.

7 R. Frankson, K. Kunkel, S. Champion, and D. Easterling, "2017: South Dakota State Climate Summary," NOAA Technical Report NESDIS 149-SD, https://statesummaries.ncics.org.

8 Threaded Station Extremes, http://threadex.rcc-acis.org.

9 US Department of the Interior, Bureau of Land Management, General Land Office Records, Land Patent, Document 01486, https://glorecords.blm.gov; Land Status Record for South Range 22 East of the Black Hills Meridian, US Department of the Interior, Bureau of Land Management, https://glorecords.blm.gov; Richard Edwards, Jacob K. Friefeld, and Rebecca S. Wingo, *Homesteading the Plains: Toward a New History* (Lincoln: University of Nebraska Press, 2017), 113–15.

10 Interview with Aliya Hassen, 12.

11 Nabeel Abraham and Andrew Shryock, eds., *Arab Detroit: From Margin to Mainstream* (Detroit: Wayne State University Press, 2000), 317–18.

12 Kristin L. Hoganson, *The Heartland: An American History* (New York: Penguin, 2019), 12–13.

13 Karen V. Hansen with Grey Osterud, "Landowning, Dispossession and the Significance of Land among Dakota and Scandinavian Women at Spirit Lake, 1900–29," *Gender and History* 26, no. 1 (2014): 106.

14 Eric Renshaw, *Forgotten Sioux Falls* (Charleston, SC: Arcadia, 2012); Henry F. Thompson, general editor, *A New South Dakota History*, 2nd ed. (Sioux Falls, SD: Center for Western Studies, 2009), 172, 176–77.

15 *US City Directories, 1822–1995*, www.ancestry.com.

16 *South Dakota, State Census, 1915*, www.ancestry.com.

17 Interview with Aliya Hassen, 15, 17, 18, 22.

18 *Sioux Falls Argus-Leader*, Aug. 31, 1911, 6. One article refers to a Muslim cemetery, but this may have been a Muslim section of Mt. Pleasant. See *Sioux Falls Argus-Leader*, Feb. 4, 1916, 12.

19 *Sioux Falls Argus-Leader*, Dec. 22, 1913, 3.

20 Interview with Aliya Hassen, 19, 22.

21 Ibid., 10, 20, 24.

22 Lori Ann Lahlum, "'Everything was changed and looked strange': Norwegian Women in South Dakota," *South Dakota History* 35, no. 3 (Fall 2005): 189–216.

23 Interview with Aliya Hassen, 24.

24 "Divorce Muddle," *Sioux Falls Argus-Leader*, Sept. 27, 1913, 3; "City Briefs," *Sioux Falls Argus-Leader*, Oct. 1, 1913, 10.

25 *US City Directories, 1822–1995*, www.ancestry.com.

26 *Sioux Falls City Directory*, 1914, *US City Directories, 1822–1995*, www.ancestry.com; *Sanborn Fire Insurance Map from Sioux Falls*.

27 Mark Hufstetler and Michael Bedeau, "South Dakota's Railroads: An Historic Context," South Dakota State Historic Preservation Office (Pierre, South Dakota, 1998, rev. 2007), 43–44, https://history.sd.gov.

28 *Sioux Falls Argus Leader*, Oct. 23, 1912, 6.

29 "No Swearing by the Koran," *Sioux Falls Argus-Leader*, Mar. 17, 1911, 8; John S. McClintock, *Pioneer Days in the Black Hills* (Norman: University of Oklahoma Press, 2000 [orig. 1939]), 336.

30 Gualtieri, *Between Arab and White*, 33–37; Holly Edwards, ed., *Noble Dreams, Wicked Pleasures: Orientalism in America, 1870–1930* (Princeton, NJ: Princeton University Press, 2000); Mark Twain, *Innocents Abroad* (Hartford, CT: American Publishing Company, 1869).

31 *Sioux Falls Argus-Leader*, July 29, 1914, 8;

32 "A Mohammedan Conspiracy," *Thanhouser Films: An Encyclopedia and History*, www.thanhouser.org.

33 "Gossip from the Capital," *Sioux Falls Argus-Leader*, Aug. 23, 1906, 2; "Christians Killed in Persia," *Sioux Falls Argus-Leader*, July 24, 1900, 2; "Moslems Called to Join Holy War," *Sioux Falls Argus-Leader*, May 8, 1912, 1; "Glad to Throw Aside Veils," *Sioux Falls Argus-Leader*, Jan. 6, 1909, 2; "Chance for Muslim Girls," *Sioux Falls Argus-Leader*, Dec. 27, 1906, 8.

34 Modupe Labode, personal correspondence, Jan. 24, 2021.

35 "An Egyptian Viewpoint," *Sioux Falls Argus-Leader*, May 31, 1010, 4.

36 "Religion and Trousers," *Sioux Falls Argus-Leader*, Jan. 26, 1907, 10.

37 "No Bearing on Situation," *Sioux Falls Argus-Leader*, Mar. 10, 1906, 11.

38 George W. Kingbury, *South Dakota: Its History and Its People*, vol. 9 (Chicago: Clarke Publishing, 1915), 895–96.

39 "An Interesting Discourse," *Sioux Falls Argus-Leader*, Nov. 11, 1912, 5.

40 "Mohammedan in History," *Sioux Falls Argues Leader*, Nov. 7, 1912, 3.

41 "In Darkness and Despair," *Sioux Falls Argus-Leader*, July 24, 1911, 3.

42 *Sioux Falls Argus Leader*, Feb. 24, 1913, 5.

43 *US City Directories, 1822–1995*, www.ancestry.com.

44 "Young Syrians vs. Young Americans; The Syrian People Will Make a Fight for Their Rights," *Sioux Falls Argus-Leader*, May 2, 1912, 3; *US, Army Transport Service, Passenger Lists, 1910–1939*, www.ancestry.com.

45 "Municipal Court," *Sioux Falls Argus-Leader*, Feb. 21, 1914, 12; *US City Directories, 1822–1995*, www.ancestry.com.

46 "True Americanism," *Sioux Falls Argus-Leader*, June 16, 1915, 4.

47 Andrew Cayton and Susan Gray, eds., *The Identity of the American Midwest: Essays on Regional History* (Bloomington: Indiana University Press, 2007), 150; and compare Werner Sollors, *Beyond Ethnicity: Consent and Descent in American Culture* (New York: Oxford University Press, 1987), and R. Laurence Moore, *Religious Outsiders and the Making of Americans* (New York: Oxford University Press, 1987).

48 Sally Howell, *Old Islam in Detroit: Rediscovering the Muslim American Past* (New York: Oxford University Press, 2014); Abdo Elkholy, *The Arab Moslems in the United States: Religion and Assimilation* (New Haven, CT: College and University Press, 1966).

49 Interview with Aliya Hassen, 14, 18, 21, 23.

50 "Wed in Syria," *Cedar Rapids Evening Gazette*, Aug. 12, 1897, 5.

51 "Old Courthouse Museum," www.siouxlandmuseums.com.

52 "Mohammedans Celebrate: Sioux Falls Witnesses a Novel Parade by Syrian Lodge of Bedr-El-Moneer," *Sioux Falls Argus-Leader*, July 5, 1916, 7.

53 Ibid.

54 *Sioux Falls City Directory*, 1916, www.ancestry.com.

55 "Organize First Lodge of Syrians in State," *Sioux Falls Argus-Leader*, Mar. 8, 1916, 5.

56 "Curbstone Opinions," *Sioux Falls Argus-Leader*, Mar. 9, 1916, 8.

57 "Why the 'Holy War' Failed," *Sioux Falls Argus-Leader*, Oct. 26, 1917, 4.

58 Interview with Aliya Hassen, 24.

59 "Face to Face with Kaiserism," *Sioux Falls Argus-Leader*, Mar. 29, 1918, 4, and Jan. 10, 1919, 12.

60 "M'Kennan Hospital Here Received 1,070 Patients during Year," *Sioux Falls Argues-Leader*, Mar. 26, 1917, 3.

61 "US Espionage Act, 1917," www.firstworldwar.com.

62 David M. Kennedy, *Over Here: The First World War and American Society* (New York: Oxford University Press, 2004), 80.

63 Joe P. Kirby, "The Case of German Socialist Farmers," *South Dakota History* 42, no. 3 (Fall 2012): 237–55.

64 LaVern J. Rippley, *South Dakota History* 27, no. 3 (Fall 1997): 107–32.

65 Merle J. F. Funk, "Divided Loyalties: Mennonite and Hutterite Responses to the United States at War, Hutchinson County, South Dakota, 1917–1918," *Mennonite Life* 52, no. 4 (Dec. 1997): 24–32.

66 Interview with Aliya Hassen, 24.

67 "Syrian Colony Is Very Patriotic," *Sioux Falls Argus-Leader*, June 21, 1918, 7.

68 "Syrian Citizens Raise Big R.C. Fund," *Sioux Falls Argus-Leader*, June 24, 1918, 8.

69 *US, World War I Draft Registration Cards, 1917–1918*, www.ancestry.com.

70 *US, World War I Soldier Naturalizations, 1918*, www.ancestry.com.

71 *Lists of Outgoing Passengers, 1917–1938*, www.ancestry.com.

72 *Sioux Falls City Directory*, 1918, 557, www.ancestry.com.

73 "The Meuse Argonne Offensive," National Archives, www.archives.gov; "91st Division American Expeditionary Force, World War I," 91st Division Publication Committee (San Mateo, CA, 1919), as reprinted in *New River Notes*, www.newrivernotes.com.

74 "91st Division American Expeditionary Force."

75 "Learns Details Chamie's Death," *Sioux Falls Argus-Leader* Jan. 7, 1919.

76 South Dakota, State Census, 1915, www.ancestry.com; *Find a Grave*, Pvt Joe Chamie (22 Feb 1887–17 Oct 1918), No. 55956888, Meuse-Argonne American Cemetery and Memorial, Romagne-sous-Montfaucon, Departement de la Meuse, Lorraine, France, www.findagrave.com.

CHAPTER 2. HOMESTEADING WESTERN NORTH DAKOTA

1 Climate-Data.Org, "El Bire," https://en.climate-data.org; National Oceanic and Atmospheric Administration (NOAA) Williston, ND, Station, http://threadex. rcc-acis.org; NOAA, Williston, ND, Station, http://tp.ncdc.noaa.gov.

2 "Lost in Storm," *Ross Valley News*, Jan. 6, 1911, 1.

3 Interview with Sam Omar by Everal J. McKinnon, Works Progress Administration, North Dakota Writers' Project, Ethnic Group Files, Series 30559, Roll 3, State Historical Society of North Dakota. Sam Omar's recollections are part of the WPA ethnic history interviews conducted in the late 1930s in North Dakota. Though states throughout the country recorded the memories of their "ethnic" populations, Georgia and North Dakota were the only states whose oral histories offer significant evidence of past Muslim inhabitants.

4 "The Ships List," www.theshipslist.com; *New York Passenger and Crew Lists (including Castle Garden and Ellis Island), 1820–1957*, www.ancestry.com; Interview with Sam Omar.

5 Interview with Sam Omar; "Declaration of Intention," Records of the Bureau of Land Management, National Archives Building, Washington, DC. Thanks to Rana Razek for sharing a copy of the land file.

6 Elwyn B. Robinson, *History of North Dakota* (Fargo: Institute for Regional Studies at North Dakota State University, 1995), 236.

7 Ibid., 242.

8 Mary Wilma M. Hargreaves, *Dry Farming in the Northern Great Plains* (Cambridge, MA: Harvard University Press, 1957), especially 439–41.

9 *Ross Valley News*, Jan. 1, 1904, 1.

10 *1910 United States Federal Census*, www.ancestry.com.

11 Robinson, *History of North Dakota*, 244.

12 William C. Sherman, Paul L. Whitney, and John Guerrero, *Prairie Peddlers: The Syrian-Lebanese in North Dakota* (Bismarck, ND: University of Mary Press, 2002), 123, 127. In their appendices, Sherman, Whitney, and Guerrero include raw data for Syrians immigrants from US census, naturalization, homestead claim, name change, and US military records.

13 Interview with Hassyn Alla Juma by Everal J. McKinnon, Works Progress Administration, North Dakota Writers' Project, Ethnic Group Files, Series 30559, Roll 3, State Historical Society of North Dakota.

14 *US, Indexed County Land Ownership Maps, 1860–1918*, www.ancestry.com; Richard Edwards, Jacob K. Friefeld, and Rebecca S. Wingo, *Homesteading the Plains: Toward a New History* (Lincoln: University of Nebraska Press, 2017), 113; US Department of Interior, Bureau of Land Management, Certificate No. 12749 "Township I55 North Range 92 West of the 5th Principal Meridian, North Dakota," https://glorrecords.blm.gov.

15 Sherman et al., *Prairie Peddlers*, 129.

16 Ibid., 34.

17 Ibid., 154. See also "North Dakota State News," *Ward County Independent*, Apr. 29, 1903, 3.

18 "Homestead Application 20167," Mar. 24, 1903; "United States Land Office Explanatory Affidavit," May 28, 1904; Letter to Commissioner of the General Land Office, May 28, 1904; Affidavit by Sam Omar, Glenburn, North Dakota, Mar. 8, 1905, Records of the Bureau of Land Management, National Archives Building, Washington, DC.

19 "Homestead Proof—Testimony of Witness," Records of the Bureau of Land Management, National Archives Building, Washington, DC. The distance is measured on Google Earth from Ross to the 5th Median, Township 155 North, Range 92 West, data recorded on Sam Omar's land patent.

20 Norman K. Risjord, *Dakota: The Story of the Northern Plains* (Lincoln: University of Nebraska Press, 2012), 173.

21 John Hudson, "Frontier Housing in North Dakota," *North Dakota History* 42, no. 4 (1975): 4–15; Interview with Side Abdallah by Everal J. McKinnon, Works Progress Administration, North Dakota Writers' Project, Ethnic Group Files, Series 30559, Roll 3, State Historical Society of North Dakota.

22 Robinson, *History of North Dakota*, 2–9.

23 Jerry Zwald, Garner, Iowa, personal correspondence, Dec. 2019.

24 Interview with Sam Omar.

25 "Notice of Publication," "Homestead Proof-Testimony of Clamant," "Homestead Proof-Testimony of Witness," "Receiver's Office Receipt," Dec. 17, 1906, Land File; US Department of Interior, Bureau of Land Management, Certificate No. 12749, https://glorecords.blm.gov.

26 Robinson, *History of North Dakota*, 247.

27 Ibid., 248.

28 Ibid.

29 Interviews with Mary Juma, Mike Abdalla, Side Abdallah, Works Progress Administration, North Dakota Writers' Project, Ethnic Group Files, Series 30559, Roll 3, State Historical Society of North Dakota.

30 Interview with Boaley Farhat by Everal J. McKinnon, Oct. 31, Nov. 1, 3, 1939, North Dakota Ethnic Files, Works Progress Administration.

31 Ibid.; Perry Piper, "Sulky Plow," *Farm Collector*, www.farmcollector.com; "Farhat, Bo Aley," Patent No. 202179, May 29, 1911, US Bureau of Land Management, May 29, 1911, https://glorecords.blm.gov; *US Indexed County Land Ownership Maps, 1860–1918*, www.ancestry.com.

32 Interview with Mike Abdallah by Everal McKinnon, Ross, North Dakota, [1939]; *North Dakota, Naturalization Index, 1874–1963*, www.ancestry.com; Bureau of Land Management, Patent No. 591371, July 9, 1917, https://glorecords.blm.gov.

33 "Crops Grow without Rain," *Bottineau Courant*, July 31, 1908, 6.

34 "Syrian Peas," *North Lemmon State-Line Herald*, Feb. 24, 1911, 5.

35 "New Kind of Pea," *Sioux Falls Argus-Leader*, Jan. 23, 1911, 6.

36 Hargreaves, *Dry Farming*, 185–86.

37 Interview with Mike Abdallah.

38 Interview with Boaley Farhat.

39 Robinson, *History of North Dakota*, 264–66, 272–76; Risjord, *Dakota*, 190.

40 H. Elaine Lindgren, *Land in Her Own Name* (Fargo: North Dakota Institute for Regional Studies, 1991), 23.

41 Rana Razek, personal correspondence, Nov. 18, 2019. Razek points out that William Sherman missed the presence of this Muslim woman homesteader; see further Sherman et al., *Prairie Peddlers*, 129.

42 *Border Crossings: From Mexico to U.S., 1895–1964*, www.ancestry.com.

43 Bureau of Land Management, https://glorecords.blm.gov.

44 North Dakota Naturalization Records Index, https://library.ndsu.edu.

45 Bureau of Land Management, "Isha Mostaf," https://glorecords.blm.gov; North Dakota Hometown Locator, https://northdakota.hometownlocator.com.

46 *U.S., Indexed County Land Ownership Maps, 1860–1918*, www.ancestry.com.

47 *U.S., Army Transport Service, Passenger Lists, 1910–1939*, www.ancestry.com.

48 The two daughters stayed in Ottoman Syria and then in Lebanon. But the family stayed in touch, and in the early 1970s, Mary and Hassen's son, Charles, bought a plane ticket for the one living sister to visit them in North Dakota. It was the first and only time that the brother and sister met. Interview with Mr. Charlie Juma Sr. (Stanley) by Larry Sprunk, Mar. 15, 1976, Tape Number 24, North Dakota Oral History Project, State Historical Society of North Dakota.

49 Interview with Mary Juma by Everal J. McKinnon, trans. Sada Cader Juma, Works Progress Administration, North Dakota Writers' Project, Ethnic Group Files, Series 30559, Roll 3, State Historical Society of North Dakota; Interview with Charlie Juma.

50 Interview with Mary Juma; "Homestead Application 14719," "Homestead Proof," and "Homestead Proof-Testimony of Claimant," Bureau of Land Management, National Archives Building, Washington, DC.

51 Alixa Naff, *Becoming American: The Early Arab Immigrant Experience* (Carbondale: Southern Illinois University Press, 1985), 169–71.

52 Ibid., 130.

53 Charlotte Marie Albrecht, "Peddling an Arab American History: Race, Gender, and Sexuality in Early Syrian American Communities," PhD diss., University of Minnesota, 2013.

54 "Syrians of Mount Lebanon Make Home in West St. Paul," *St. Paul Globe*, Mar. 22, 1903, 23. Thanks to Rana Razek for sharing this citation.

55 Interview with Mary Juma; "Homestead Application 14719," "Homestead Proof," and "Homestead Proof-Testimony of Claimant"; Interview with Charlie Juma.

56 Interview with Mary Juma.

57 *Ross Valley News*, Jan. 15, 1915, 1; Interview with Charlie Juma.

58 "Our Schools," *Ross Valley News*, Sept. 18, 1914, 1.

59 L. J. Meiers, ed., "School Notes," *Ross Valley News*, Jan. 15, 1915, 5.

60 Interview with Mary Juma; Interview with Charlie Juma.

61 Interview with Hassyn Alla Juma; Interview with Mike Abdallah.

62 Interview with Mike Abdallah.

63 C. Nijland, "Mahjar Literature," *Encyclopedia of Arabic Literature*, vol. 2, ed. Julie Scott Meisami and Paul Starkey (London: Routledge, 1998), 492–93.

64 Sollors, *Beyond Ethnicity*; Interview with Charlie Juma.

65 Interview with Hassyn Alla Juma; Interview with Mary Juma.

66 Interview with Mike Abdallah; *Ward County Independent*, July 13, 1904, 6; Sherman et al., *Prairie Peddlers*, 179–80.

67 Rayford W. Logan, *The Betrayal of the Negro: From Rutherford B. Hayes to Woodrow Wilson* (New York: Da Capo, 1997).

68 Ibram X. Kendi, *Stamped from the Beginning: The Definitive History of Racist Ideas in America* (New York: Bold Type Books, 2016).

69 "Syrian War for Citizenship," *Williston Graphic*, Oct. 14, 1909, 9.

70 "Syrian Citizen," *Grand Forks Evening Times*, Nov. 5, 1909, 1.

71 "Asks Reason for Syrian Exclusion," *Grand Forks Evening Times*, Nov. 20, 1909, n.p.

72 "Syrians in N.D. Barred by Ruling," *Fargo Forum and Daily Republican*, Nov. 3, 1909, 10.

73 Robinson, *History of North Dakota*, 245.

74 For analysis of how Syrians understood and advocated for their whiteness as part of the effort to become citizens, see Gualtieri, *Between Arab and White*, 52–80.

75 For examples, see "A Syrian John L.," *Langdon Courier Democrat*, July 14, 1892, 7; "Church Solicitor Is Banned for a Theft," *Grand Forks Evening Tribune*, Feb. 12, 1912, 5; "Trouble for Syrian Peddler," *Bismarck Daily Tribune*, Sept. 19, 1913, 2; "Arrest Syrian for Crime in Canada," *Bismarck Daily Tribune*, Jan. 19, 1915, 3; "Bringing In Cheap Labor," *Wahpeton Times*, Jan. 25, 1912, 2; "Syrian Held Up for a Belt Containing $8,500," *Washburn Leader*, Jan. 25, 1902, 8; "Reported Sold Girls," *Grand Forks Evening Tribune*, Jan. 15, 1907, 1; "Rioting in New York," *Bismarck Daily Tribune*, Oct. 25, 1905, 4; "Arrest Conspirator," *Bismarck Daily Tribune*, July 17, 1911, 5; "Denies the Charge Does Joe Sally," *Bismarck Daily Tribune*, July 27, 1911, 1; "Syrian Arrested for Beating Wife," *Bismarck Daily Tribune*, Feb. 6, 1910, 3; "Slayer of Boy May Have Been Syrian Avenger," *Bismarck Daily Tribune*, Jan. 14, 1910, 1; "For Embezzlement," *Grand Forks Evening Times*, Dec. 12, 1906, 3.

76 Fahrenthold, *Between the Ottomans and the Entente*.

77 *Nonpartisan Leader* (Fargo, ND), July 6, 1916, https://chroniclingamerica.loc.gov.

78 Susan Wefald, "Remembering 'Our Boys': North Dakota's World War I Monuments and Memorials (1918–1941)," *North Dakota History* 83.1 (Summer 2018): 20–36.

79 Daniel Sauerwein, "Letters from 'Over There': How North Dakota Soldiers Viewed the Great War," State Historical Society of North Dakota Blog, https://blog.statemuseum.nd.gov.

80 Joseph T. Stuart, "North Dakota and the Cultural History of the Great War," *North Dakota History* 83, no. 2 (Winter 2018): 3–17.

81 Interview with Boaley Farhat.

82 Interview with Hassyn Alla Juma; *North Dakota, Naturalization Index, 1874–1963*, www.ancestry.com; *Roster of the Men and Women Who Served in the Army or Naval Service (including the Marine Corps) of the United States of Its Allies from the State of North Dakota in the World War, 1917–1918. Vols. I–IV* (Bismarck, ND: Bismarck Tribune Co., 1931).

83 Interview with Kassam Ramedem by William A. Glenn, Oct. 23, 26, 27, 1939; North Dakota Ethnic Files; *History of the Fortieth (Sunshine) Division* (Los Angeles: C. S. Hutson, 1920), https://history.army.mil; *US World War I Draft Registration Cards, 1917–1918* and *US Army Transport Service, Passenger Lists, 1910–1939*, www.ancestry.com.

CHAPTER 3. PEDDLING IN CEDAR RAPIDS, IOWA, A TOWN OF ETHNIC TRADITION

1 *Iowa, Federal Naturalization Records, 1856–1937*, www.ancestry.com.

2 Google Maps, www.google.com; "Joub Jannine," www.localliban.org; "Joub Jannine Weather Averages," www.worldweatheronline.com.

3 "Personal," *Cedar Rapids Gazette*, Sept. 23, 1903, 3.

4 *US City Directories, 1822–1995*, www.ancestry.com. Names of Syrians were frequently misspelled, but there is another reason for the multiple spellings of a name. There was no one way to transliterate it from Arabic, and so it might be rendered in a number of different combinations. Hassen, which we might assume is Hasan, could actually be a spelling for Husayn. In Arabic, the family name, Sheronick, is spelled "sheen-ra'-alif-nun-qaf" according to a signature on the naturalization papers. *Sanborn Fire Insurance Map from Cedar Rapids, Linn County, Iowa*, Sanborn Map Company, 1913, www.loc.gov; *Iowa State Census, 1905*, www.ancestry.com.

5 Jon Teaford, "The Development of Midwestern Cities," in *Finding a New Midwestern History*, 215; Brie Swenson Arnold, "An Opportunity to Challenge the 'Color Line': Gender, Race, Ethnicity, and Women's Labor Activism in Late Nineteenth-Century Cedar Rapids, Iowa," *Annals of Iowa* 74 (Spring 2015): 103–5; Pam Stek, "The 1898 American Cereal Company Strike in Cedar Rapids: Gender, Ethnicity, and Labor in Late Nineteenth-Century Iowa," *Annals of Iowa* 74 (Spring 2015): 146–52; Iowa State Data Center, www.iowadatacenter.org.

6 George Henry and the History Center, *Cedar Rapids, Iowa* (Charleston, SC: Arcadia, 2001), 102; George T. Henry and Mark H. Hunter, *Cedar Rapids: Downtown and Beyond* (Charleston, SC: Arcadia, 2005), 9, 11, 14.

7 State Historical Society of Iowa, *Iowa: A Guide to the Hawkeye State* (New York: Hastings House, 1949), 187, 189, 194; Henry and Hunter, *Cedar Rapids: Downtown and Beyond*, 77, 87.

8 George T. Henry and Mark W. Hunter, *Cedar Rapids: Then and Now* (Charleston, SC: Arcadia, 2003), 9, 15, 21, 22, 66, 91–96; Henry and Hunter, *Cedar Rapids: Downtown and Beyond*, 6, 28, 58, 77, 93; Henry and the History Center, *Cedar Rapids, Iowa*.

9 Henry and the History Center, *Cedar Rapids*, 31–32; *Sanborn Fire Insurance Map from Cedar Rapids*.

10 Henry and Hunter, *Cedar Rapids: Downtown and Beyond*, 84–85, 93, 95.

11 "Personal and Local," *Cedar Rapids Evening Gazette*, Dec. 9, 1890, 3.

12 Henry and Hunter, *Cedar Rapids: Downtown and Beyond*; "Wed in Syria," *Cedar Rapids Evening Gazette*, Aug. 12, 1897, 5.

13 Thanks to Charles Louis Richter for helping me find this information; see further "What Other Peoples East," *Kansas City Times*, July 13, 1908, 9. This article and the one in the *Cedar Rapids Evening Gazette* are almost copies of one another, adjusted for whatever ethnic groups were living in each respective locale.

14 "Never Forget Native Dishes," *Cedar Rapids Evening Gazette*, July 15, 1908, 5.

15 Ibid.

16 "Syrian Peddlers," *Cedar Rapids Evening Gazette*, May 12, 1894, 5.

17 "An Assyrian Mixup," *Cedar Rapids Evening Gazette*, Nov. 22, 1909, 13.

18 "A Victory for Ferris," *Cedar Rapids Gazette*, Mar. 27, 1907, 29; "Supervisors Proceedings," *Cedar Rapids Evening Gazette*, June 9, 1910, 8.

19 "Overstepped His Authority," *Cedar Rapids Evening Gazette*, Oct. 22, 1909, 8.

20 "The Romance Was Untrue," *Cedar Rapids Evening Gazette*, Oct. 18, 1902. 2.

21 "Wholesale Smuggling," *Cedar Rapids Evening Gazette*, Aug. 19, 1902, 1.

22 "Syrian Probe Comes to Head," *Cedar Rapids Evening Gazette*, Mar. 11, 1910, 9; "Joseph George Pleads Guilty and Fined $500," *Cedar Rapids Evening Gazette*, Apr. 8, 1910, 5.

23 "Armenians Commit Horrible Atrocities," *Cedar Rapids Evening Gazette*, Jan. 20, 1906, 1; "Treaty with Sulu," *Cedar Rapids Evening Gazette*, Sept. 29, 1899, 7; "A Move in Manchuria," *Cedar Rapids Evening Gazette*, Nov. 6, 1900, 6; "Banish Dogs from Houses," *Cedar Rapids Evening Gazette*, July 9, 1904, 5.

24 "Universal War," *Cedar Rapids Evening Gazette*, Jan. 6, 1896, 4.

25 "Mohammedan No Good," *Cedar Rapids Evening Gazette*, Apr. 25, 1902, 8.

26 "Story of the Arabian Nights," *Cedar Rapids Evening Gazette*, Jan. 22, 1910, 6.

27 "Moslem World Celebrates End of Its Lenten Season," *Cedar Rapids Evening Gazette*, Aug. 11, 1915, 5.

28 Ibid.; "Cedar Rapids Boy Tells of Religious Awakening in India," *Cedar Rapids Evening Gazette*, Jan. 31, 1914, 10.

29 "The Mohammedan Lent," *Cedar Rapids Evening Gazette*, July 1, 1916, 4.

30 Interview with Najibe [Negebe] Sheronick by Alixa Naff, Naff Collection, National Museum of American History, June 6, 1980, 8.

31 Ibid.; *New York, Passenger and Crew Lists (including Castle Garden and Ellis Island), 1820–1957*, www.ancestry.com.

32 *McCoy's Cedar Rapids City Directory 1912* (Rockford, IL: McCoy, 1912), www. ancestry.com.

33 Nelson, Paul C. "Rise and Decline of the Rock Island Passenger Train in the 20th Century," *Annals of Iowa* 41 (1971): 654, 657.

34 *Sanborn Fire Insurance Map from Cedar Rapids.*

35 Naff, *Becoming American,* 269–70.

36 "Syrian Colony in Court," *Cedar Rapids Evening Gazette,* Mar. 21, 1907, 6.

37 Interview with Najibe Sheronick, 11.

38 Hussien Ahmed Sheronick, "A History of the Cedar Rapids Muslim Community: The Search for an American Islamic Identity," honors thesis, Coe College, Cedar Rapids, Iowa, May 3, 1988.

39 Farenthold, *Between the Ottomans and the Entente,* 6.

40 Interview with Mike Aossey by Alixa Naff, June 20, 1980, Box 273, Naff Collection.

41 "Wed in Syria," *Cedar Rapids Evening Gazette,* Aug. 12, 1897, 5.

42 *1910 United States Federal Census,* www.ancestry.com.

43 "Total Population for Iowa's Incorporated Places: 1850–2010," www.iowadatacenter.org.

44 Interview with Mike Aossey, 11, 20.

45 Interview with Mike Aossey.

46 Ibid.

47 Ibid.

48 Ibid.

49 Ibid.

50 Ibid., 19, 22.

51 Ibid, 19.

52 Harrison John Thornton, *The History of the Quaker Oats Company* (Chicago: University of Chicago Press, 1933), 178.

53 Ibid., 153–58.

54 Interview with Mike Aossey.

55 Ibid.; "Ford River Rouge Plant Firehouse," www.fordmotorhistory.com.

56 *U.S., World War I Draft Registration Cards, 1917–1918,* www.ancestry.com.

57 *Sanborn Fire Insurance Map from Cedar Rapids.*

58 "'Talk Religion and Use Billiard Cues to Drive Arguments," *Cedar Rapids Evening Gazette,* July 6, 1914, 9.

59 Nancy Ruth Derr, "Iowans during World War I: A Study of Change under Duress," PhD diss., George Washington University, 1979, 228.

60 Ibid., 222–65; Stephen J. Frese, "Divided by a Common Language: The Babel Proclamation and Its Influence in Iowa History," *History Teacher* 39, no. 1 (Nov. 2005): 59–68.

61 "Cedar Rapids Plan in War Activities Likely to Be Adopted in Other Cities," *Cedar Rapids Evening Gazette,* July 13, 1918, 11.

62 "Syrians Gave Freely," *Cedar Rapids Evening Gazette*, June 11, 1918, 11.

63 Derr, "Iowans during World War I," 1.

64 *U.S., World War I Draft Registration Cards, 1917–1918*. www.ancestry.com; *Iowa, Federal Naturalization Records, 1856–1937*, www.ancestry.com.

65 Interview with Abdullah Igram by Alixa Naff, Oct. 23, 1980, Cedar Rapids, Iowa, Naff Collection, National Museum of American History, 1, 2, 4, 8, 9, 10, 14.

66 Allen W. Hatheway, "History and Chronology of Manufactured Gas," *Former Manufactured Gas Plants*, www.hatheway.net; "Council Committee Reports Favorably to Gas Corporation," *Cedar Rapids Evening Gazette*, July 8, 1918, 9; "Gas Company Asks Higher Prices for Product Here," *Cedar Rapids Evening Gazette*, May 17, 1918, 15.

CHAPTER 4. MICHIGAN CITY, INDIANA, AND SYRIAN MUSLIM INDUSTRIAL WORKERS

1 "Michigan City Climate History," www.myweather2.com; "Indiana's Lake Michigan Programs," www.in.gov; Laurie Radke et al., *The Portable LaPorte County* [1978], Michigan City Public Library, www.mclib.org.

2 Radke, *The Portable LaPorte County*; "Our Heritage (1976)."

3 "An Interview with Hussien Hussien Ayad by John P. Brennan," Public Library of Michigan City Indiana, n.d., 2, 8.

4 Elisabeth M. Marsh, "Making American Lives: Immigrants and Americanization in Michigan City, Indiana, 1880–1941," PhD diss., Indiana University, 2012, 24, 26, 37, 40.

5 Ibid., 42.

6 Abdul Jalil Al-Tahir, "The Arab Community in the Chicago Area: A Comparative Study of the Christian-Syrians and the Muslim-Palestinians," PhD diss., University of Chicago, 1952.

7 Elizabeth M. Munger, "Michigan City's First Hundred Years," Michigan City, Indiana, Public Library, 78.

8 Bob Kaser with Henry Lange, "Lakefront Legacy," in "Our Heritage (1976)."

9 RoseAnna Mueller, *Michigan City* (Charlestown, SC: Arcadia, 2005), 102.

10 "100 Years Ago, the Most Famous Landmark in Indiana Vanished," Jan. 5, 2020, https://orangebeanindiana.com.

11 Marsh, "Making American Lives," 69–89, 97.

12 Ibid., 112–13; "Turk Insults Woman," *Michigan City Evening Dispatch*, July 5, 1907, 1; "Syrian Picked Pretty Flowers," *Michigan City Evening Dispatch*, July 5, 1907, 1.

13 Marsh, "Making American Lives," 115–16.

14 *South Bend Tribune*, Mar. 30, 1910, 1.

15 Marsh, "Making American Lives," 114, 117; "Lay Blame to Turks," *Michigan City Evening-Dispatch*, July 22, 1908, 1; 1905 *Michigan City Directory*, www.ancestry.com.

16 "Mean Battle," *Brazil Daily Times*, July 8, 1908, 4.

17 "A Straw Boss Made Charges," *Michigan City Evening News*, Feb. 26, 1914, 1.

18 "Both Turk and Syrian under Federal Ban," *Indianapolis News*, Oct. 8, 1909, 11.

19 "Will Deport 200 Syrians," *Times* (Munster, IN), Jan. 30, 1913, 4.

20 *US City Directories, 1822–1995*, www.ancestry.com; *Sanborn Fire Insurance Map from Michigan City, La Porte County, Indiana*, Sanborn Map Company, May 1912, www.loc.gov; "Historical Slide Collection," Michigan City Library, www.mclib. org.

21 "Interview with Hussien Hussien Ayad"; *Sanborn Fire Insurance Map from Michigan City*.

22 "Two Poolroom Men Are Fined," *Michigan City Evening News*, Jan. 29, 1914, 1.

23 *Sanborn Fire Insurance Map from Michigan City*.

24 "Interview with Hussien Hussien Ayad," 3–4.

25 "Jewish Quintet Beats Baptists," *Michigan City Evening News*, Feb. 27, 1914, 1; "Jewish Relief Day Observed," *Michigan City Evening News*, Jan. 17, 1916, 1.

26 Linda K. Jacobs, "'Playing East': Arabs Play Arabs in Nineteenth Century America," *Mashriq & Mahjar* 2, no. 2 (2014): 79–110.

27 "Jack Leon Fails to Appear Here," *Michigan City Evening News*, Jan. 13, 1914, 1.

28 "The Terrible Turk," *Michigan City Evening News*, Jan. 12, 1914, 2; "Hussane in Another Win," *Michigan City Evening News*, Feb. 17, 1914, 1; "The Orpheum," www.cinematreasures.org; "Hussane and Zybszko," *Michigan City Evening News*, Mar. 30, 1914, 1; "Big Wrestler Arrives Here," *Michigan City Evening News*, Apr. 13, 1914, 1; "Scloom Deals Costello," *Michigan City Evening News*, Apr. 14, 1914, 1.

29 *US City Directories, 1822–1995 and US Social Security Applications and Claims Index, 1936–2007*, www.ancestry.com.

30 Interview with Mary Shamey by Alixa Naff, Naff Collection, May 30, 1980, 1–9; Google Earth, www.google.com; National Oceanic and Atmospheric Administration (NOAA), www.ncdc.noaa.gov.

31 Interview with Mary Shamey, 14, 19, 20, 23.

32 Interview with Kamel Osman by Alixa Naff, Taylor, Michigan, June 4, 1980, Naff Collection, National Museum of American History, 19, 20; *Indiana, Birth Certificates, 1907–1940 and Indiana, Select Marriages Index, 1748–1993*, www. ancestry.com.

33 Interview with Kamel Osman, 18, 19, 31.

34 "City's First Conscript," *Michigan City Evening News*, Aug. 8, 1917, 4; *World War I Draft Registration Cards, 1917–1918*, www.ancestry.com.

35 "Draft List Is Certified," *Michigan City Evening News*, Aug. 15, 1917, 1.

36 "Thousands at Farewell of Departing Youths," *Michigan City Evening News*, Sept. 26, 1917, 1.

37 "More Soldiers to Go Friday," *Michigan City Evening News*, Mar. 27, 1918, 1.

38 "Military Event Burial of Hero," *Michigan City Evening News*, Apr. 10, 1918, 4; "Dedicate Flag Syrian Church," *Michigan City Evening News*, May 29, 1918, 8.

39 "Verdict Favors Joseph Allie," *Michigan City Evening News*, Apr. 10, 1918, 4.

40 World War I Draft Registration Cards, 1917–1918, www.ancestry.com; "Names of Men Next to Entrain," *Michigan City Evening News*, Apr. 17, 1918, 1; "Joe Allie Writes from Camp," *Michigan City Evening News*, July 13, 1918, 8; US Army Transport Service, Passenger Lists, 1910–1939, www.ancestry.com; *Michigan City Evening News*, n.d., 1919.

41 "Islam in Michigan City: Past and Present," Michigan City Islamic Center, Michigan City, Indiana, Public Library, n.d.

CHAPTER 5. MUSLIM LIFE AND THE AGRICULTURAL DEPRESSION IN NORTH DAKOTA

1 Interview with Boaley Farhat; Charles Ellis Dickson, "Prosperity Rides on Rubber Tires: The Impact of the Automobile on Minot during the 1920s," *North Dakota Historical Quarterly* 53 (1986): 14–23; *Standard Atlas of Mountrail County, North Dakota* (1917), p. 12, www.digitalhorizonsonline.org.

2 *North Dakota, Select County Marriage Records, 1872–2017, 1910 US Federal Census*, www.ancestry.com; Interview with Boaley Farhat.

3 Interview with Side Abdallah; Interview with Hassyn Alla Juma.

4 Stacy D. Fahrenthold, "Making Nations, in the Mahjar: Syrian and Lebanese Long-Distance Nationalisms in New York City, São Paulo, and Buenos Aires, 1913–1929," PhD diss., Northeastern University, 2014, 162–63.

5 Interview with Sam Omar; "Local Syrians Make Effort to Help Sufferers Overseas," *Bismarck Tribune*, Dec. 29, 1925, 2.

6 William C. Pratt, "Rural Radicalism on the Northern Plains, 1912–1950," *Montana: The Magazine of Western History* 42, no. 1 (Winter 1992): 42–55.

7 Robert P. Wilkins, "The Nonpartisan League and Upper Midwest Isolationism," *Agricultural History* 39, no. 2 (April 1965): 102–9.

8 "County Goes for Wilson," *Ross Valley News*, Nov. 10, 1916, 1.

9 Scot A. Stradley, "Senator Lynn Joseph Frazier and Federal Agricultural Policy, 1923–1939," *North Dakota History* 66, no. 3/4 (1999): 30–33; *Ward County Independent*, Oct. 13, 1921, 7; Robinson, *History of North Dakota*, 338, 342.

10 Robinson, *History of North Dakota*, 372–74, 381.

11 Ibid.; Stradley, "Senator Lynn Joseph Frazier," 30, 34–35.

12 Leslie Dibble, Marie Dibble, Ruth Meiers, Gertrude Reep, and W. Ray Stewart, *Tales of Mighty Mountrail: A History of Mountrail County, North Dakota*, vol. 1 (Dallas: Taylor Publishing, 1979), 26–29.

13 "Insurance Cost on Storage Is Reduced," *Bismarck Tribune*, June 18, 1930, 9.

14 "Farmers Union Is Meeting at Minot," *Bismarck Tribune*, Nov. 10, 1930, 6.

15 Robinson, *History of North Dakota*, 386–88.

16 Dickson, "Prosperity Rides on Rubber Tires," 20.

17 Harry C. McDean, "Federal Farm Policy and the Dust Bowl: The Half-Right Solution," *North Dakota History* 47, no. 3 (Summer 1980): 21–31.

18 Interview with Mike Abdallah.

19 Sherman et al., *Prairie Peddlers*.

20 Originally this was described as the NE1/4 SE1/4 of Section 28 on the Mountrail County Plat map. Today it is parcel 190013401, also known as geographic township T156N R92W. Sidwell's Portico, https://portico.mygisonline.com.

21 "The Assyrian Moslem of Ross," in *Tales of Mighty Mountrail*, 104–5.

22 Interview with Side Abdallah.

23 Robinson, *History of North Dakota*, 543.

24 Schuessler, "Little Mosque"; Interview with Mary Juma.

25 Robinson, *History of North Dakota*, 544.

26 Interview with Sam Omar.

27 "Ross Twp," *Tales of Mighty Mountrail*, 221.

28 "Charles Amid Abdallah, 1921–1930," www.findagrave.com; "Moslem Cemetery," www.findagrave.com.

29 *Montana, Birth Records, 1897–1988*, www.ancestry.com; *1930 United States Federal Census*, www.ancestry.com; *1940 United States Federal Census*, www.ancestry.com.

30 *U.S., Social Security Applications and Claims Index, 1936–2007*, www.ancestry.com; *1940 United States Federal Census*, www.ancestry.com.

31 Interview with Mike Abdallah.

32 *1940 United States Federal Census*, www.ancestry.com; Interview with Hassyn Alla Juma.

33 Robinson, *History of North Dakota*, 402–5; Interview with Charlie Juma.

34 Robinson, *History of North Dakota*, 398–400.

35 Interview with Mike Abdallah; *1940 United States Federal Census*, www.ancestry.com.

36 Interview with Mike Abdallah; "Toby Abdallah," www.findagrave.com; "Grafton State School," *Asylum Projects*, www.asylumprojects.org; US Department of the Interior National Park Service, National Register of Historic Places Registration Form, "North Dakota Institution for the Feeble-Minded," Sept. 23, 1996, https://npgallery.nps.gov; Lutz Kaelber, "Eugenic Sterilizations in the United States: North Dakota," www.uvm.edu.

37 Interview with Boaley Farhat.

38 Interview with Sam Omar.

39 Robinson, *History of North Dakota*, 406.

40 Interview with Mary Juma; Interview with Charlie Juma.

41 Interview with Mike Abdallah.

42 *Tales of Might Mountrail*, 26–27.

43 Robinson, *History of North Dakota*, 406–9.

44 Geoff Cunfer, "The New Deal's Land Utilization Program in the Great Plains," *Great Plains Quarterly* 21, no. 3 (Summer 2001): 193–210.

45 "Closing Dates on Loans Is Extended," *Bismarck Tribune*, Dec, 22, 1941; 1, "Set Latest Date for AAA Soil Payments," *Bismarck Tribune*, Dec. 9, 1942, 3; "Grant County Elects 1943 Farm Leaders," *Bismarck Tribune*, Nov. 20, 1942, 6; Robinson, *History of North Dakota*, 416–19.

46 Robinson, *History of North Dakota*, 390–2, 421–39; Lawrence H. Larsen, "Gerald Nye and the Isolationist Argument," *North Dakota History* 47, no. 1 (1980): 25–27.

47 *1940 United States Federal Census, US WWII Draft Cards Young Men, 1940–1947, and U.S., Department of Veterans Affairs BIRLS Death File, 1850–2010*, www. ancestry.com.

48 Robinson, *History of North Dakota*, 424–25, 428–29; Interview with Charlie Juma.

49 *Tales of Mighty Mountrail*, 26–29; Robinson, *History of North Dakota*, 425, 431–33.

50 During the Trump era, the legacy of the mosque on the prairie attracted international press coverage as a symbol of Islam's long history in the United States. See Cary Beckwith, "Of Mosques and Men," *New Republic*, January 31, 2016, www. newrepublic.com; Ryan Schuessler, "Little Mosque on the Prairie Reveals a Century of Religious Coexistence," *Guardian*, July 18, 2016, www.theguardian. com; and Samuel G. Freedman, "North Dakota Mosque a Symbol of Muslims' Long Ties in America," *New York Times*, May 27, 2016, www.nytimes.com.

CHAPTER 6. CEDAR RAPIDS' GROCERY BUSINESS AND THE GROWTH OF A MUSLIM MIDWESTERN TOWN

1 *Iowa, State Census Collection, 1836–1925, 1920 US Census; Iowa, Marriage Records, 1880–1951; Iowa, Federal Naturalization Records, 1856–1937*, www.ancestry.com.

2 Clarence A. Andrews, "Cedar Rapids in the Roaring Twenties," *Palimpset* (Spring 1987): 32–38; *McCoy's Cedar Rapids City Directory*, 7, www.ancestry.com.

3 George Henry and the History Center, *Cedar Rapids, Iowa* (Charleston, SC: Arcadia, 2001), 85–86.

4 "First Case Is Tried in New Superior Court Room," *Cedar Rapids Evening Gazette and Republican*, Dec. 21, 1928, 16.

5 *US City Directories, Cedar Rapids, Iowa, 1925 and 1935*, www.ancestry.com.

6 "Real Estate Transfers," *Cedar Rapids Evening Gazette*, June 23, 1926, 5.

7 Interview with Fatima Igram by Laura Derr, transcribed by Imelda K. Collins, Junior League of Cedar Rapids, Feb. 6, 1985, www.historycenter.org, 21.

8 Ibid., 25; *Cedar Rapids Evening Gazette and Republican*, Sept. 21, 1928, 24, Jan. 4, 1929, 17; Apr. 19, 1929, 30; Nov. 22, 1929, 18; May 1, 1931, 15; July 24, 1931, 16.

9 "Urbana Man Back from Europe Trip," *Cedar Rapids Evening Gazette*, Sept. 16, 1922, 3. In 1920, thirty-four-year-old Abdo along with his twenty-three-year-old brother William (or Yahya)—but not Mike—was a boarder at the sixty-year-old Thomas Allbones's home. That same year, on November 24, Abdo became a naturalized US citizen.

10 *New York, Passenger and Crew Lists (including Castle Garden and Ellis Island), 1820–1957*, www.ancestry.com.

11 "Vinton Man Leaves for Assyria to Visit Kin," *Cedar Rapids Evening Gazette*, June 14, 1926, 6.

12 Interview with Hasibe and Abe Aossey by Alixa Naff, Cedar Rapids, Iowa, June 17, 1980, Naff Collection, National Museum of American History, 2–4, 7, 20.

13 Mae M. Ngai, "The Architecture of Race in American Immigration Law: A Reexamination of the Immigration Act of 1924," *Journal of American History* 86, no. 1 (1999): 67–92.

14 Gualtieri, *Between Arab and White*.

15 *Cedar Rapids Evening Gazette*, Mar. 1, 1927, 12.

16 "Vinton Man Given the Right to Enter the Country by Davis," *Cedar Rapids Evening Gazette*, Mar. 8, 1927, 1.

17 "Hearing Held Here on Immigrant Registry Plea of Local Men," *Cedar Rapids Gazette*, Aug. 9, 1940, 5.

18 Interview with Abdullah Igram; *Iowa, State Census Collection, 1836–1925, 1920 US Census; Iowa, Marriage Records, 1880–1951; Iowa, Federal Naturalization Records, 1856–1937; New York, Passenger and Crew Lists (including Castle Garden and Ellis Island), 1820–1957; 1930 United States Federal Census; US City Directories, 1822–1995*, www.ancestry.com; "*Majestic 2*," https://greatships.net.

19 Naomi Doebel, "New Harrison Building Opens Tuesday with Latest Conveniences and Modern Equipment," *Cedar Rapids Evening Gazette and Republican*, Aug. 31, 1930, 5; see also Mar. 8, 1930, 12; May 18, 1931, 3; Apr. 4, 1931; Oct. 17, 1931, 5.

20 "Two Holdups Inside of Half Hour," *Cedar Rapids Gazette and Republican*, Dec. 7, 1930, 1.

21 *Cedar Rapids Gazette and Republican*, Feb. 1, 2931, 1.

22 *Cedar Rapids Evening Gazette and Republican*, July 17, 1931, 4; Phone conversation, Clerk of Court, Linn County, Iowa, June 18, 2020.

23 Glenda Riley, "Divorce Records: Linn County, Iowa, 1928–1944," *Annals of Iowa* 50 (1991): 787–800.

24 "Hassan A. Igram," *Cedar Rapids Gazette*, Mar. 31, 1980, 2A; *Iowa, Marriage Records, 1880–1951, US City Directories, 1822–1995*, www.ancestry.com.

25 *Cedar Rapids Gazette*, Dec. 21, 1933, 13.

26 "Sixteen Are Injured in Auto Accidents," *Cedar Rapids Evening Gazette*, Apr. 2, 1928, 1.

27 "Thieves Have Little Sympathy at Vinton," *Cedar Rapids Evening Gazette and Republican*, Apr. 5, 1928, 3.

28 *Iowa, Marriage Records, 1880–1951*, www.ancestry.com; "Divorce Petitions," *Cedar Rapids Gazette*, Nov. 1, 1944, 4; Interview with Mike Aossey, 20. They later married a second time, but that marriage also ended in divorce.

29 Interview with Najibe Sheronick, 1–20; "Negebe H. Sheronick," *Cedar Rapids Gazette*, June 9, 1989, 14.

30 Interview with Fatima Igram, 7–14.

31 Ray Anderson, "Mohammedan Farmer of Fayette Lives Up to Christian Principles by Pinning His Faith on 260-Year-Old Koran," *Cedar Rapids Evening Gazette and Republican*, July 27, 1930, 5.

32 Interview with Fatima Igram, 1–7; Housein Hamad, *Cedar Rapids Gazette*, Feb. 18, 1971, 3, 29.

33 Interview with Abdullah Igram, 18, 22; Interview with Fatima Igram, 7–14, 26, 28, 29, 32.

34 *Cedar Rapids Gazette*, Feb. 20, 1932, 10; Oct. 12, 1934, 15; July 19, 1935; May 7, 1939, 30.

35 Interview with Fatima Igram, 23–24; Interview with Abdullah Igram, 28.

36 Andrews, "Cedar Rapids," 36.

37 Interview with Fatima Igram, 16.

38 *Cedar Rapids Gazette*, May 17, 1939, 10; Mar. 3, 1938, 20; Jan. 13, 1938, 21.

39 "Divine Science Group," *Cedar Rapids Gazette*, Oct. 13, 1938.

40 "P.T.A. Meetings," *Cedar Rapids Gazette*, Mar. 19, 1939, 22.

41 Interview with H. K. and Laila Igram by Alixa Naff, Cedar Rapids, June 18, 1980, Naff Collection, National Museum of American History.

42 Ibid., 19; Interview with Abdullah Igram, 19; "The Olympic," www.theolympiccr.com.

43 Telephone conversation with Mike Karoub by Alixa Naff, Naff Collection, National Museum of American History, Nov. 10, 1980; Hussien Ahmed Sheronick, "A History of the Cedar Rapids Muslim Community: The Search for an American Islamic Identity," honors thesis, Coe College, May 3, 1988, 31.

44 Interview with Hasibe Aossey by Alixa Naff, Naff Collection, National Museum of American History, 21, 23A.

45 Interview with Fatima Igram, 10; Interview with Hasibe Aossey; Interview with Najibe Sheronick.

46 *Cedar Rapids Gazette*, Feb. 21, 1934, 16; "1,100 Attend Rose of Fraternity Dinner," *Cedar Rapids Gazette*, Nov. 15, 1934, 15.

47 *Cedar Rapids Gazette*, Feb. 16, 1936, 27, and Feb. 13, 1939, 12.

48 Interview with Najibe Sheronick, 19.

49 Sheronick, "History of Cedar Rapids Muslim Community," 131–38.

50 "Local Bldg. Permits during the Last Week," *Cedar Rapids Gazette*, Mar. 17, 1935, 18.

51 *Cedar Rapids Gazette*, May 12, 1935, 32.

52 *Sanborn Fire Insurance Map from Cedar Rapids, Linn County, Iowa*, Sanborn Map Company, 1949, www.loc.gov.

53 Sheronick, "History of Cedar Rapids Muslim Community," 35.

54 Ibid., 33.

55 "Moslem Church to Be Dedicated This Afternoon," *Cedar Rapids Gazette*, June 16, 1935, 23.

56 Interview with Fatima Igram, 11–18; Sheronick, "History of Cedar Rapids Muslim Community," 34–35.

57 "Moslem Prayers Recorded in C.R.," *Cedar Rapids Gazette*, Feb. 11, 1945, 28.

58 Bill R. Douglas, "Making Iowa Safe for Differences: Barnstorming Iowa on Behalf of Religious Tolerance, 1936–1943," *Annals of Iowa* 75 (2016): 234–59.

59 "Rose of Fraternity Lodge Has Program," *Cedar Rapids Gazette*, Nov. 25, 1935, 10.

60 *Cedar Rapids Gazette*, June 18, 1938, 2.

61 *Cedar Rapids Gazette*, Jan. 12, 1936, 7; see also Interview with Abdullah Igram, 18–19.

62 "First Anniversary of Moslem Temple Here Observed," *Cedar Rapids Gazette*, July 2, 1936, 16.

63 Interview with Fatima Igram, 19–20.

64 "Funeral for Hassan Sheronick on Thursday," *Cedar Rapids Gazette*, Nov. 27, 1934, 7.

65 "Aossey Babe Dies," *Cedar Rapids Gazette*, Feb. 25, 1936, 21.

66 "Rose of Fraternity to Celebrate Third Anniversary of Local Moslem Temple," *Cedar Rapids Gazette*, June 19, 1937, 7.

67 "Local Moslem Will Join in Celebration of Their Pilgrims' Day," *Cedar Rapids Gazette*, Dec. 1, 1937, 12.

68 "Ramadan Holiday to Be Celebrated by Moslems," *Cedar Rapids Gazette*, Nov. 20, 1938, 13.

69 Fred Henson, "Couple in Their Seventies Brave Atlantic to See Their Son," *Cedar Rapids Gazette*, Oct. 15, 1939, 2.

70 *McCoy's Cedar Rapids City Directory 1937*, www.ancestry.com.

71 "Unity Meeting Held at the Moslem Temple," *Cedar Rapids Gazette*, Jan. 29, 1939, 3.

72 "Moslem Group Answers Complaints to Council, Says Meetings Orderly," *Cedar Rapids Gazette*, June 30, 1936, 7.

73 "Honored on Birthday," *Cedar Rapids Gazette*, Sept. 5, 1938, 9.

74 Interview with Mike Aossey, 14, 16, 18, 20.

75 *Cedar Rapids Gazette*, May 4, 1935.

76 Henson, "Couple in Their Seventies Brave Atlantic," 2.

77 "I.Y.A.," *Cedar Rapids Gazette*, Dec. 1, 1940, 22.

78 "Islamic Youth to Install Officers at Temple Sunday," *Cedar Rapids Gazette*, May 12, 1940, 8.

79 "Two Boys Publish Newspaper about Moslems in the U.S.," *Cedar Rapids Gazette*, June 8, 1941, 13.

80 "Dramatic Guild of Wilson School to Give Three-Act Comedy," *Cedar Rapids Gazette*, Nov. 5, 1944, 22.

81 "New Igram Store to Open Saturday," *Cedar Rapids Gazette*, Oct. 17, 1941, 15.

82 *Cedar Rapids Gazette*, Oct. 13, 1941, 14; Oct. 14, 1941, 3.

83 Justus D. Doenecke, "Verne Marshall's Leadership of the No Foreign War Committee, 1940," *Annals of Iowa* 41, no. 7 (1973): 1153–72.

84 *Cedar Rapids Gazette*, Feb. 16, 1943, 14; Apr. 14, 1944, 13; June 3, 1945, 10.

85 "Roosevelt High Pupils to Buy Defense Bond," *Cedar Rapids Gazette*, Dec. 21, 1941, 31.

86 *US WWII Draft Cards Young Men, 1940–1947, Iowa, World War II Bonus Case Files, 1947–1954*, www.ancestry.com; Jennifer Ann Rivera Silverman, ""The

Exigencies of War': The Army Specialized Training Program and Washington University, 1942–1945," PhD diss., Washington University in St. Louis, 2015, vii; 89th Infantry Division of World War II, "ASTP: The Army's Waste of Manpower," www.89infdivww2.org; George Raynor Thompson and Dixie R. Harris, *The Signal Corps: The Outcome (Mid-1943 through 1945)* (Washington, DC: Center for Military History, 1991); Rebecca Robbins Raines, Signal Corps (Washington, DC: Center for Military History, 2005), 68.

87 Louise Lux, "Women in War Work," *Cedar Rapids Gazette*, Sept. 13, 1943, 8; "Ichey Mary Rahal Sheronick," www.findagrave.com.

CHAPTER 7. FROM SIOUX FALLS AND MICHIGAN CITY TO DETROIT, CAPITAL OF THE MUSLIM MIDWEST

1 Interview with Aliya Hassen, 22, 26; Pamela Short, "Summary of *The Sage Hen*," www.imdb.com; "The Olympic Theater," Greetings from Sioux Falls, www.greetingsfromsiouxfalls.com; Google Maps, www.google.com; *Sioux Falls Argus-Leader*, Feb. 26, 1921, 22, 23, 26; *1921 Sioux Falls City Directory*, www.ancestry.com.

2 *Fourteenth Census of the United States*, 1920, www2.census.gov; Gary D. Olson, "The William Brown Incident: Racism and Vigilantism in Sioux Falls," *South Dakota History* 35, no. 2 (2005): 137–51.

3 "Recall Permit to Build Store on East Sixth," *Sioux Falls Argus-Leader*, Feb. 24, 1920, 8.

4 "Commission Firm in Refusing Permit," *Sioux Falls Argus-Leader*, Mar. 2, 1920, 4.

5 See, for example, "Moslems Seek to Rule the World," *Sioux Falls Argus-Leader*, Apr. 3, 1922, 31, and "Back to the Harem Cry Old Turks, Quoting Koran: Misogznic [*sic*] Moslems Would Legalize Restoration of Polygamous Relations in Nation," *Sioux Falls Argus-Leader*, Sept. 15, 1923, 1.

6 *Sioux Falls Argus-Leader*, Nov. 5, 1920, 13.

7 Clara E. Laughlin, "Men Are Like That," *Sioux Falls Argus-Leader*, Sept. 26, 1921, 10.

8 Rex C. Myers, "An Immigrant Heritage: South Dakota's Foreign-Born in the Era of Assimilation," South Dakota Historical Society Press, 1989, www.sdhspress.com.

9 "Municipal Court," *Sioux Falls Daily Argus*, Mar. 26, 1920, 13.

10 "Municipal Court," *Sioux Falls Argus-Leader*, Mar. 11, 1924, 3.

11 "Swiden Pleads Guilty Encouraging Boys to Steal Railway Coal," *Sioux Falls Argus-Leader*, Nov. 17, 1922.

12 "Permit Side to Attend Funeral of His Brother," *Sioux Falls Argus-Leader*, Feb. 16, 1920, 8; see also Feb. 12, 1920, 9.

13 Interview with Aliya Hassen, 14.

14 "After Converts Muhammadanism," *Sioux Falls Argus-Leader*, Apr. 19, 1921, 7.

15 Interview with Aliya Hassen, 18, 23, 27; James Barr, "General Gouraud: 'Saladin, We're Back!' Did He Really Say It?" *Syria Comment*, May 27, 2016, www.joshualandis.com.

16 Dedication Page, "Records," Aliya Hassen Papers, Bentley Historical Library, University of Michigan, 1923–1940 Folder.

17 "New Teachers Are Assigned," *Sioux Falls Argus-Leader*, Sept. 3, 1923, 9.

18 "Many Teachers in City Schools Sign Contracts," *Sioux Falls Argus-Leader*, June 13, 1924, 7.

19 *Sioux Falls Argus-Leader*, Sept. 26, 1924, 20.

20 "Educational Advantages; Latest Types of Buildings," *Sioux Falls Argus-Leader*, Jan. 1, 1924, 37; "Four New Teachers in S.F. Schools," *Sioux Falls Argus-Leader*, Feb. 5, 1924, 13.

21 "Records Given for Prizes in Music Competition," *Sioux Falls Argus-Leader*, May 12, 1924, 12.

22 Renshaw, *Forgotten Sioux Falls*, 73–74.

23 Antoinette Donnelly, "Mothers to Blame for Daring Stunts of Flappers," *Sioux Falls Argus-Leader*, Sept. 23, 1921, 7.

24 Interview with Aliya Hassen, 23A.

25 "Records," Aliya Hassen Papers, 78.

26 *US, Social Security Applications and Claims Index, 1936–2007*, www.ancestry.com.

27 "Records," Aliya Hassen Papers, 131–32.

28 See, for example, Edward E. Curtis IV and Danielle Brune Sigler, eds., *The New Black Gods: Arthur Huff Fauset and the Study of African American Religions* (Bloomington: Indiana University Press, 2009).

29 At some later point, these lines were revised to repeat the first part of the *adhan*, or call to prayer: "There is no god but God; Muhammad is the Messenger of God." But Aliya's first version—"there is no god except Him"—is a typical prayer uttered by Muslims, too.

30 "Records," Aliya Hassen Papers, 114–115.

31 Ibid., 116–18, 167.

32 Ibid., 87, 106–7, 119, 141.

33 Philip P. Mason, *Rum Running and the Roaring Twenties: Prohibition on the Michigan-Ontario Waterway* (Detroit: Wayne State University Press, 1995), 71–72, 75, 94.

34 "Records," Aliya Hassen Papers, 120.

35 Mark Jay and Philip Conklin, *A People's History of Detroit* (Durham, NC: Duke University Press, 2020), 78; Howell, *Old Islam in Detroit*, 33, 55, 89, 105.

36 *US City Directories*, 1920 US Census, www.ancestry.com.

37 "Ford Rouge," www.thehenryford.org.

38 Jay and Conklin, *People's History of Detroit*, 79.

39 Interview with Aliya Hassen, 21; *1930 United States Federal Census, Michigan, Marriage Records, 1867–1952*, www.ancestry.com.

40 *US City Directories, 1822–1995, 1930 Federal Census*, www.ancestry.com.

41 B. H. Lee, "Divorce Law Reform in Michigan," *University of Michigan Journal of Law Reform* 5 (1972): 409–25, https://repository.law.umich.edu; Sonja Hunter,

"The Rise of Divorce in Michigan," Feb. 28, 2013, https://kalamazoogenealogy. blogspot.com.

42 *Michigan, Divorce Records, 1897–1952*, www.ancestry.com.

43 Alex Baskin, "The Ford Hunger March—1932," *Labor History* 13, no. 3 (1972): 331–60.

44 Interview with Aliya Hassen, 25, 26, 28.

45 *US, World War II Draft Registration Cards, 1942, Michigan, Marriage Records, 1867–1952*, www.ancestry.com.

46 "Effort to Collect Gambling Debt Results in Stabbing," *Detroit Free Press*, Aug. 28, 1933, 7; Interview with Aliya Hassen, 20.

47 "Returned Here for Burial," *Lafayette Sun*, Nov. 17, 1948, 1.

48 Interview with Aliya Hassen, 28.

49 *US City Directories, 1822–1995*, www.ancestry.com.

50 *Sanborn Fire Insurance Map from Sioux Falls, Minnehaha County, South Dakota*, Sanborn Map Company, 1916, www.loc.gov.

51 "Bankrupt Sale," *Sioux Falls Argus-Leader*, Feb. 6, 1912, 3; Feb. 8, 1912, 5.

52 "Qaraaoun," www.localiban.org; *Argus-Leader*, Feb. 8, 1912, 5.

53 Jay and Conklin, *People's History of Detroit*, 95.

54 *US WWII Draft Cards Young Men, 1940–1947; New York, Passenger and Crew Lists (including Castle Garden and Ellis Island), 1820–1957*, www.ancestry.com; Interview with Osman Chamie, Naff Collection, National Museum of American History, 2, 4, 6, 8, 9, 28.

55 Jay and Conklin, *People's History of Detroit*, 92, 95.

56 Anan Ameri and Yvonne Lockwood, *Arab Americans in Metro Detroit* (Charleston, SC: Arcadia, 2001), 95.

57 "Ford Wage Increase Totals 13 Millions," *Battle Creek Enquirer*, May 17, 1941, 1.

58 Interview with Osman Chamie.

59 Interview with Kamel Osman, 4.

60 Ibid., 19–20.

61 Jay and Conklin, *People's History of Detroit*, 88.

62 Interview with Kamel Osman, 20, 28.

63 Jay and Conklin, *People's History of Detroit*, 80.

64 Interview with Osman Chamie, 34–37.

65 *US City Directories*, www.ancestry.com; Interview with Mary Shamey, 14.

66 Interview with Mary Shamey, 14, 18, 19, 20A, 21, 23, 31.

67 Ameri and Lockwood, *Arab Americans in Metro Detroit*, 94; Interview with Mary Shamey, 20, 20A, 21.

68 Sami Asmar, "The Two Tenors of Arabic Music," March 11, 2000, www.turath.org.

69 Interview with Mary Shamey, 22, 23A, 32.

70 Ibid., 16; Interview with Kamel Osman, 16.

71 "Muslims Dedicate Temple to Fulfill 20-Year Dream," *Detroit Free Press*, May 31, 1937, 4.

72 "Group Files Protest in Lebanese Strife," *Detroit Free Press*, Nov. 28, 1943.

73 "Jews Prosper in Her Native Iraq, She Says," *Detroit Free Press*, Jan. 29, 1939, 8.

74 Hani Bawardi, *The Making of Arab Americans: From Syrian Nationalism to U.S. Citizenship* (Austin: University of Texas Press, 2014).

75 Howell, *Old Islam in Detroit*, 97, 118–19, 122.

76 "Peace Be with You the Cry as Season of Fasting Closes," *Detroit Free Press*, Nov. 13, 1939, 4.

77 The figure is repeated in multiple issues of the *Free Press*, including Nov. 13, 1939, 4.

78 Jay and Conklin, *People's History of Detroit*, 96–101.

79 "Invasion Stirs Detroiters to New Heights of Patriotism," *Detroit Free Press*, June 11, 1944, 37.

80 *US World War II Draft Cards Young Men, 1940–1947*, and *US World War II Army Enlistment Records, 1938–1946*, www.ancestry.com.

81 Major General H. L George to First Sgt. Ali Said, Feb. 4, 1943, Haragely Papers, Bentley Historical Museum, University of Michigan.

82 "Reporter's Notebook," Nov. 20, 1943, Haragely Papers.

83 Major James F. Smith to Mrs. Sarah Said, Nov. 8, 1946, Haragely Papers.

CONCLUSION

1 "Sixth Annual Convention, The Federation of Islamic Associations in the United States and Canada, 1957," Bentley Historical Library, University of Michigan; Howell, *Old Islam in Detroit*, 158.

2 "Vet Leads Moslems in Fight for Recognition," *Toledo Blade*, July 5, 1953, 11; Interview with Abdullah Igram, 17; Lily Rothman, "The Khan Family and American History's Hidden Muslim Soldiers," *Time*, Aug. 3, 2016, www.time.com. The original story appeared on July 13, 1953.

3 May Alhassen, "Aliya Hassen," *Encyclopedia of Muslim-American History*, vol. 1 (New York: Facts on File, 2010), 232–33.

4 Edward E. Curtis IV, "The Black Muslim Scare of the Twentieth Century: The History of State Islamophobia and Its Post-9/11 Variations," *Islamophobia in America*, ed. Carl W. Ernst (New York: Palgrave, 2013), 75–106.

5 "Moslem Group Snubbed by Acting Detroit Mayor," *Chicago Tribune*, Aug. 3, 1957, 13; "Acting Mayor of Detroit Snubs International Islamic Meeting," *Ironwood Daily Globe*, Aug. 3, 1957, 1; "Snub by Miriani Incenses Moslems," *Detroit Free Press*, Aug. 3, 1957, 1.

6 Edward E. Curtis IV, *Muslim American Politics and the Future of US Democracy* (New York: New York University Press, 2019).

7 Edward E. Curtis IV, *Muslims in America: A Short History* (New York: Oxford, 2009); Howell, *Old Islam in Detroit*.

INDEX

ABOUT THE AUTHOR

EDWARD E. CURTIS IV traces his Midwestern Syrian heritage to the Hamaway and Samaha families, who first settled in the region during the late 1800s. His decision to study Islam and Arabic as a first-year college student was inspired by his experience growing up as an Arab American in Southern Illinois. Since then, he has written or edited a dozen books, mainly about Islam and Muslims in the United States and in the African Diaspora. His previous works include *Muslims in America: A Short History* and *Muslim American Politics and the Future of US Democracy*. Curtis is the William M. and Gail M. Plater Chair of the Liberal Arts at the Indiana University School of Liberal Arts in Indianapolis.